Notational Analysis of Sport

Notational Analysis of Sport

Mike Hughes

Centre for Notational Analysis
University of Wales Institute
Cardiff, UK

and

Ian Franks

School of Human Kinetics
University of British Columbia
Vancouver, Canada

E & FN SPON
An Imprint of Chapman & Hall

London · Weinheim · New York · Tokyo · Melbourne · Madras

Published by E & FN Spon, an imprint of Chapman & Hall,
2–6 Boundary Row, London SE1 8HN, UK

Chapman & Hall, 2–6 Boundary Row, London SE1 8HN, UK

Chapman & Hall GmbH, Pappelallee 3, 69469 Weinheim, Germany

Chapman & Hall USA, 115 Fifth Avenue, New York, NY 10003, USA

Chapman & Hall Japan, ITP-Japan, Kyowa Building, 3F, 2-2-1 Hirakawacho, Chiyoda-ku, Tokyo 102, Japan

Chapman & Hall Australia, 102 Dodds Street, South Melbourne, Victoria 3205, Australia

Chapman & Hall India, R. Seshadri, 32 Second Main Road, CIT East, Madras 600 035, India

First edition 1997

© 1997 M. Hughes and I.M. Franks

Typeset in 10/12pt Palatino by Saxon Graphics Ltd, Derby
Printed in Great Britain by TJ International Ltd, Padstow, Cornwall

ISBN 0 419 18010 9

Contents

Acknowledgements

Chapter 2 was written by Peter Treadwell (Head of Graduate School) and Keith Lyons (Director for the Centre of Notational Analysis) of the University of Wales Institute, Cardiff.

A large part of the work that went into creating the knowledge base for Chapter 8 was completed by Kenneth G. More who was funded by the Social Science and Humanities Research Council of Canada.

Know your enemy as you know yourself and you need not fear one hundred battles;

Know yourself but not the enemy, for every victory gained you will also suffer a defeat;

Know neither the enemy nor yourself and you will succumb in every battle.

Sun Tzu, 652 AD

Introduction

This introductory section acts as a simple guide to the rest of the book. The aim of the book is to provide a ready manual on notational analysis.

The book is written for the sports scientist, the coach, the athlete or for anyone who wishes to apply analysis to any aspect of a performance operation. Although this book is applied directly to sport, notational analysis is a procedure that can be used in any discipline that requires assessment and analysis of performance, e.g. nursing, surgical operations, skilled manufacturing processes, unskilled manufacturing processes, haute cuisine, etc.

To cater for the anticipated spectrum of readership, the book is written to balance the needs for a practical approach, with plenty of examples, and yet provide a sound scientific analysis of the subject area. In this way it is hoped that both the practitioners of sport, the athletes and coaches, as well as the sports scientists will find the book useful.

ABOUT THIS BOOK

Like most texts the information within this book is presented in an order that is considered logical and progressive. It is not totally necessary, however, to use the book in this way. It is anticipated that at times certain sections will be needed to be used for immediate practical requirements. At the start of each chapter advice is given on how to use that chapter and also which chapters, if any, require reading and understanding beforehand.

ORGANIZATION OF THIS BOOK

Chapter 1. Why and how feedback has been used – a review of the literature

The aim of this chapter is to provide a full and complete understanding of the need for feedback. By examining the research recently completed on feedback, and the different forms it can take, conclusions are drawn as to the best ways of providing feedback to the learning or competing athlete. The objectivity and accuracy with which trained and expert observers can provide feedback is reviewed and the consequences of this research analysed.

Chapter 2. The use of video

Video is a very necessary tool both in visual feedback and notational analysis; consequently, the uses of video within sport are detailed and rationalized.

Chapter 3. Sports analysis

The aim of this chapter is to provide an insight into how sports can be broken down into their inherent logical progressions. The construction of flowcharts for different sports is examined, together with the definition of key events in these respective sports. The whole process is integrated into a complete and logical analysis for these sports. The next step is to design a data collection and data processing system, so anyone interested in designing a notation system should read this chapter first.

Chapter 4. Notational analysis – a review of the literature

This section offers as much information about notation systems as possible. The chapter is written in the form of a literature review of the research work already published in this field. Although this is written for, and by, sports scientists, it is hoped that anyone with an interest in this rapidly growing area of practice and research will find it equally interesting and rewarding.

The review is aimed at being as comprehensive as possible but, being aware that inevitably some published work will be missed, it is structured to follow the main developments in notational analysis. After tracing a historical perspective of the roots of notation, the application of these systems to sport are then developed. These early systems were all hand notation systems – their emerging sophistication is followed until the advent of computerized notation. Although the emphasis is given to the main research developments in both hand and computerized notational systems, where possible the innovations of new systems and any significant data outputs within specific sports are also assessed.

Chapter 5. How to develop a notation system

This chapter will enable you to develop your own hand notation system for any sport, no matter how simple or complicated you wish to make it – the underlying principles apply. If you are hoping to develop a computerized system, the same logical process must be followed, so this section is a vital part of that developmental process too. It will also help understanding a great deal if chapters 3 and 4 have also been read.

Chapter 6. Examples of notation systems

The best way to appreciate the intricacies of notational analysis is to examine systems for the sport(s) in which you are interested, or sports that are similar. This chapter presents a number of examples of different systems for different sports. They have been devised by students of notational analysis; and are therefore of differing levels of complexity and sophistication – but there are always lessons to be learnt even from the simplest of systems. The explanations and analyses are completed by beginners at notational analysis; coaches of these sports should not therefore be irritated at the simplistic levels of analysis of the respective sports. The encouraging aspects about these examples is the amount of information that the systems provide – even the simplest of them. Examples 1–3 are for individual sports, while examples 4–7 are for team games, which are often more difficult to notate.

Chapter 7. How to develop a computerized notation system

The aim of this chapter is to build on the logical structure already created by the analysis of sport and the structuring of decision pathways, and then go on to design flowcharts for computer programs. The next progression is to then convert these flowcharts into sets of sequential instructions and hence into programs. If you are not familiar with any computing languages, this Chapter should still be of use – for two reasons. If you are intending to learn to program there is no better way than having a specific goal for your first programs, but note that you will need help from other sources such as specific language textbooks and, almost certainly, the advice of an expert now and then. If you do not wish to gain these skills but are intending to use someone to do the programming for you, then this part of the book will prove invaluable in helping your communication with that expert. If you can already program, be patient with the simple approach, there are a number of very helpful pieces of advice, gained from years of experience, i.e. mistakes, hidden within these elementary programs.

Chapter 8. Analysis of coaching behaviours – a review

Four distinct areas are addressed in this review. The first two sections establish the background to modern research on teaching and, in particular, the development of systematic observation techniques as a means of generating valid and reliable information on teacher process variables. Intervention studies are then cited in the third section to detail the necessary contingencies for the effective use of systematic observation in the analysis and modification of instructional behaviour. The fourth section cites literature that presents a rationale for those verbal coaching behaviours that are considered most effective. Finally, an extensive bibliography of literature related to the research on coaching analysis is provided.

Summary and conclusions

A condensation of some of the main points of creating systems are presented, together with a review of some of the problems in presenting data output. Some possible sources of help are also listed for both the UK and North America.

References

These provide a thorough database of all previous published research in notational analysis of sport, and related subject material, that will enable the reader to find their way further into any particular topic or sport.

Glossary

Inevitably any technical discipline develops its own jargon, particularly those involving computers, consequently this section is included to help those readers that may be unfamiliar with some of the terms used within other passages of this book.

algorithm	A process of rules for calculating something, especially by machine.
arrays	A function capable of storing columns of data, or even rows and columns (i.e. in two-dimensional arrays) of data, under one variable name.
BASIC	A computer language (Beginners All-purpose Symbolic Instruction Code).
bit of memory	The fundamental unit of a computer's memory.
buffer	A software buffer is an area of memory set aside for data in the process of being transferred from one device, or piece of software, to another. A hardware buffer is put into a signal line to increase the line's drive capability.
byte of memory	Eight bits of memory. Data is normally transferred between devices one byte at a time.
concept keyboard	A touch-sensitive digitization pad permitting alternative, and often easier, methods of data input into a computer.
flowchart	Diagrammatic representation of the logical processes involved in solving a problem.
hardware	Computer and other peripheral machinery.
machine code	Programs produced in a computer's assembler are machine code.

peripheral	Any device connected to the central processing unit, such as the analogue port, printer port, etc., but not including the memory.
RAM	Random Access Memory – the main memory in the microcomputer.
software	The computer program.
string	Computer terminology denoting a function capable of storing any character or group of characters, e.g. words
VDU	Visual display unit.

Why and how feedback has been used – a review of the literature

1

1.1 INTRODUCTION

The aim of this chapter is to provide a full and complete understanding of the need for feedback. By examining the research recently completed on feedback, and the different forms it can take, conclusions are drawn as to the best ways of providing feedback to the learning or competing athlete. The objectivity and accuracy with which trained and expert observers can provide feedback is reviewed, and the consequences of this research analysed.

1.2 THE NEED FOR FEEDBACK

1.2.1 THE COACHING PROCESS AND ITS PROBLEMS

Traditionally, coaching intervention has been based upon subjective observations of athletes. However, several recent studies have shown that such observations are not only unreliable but also inaccurate. Franks and Miller (1986) compared coaching observations to eyewitness testimony of a criminal event. Using methodology gained from applied memory research, they showed that international-level soccer coaches could only recollect 42% of the key factors that determined successful soccer performance during one match. In another study, a forced choice recognition paradigm was used by Franks (1993), who found that experienced gymnastic coaches were not significantly better than novice coaches in detecting differences in two, sequentially presented, front hand-spring performances.

An additional finding of interest in this study was that experienced coaches produced many more false positives (detecting a difference when none existed) than their novice counterparts and were also very confident in their decisions, even when wrong. This finding led to the speculation that the training undertaken by coaches predisposes them to seek out and report errors in performances even when none exist. The evidence from these studies combined with many others from the field of applied psychology (such as experiments that investigate the reliability of eyewitness testimony of criminal events) leads one to believe that the processing of visual information through the human information processing system is extremely problematic (Neisser, 1982) if one requires an objective, unbiased accounting of past events. Hence, the solution is to collect relevant details of performance during a live event and then recall these details at the termination of that event. Although many recording devices (e.g. a tape recorder) would serve equally well as an external memory aid, the computer appears to be ideally suited for such a task.

1.2.2 FEEDBACK

Information that is provided to the athlete about action is one of the most important variables affecting the learning and subsequent performance of a skill (see Franks, 1996, for a practical review). Knowledge about the proficiency with which athletes perform a skill is critical to the learning process and in certain circumstances a failure to provide such knowledge may even prevent learning from taking place. In addition, the nature of the information that is provided has been shown to be a strong determinant of skilful performance, i.e. precise information about the produced action will yield significantly more benefits for the athletes than feedback that is imprecise (Newell, 1981).

How then does the athlete acquire this vital information about action? First, a major contributor to the athlete's knowledge base about the performance of a skill is that of intrinsic feedback. This has been defined as information that is gained from the body's own proprioceptors, such as muscle spindles, joint receptors, etc. (for a more detailed description of this internal process see Schmidt, 1988, chapters 6–8). A second source of feedback is that which augments the feedback from within the individual. This can be thought of as extrinsic information or Knowledge of Results (KR). The term Knowledge of Performance (KP) has also been used to differentiate between information about the outcome of the action (KR) and information about the patterns of actions used to complete the skill (KP). A full discussion of this issue can be gained from Gentile (1972) and Salmoni, Schmidt and Walter (1984); however, for the purposes of this discussion KR will be used to denote both knowledge of results and knowledge of performance. Magill (1989) offers perhaps the best global definition of KR, '... information provided to an individual after the completion of a response that is related to either the outcome of the response or what performance characteristics produced that out-come'.

Although intrinsic feedback is of vital importance to the performance of skill, there is very little that coaches and teachers can do to improve upon this 'hardwired' system. It remains the responsibility of the coach, therefore, to offer the best possible extrinsic feedback that will enable the athlete to accurately compare 'what was done' with 'what was intended'. Clearly, the use of video or film has the potential to provide such feed-back. The benefits of using such aids are intuitively obvious. In the case of video, the information can be played back on a TV screen only a few seconds after the event has taken place. There is no delay period that may hamper the comparison of performances being made by the athlete, the motivation to perform is enhanced by individuals wanting to see themselves on TV and, in addition, the whole performance can be stored in its entirety or edited for later analysis. The videotape can therefore provide error information, can be a reinforcer when performance is cor-rect and can be a strong motivating force.

Given the fact that video offers the potential to be an excellent source of information feedback, the research into the effects of video feedback upon the skill learning process should show positive benefits. Surprisingly, however, there are few research studies that have shown a clear superiority of using video as a form of KR that will effect the learn-ing of a skilled motor act. An excellent review of 51 studies using several sport skill examples was completed by Rothstein and Arnold (1976). While the results of these studies did not offer unequivocal support for the use of video as an essential component in the process of coaching and instruction, there was uniform agreement on one aspect, i.e. the interaction of the level of skill at which the athlete was performing and the method of giving the video feedback. Athletes that are at the early stages of learning a skill cannot improve their performance by observing videotapes without the assistance of the coach who can draw their atten-tion to the key elements of performance competency. There has also been some recent evidence (Ross *et al.*, 1985) that shows indiscriminate viewing of videotape by early learners may even retard the learning process. One possible explanation of this phenomenon may be that there is too much information for the beginner athlete to assimilate. Furthermore, these novice athletes have a good probability of paying attention to the non-critical elements of performance. The practical implication of this finding is that coaches should either edit the video-tape before showing it to their athletes, or highlight, by instruction or slow motion, the response cues that are responsible for correct perfor-mance. It does appear, however, that the need for this type of interven-tion by the coach diminishes as the skill level of the performer improves.

On a practical level, therefore, two problems seem to arise for the coach when considering the use of video feedback. The first problem is that of identifying the 'critical elements' of successful athletic performance. Then, having identified these elements, the second problem is a technological one. Can systems be developed that can provide fast and efficient feedback that pertains only to the critical elements of performance? These problems have been of central concern to the research groups at the Centre for Sport Analysis (University of British Columbia, Vancouver), Centre for Notational Analysis (University of Wales Institute, Cardiff) and the Notation Laboratories at Liverpool John Moores University. In Vancouver, Franks and his colleagues have been adopting a systems approach to the analysis of athletic performance (Franks and Goodman, 1986a). They have developed several computer-aided sport analysis systems (Franks, Goodman and Patterson, 1986; Franks and Goodman, 1986b; Franks, Wilson and Goodman, 1987; Partridge and Franks, 1993; McGarry and Franks, 1996; Partridge and Franks, 1996) that capture the critical elements of competition, store these events in a computer's memory, compute specified analyses on these data and print out the results immediately following competition. The research in Liverpool has benefited from an even more experienced base – early definitive works (Reilly and Thomas, 1976; Sanderson and Way, 1979) have set templates of systems' design in hand notation systems that have been followed by many other workers in the field. Hughes, formerly at Liverpool but now at Cardiff, has extended this wealth of experience and created computerized systems for most sports as well as researching the problems of voice interactive systems and generic systems (Hughes, 1985; Hughes and Charlish, 1988; Hughes and Cunliffe, 1986; Taylor and Hughes, 1987; Hughes and Franks, 1991; Hughes and Knight, 1993; Hughes, 1995). In developing these systems it was necessary to define and identify the critical elements of performance, and then devise an efficient data entry method, such that in certain situations a trained observer could record these events in real-time. When the demands of the complexity of the systems are such that real-time notation was not possible, then post-event analysis has been completed using the slow motion and replay facilities afforded by video. The benefits of using computers to record human athletic behaviour in this way can be summarized in terms of speed and efficiency.

Once the concept of interfacing video and computer technologies became a reality within the field of quantitative sport analysis, it was obvious that the data from athletic performance, that was stored in the computer, could be linked directly to the video image that corresponded to a particular coded athletic behaviour. Video scenes of performance could therefore be preselected and edited automatically. The advantages of using computer–video interactive systems in sport analysis has been detailed by Franks and Nagelkerke (1988). In that paper they outlined the procedures and hardware that are needed to undertake such an analysis. The observed athletic behaviour is recorded and stored along with its corresponding time. A concurrent video recording of the performance is made and a computer-produced time code is dubbed onto the second audio-channel of the videotape, giving the computer data and video data a common time base. At the commencement of the competition, the coach (or analyst) can access, via the computer, not only a digital and graphic summary of athletic performance, but can also view the video scene that corresponds to one, or a classified group of, specified athletic behaviours.

The use of such computer-aided video analysis has expanded and elaborated the coaching process, especially for team sports. While a trained observer enters a sequential history of coded events into a computer, the VCR is used to record the pictorial image of the competition. Having made the comparison between the observed data and the expected data, the coach can highlight several priority problems associated with the performance. These itemized problems are automatically edited from the tape and assembled for viewing by individuals or groups of athletes. After these video excerpts from competition have been discussed the athletes engage in a practice session organized by the coach. Recently, several analytic techniques have been developed that also examine in detail the behavioural interaction between the coach and athlete during this practice session (Franks, Johnson and Sinclair, 1988; More and Franks, 1996 More et al., 1996). It is now possible to have available feedback about athletic performance throughout this cyclical process of competition, observation, analysis and practice.

The majority of computer-aided analysis systems that have been developed to date collect data on relatively gross behavioural measures of performance. These measures include such elements as 'a shot at goal' in soccer, a 'check' in ice hockey, a 'possession change' in basketball and a 'penalty corner' in field hockey. Whereas this information, logged in the manner mentioned above, is extremely valuable to the overall improvement in performance of the various teams that use it, the need for more precise and sophisticated analysis is evident when considering the individual closed sport skills (environmental uncertainty is at a minimum) such as diving, gymnastics and golf. In these skills the movement patterns themselves are fundamental to the overall performance. For that reason, the athlete should be able to view the details of the pattern of movements that are used to produce the skill. It is also important for the athlete to be able to highlight the differences between a criterion movement pattern that is to be produced and the movement pattern that was actually completed. There are, however, several problems associated with this comparison process. First, the criterion performance itself should be a model movement pattern. Secondly, the angle of viewing must be from a position that can pick up key points in the movement pattern. Producing several simultaneous recordings from various specified angles is preferable. Thirdly, there should be a relatively short time delay between performing and viewing, and also between viewing and performing again. Fourthly, the athletes should have control over the videotapes 'slow motion', 'pause' and 'replay' functions to allow them to fully analyse the performance. Finally, the athlete must have some method of identifying the errors in his/her movement pattern in order that changes can be made on subsequent attempts.

An interesting experiment that was undertaken by Hatze (1976) speaks not only to this final problem but also may point the way for future use of audiovisual feedback techniques. Hatze developed an optimum mathematical model for a simple skilled action (kicking a can with a weighted boot while being constrained to movements of the hip, knee and ankle). From this model he determined the shortest possible time that was needed to complete the act (less than 2 s). The subject, upon whom the model was based, was asked to complete the task in as short a time as possible and was also told the optimum performance time. During the first series of trials, in which the only feedback that was given to the subject was the time of the attempted skill, the subject improved (reduced the time to complete skill) only marginally. In the second phase of the study, the subject was shown his own performance superimposed upon the optimum performance of the model (a constructed mannequin). The improvement in performance was dramatic. After only three trials the subject's performance had reached the criterion time, hence the optimum movement pattern. It was evident when viewing the earlier attempts of the subject's performance, before a model was available, that several ineffective movement strategies were being tested. These strategies involved varying the joint angles that were free to move. Once a model was used to highlight the errors in the movement pattern for the subject, the correct movement pattern was achieved.

These methods of giving comparative feedback have not been studied extensively, mainly because of the problems associated with developing the mathematical model and the technique of video superimposition. Whereas the latter of these two problems is now easily overcome (there are several 'special effects generators' that allow one to superimpose images and also split the screen into two images), the former still presents practical problems. In Hatze's study the motor task was simple and involved only a few degrees of freedom (the task constrained the number of usable joints). However, in real-world sports skills such as diving, gymnastics or golf the number of degrees of freedom associated with a pattern of multijoint co-ordination is extremely large, and would cause many problems for the mathematician and biomechanist if they were to try and model an optimum performance. Also, the optimum performance can only be calculated for each individual and their own body type at that particular time. Changes in body type (muscle development) due to training would require a further recalculation and a new optimum performance. The problems associated with the determination of this optimum performance are at the present time prohibitive, making the construction of a model similar to that used by Hatze impractical.

The effects of various types of KR and the scheduling of giving that KR has been the concern of much recent research (Young and Schmidt, 1992), and it appears that meaningful, quantitative KR, given as a summary at selected intervals after the performance, is an important determinant in learning a skilful motor act. For that reason it would appear to be the responsibility of coaches to provide the best KR possible. A new area of research has evolved that addresses the ways in which computer technology can help in the process of coaching athletes, an integral component of this process being the acquisition and delivery of highly reliable KR.

1.3 THE NEED FOR OBJECTIVE INFORMATION

The essence of the coaching process is to instigate observable changes in behaviour. The coaching and teaching of skill depends heavily upon analysis in order to effect an improvement in athletic performance. It is clear from the previous arguments in Section 1.2, that informed and accurate measures are necessary for effective feedback and hence improvement of performance. In most athletic events analysis of the performance is guided by a series of qualitative assessments made by the coach. Franks, Goodman and Miller (1983a,b) defined a simple flowchart of the coaching process (see Figure 1.1).

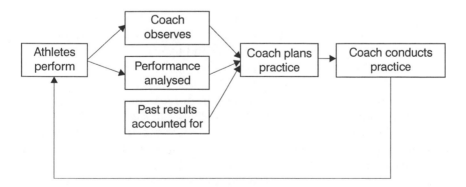

Figure 1.1   A simple schematic diagram representing the coaching process.

The schema in Figure 1.1 outlines the coaching process in its observational, analytical and planning phase. The game is watched and the coach will form a conception of positive and negative aspects of the performance. Often the results from previous games, as well as performances in practice, are considered before planning in preparation of the next match. The next game is played and the process repeats itself. There are, however, problems associated with a coaching process that relies heavily upon the subjective assessment of game action.

During a game many occurrences stand out as distinctive features of action. These range from controversial decisions given by officials to exceptional technical achievements by individual players. While these types of occurrences are easily remembered, they tend to distort the coaches' assessment of the game in total. Most of the remembered features of a game are those that can be associated with **highlighted** features of the play.

Human memory systems have limitations and it is almost impossible to accurately remember all the events that take place during an entire competition. Studies by Franks and Miller (1986, 1991) have shown that soccer coaches are less than 45% correct in their post-game assessment of what occurred during 45 min of a soccer game While there is considerable individual variability, this rapid forgetting is not surprising, given the complicated process of committing data to memory and subsequently retrieving it. Events that occur only once in the game are not easily remembered and forgetting is rapid. Furthermore, emotions and personal biases are significant factors which affect storage and retrieval processes of memory.

In most team sports an observer is unable to view, and assimilate, all the action taking place on all the playing area. Since the coach can only view parts of game action at any one time (usually the critical areas), most of the peripheral play action is lost. Consequently, the coach must then base post-match feedback on only partial information about a team's, unit's or individual's performance during the game. This feedback is often inadequate and, as such, the opportunity is missed to fully aid the possible improvement of players and teams.

Problems that are associated with subjective assessments would seem to present the coach with virtually insurmountable difficulties. The whole process of coaching, i.e. gaining improvement of performance of the athlete, hinges on the observational abilities of the coach. Despite the importance of observation within the coaching process, very little research has been completed in the specific area of observational accuracy. Hoffman, and his co-workers (Armstrong and Hoffman, 1979; Skrinar and Hoffman, 1979; Imwold and Hoffman, 1983) attempted to define the different observational processes 'expert' and 'novice' coaches exhibit while monitoring athletic performances such as gymnastics, golf and softball. One conclusion made was that 'experts' (experienced coaches) do not appear to have any standard and predefined system of monitoring performance, and therefore a diagnostic strategy that can be used to train pre-service and in-service coaches remains as yet elusive.

Despite this dearth in the literature of the sport science discipline, there has been a considerable body of applied research that quantitatively measured the accuracy of observers in criminal eyewitness situations. There are a number of similarities between the situation of the coach observing an athletic performance and that of the eyewitness to the criminal event. Wells and Loftus (1984) prefaced their text on eyewitness testimony by stating that, 'Testimony by an eyewitness can be an event of profound importance'. This is equally true for both criminal and sporting situations. The accurate analysis of competition is fundamental to the entire coaching process and underlies improvement in performance; consequently, the research completed on eyewitness testimony is very relevant to the sport coach/scientist.

Generally, it appears that eyewitnesses to criminal events are unreliable and in some cases inaccurate. One reason that was recently put forward by Clifford and Hollin (1980) was the high level of arousal that violent crime instilled in its victims. They found that the accuracy of eyewitness testimony was less accurate following the witnessing of a violent incident and also the decrease in accuracy appeared to be a function of the number of the perpetrators involved in the crime, especially under violent conditions. A further factor influencing the accuracy of the witnessing of the event was the seriousness of the crime, defined by the value of the material stolen. Leippe, Wells and Ostrom (1978) examined crime seriousness as a determinant of accuracy in eyewitness identification. The witness observed a staged theft, in which either an expensive or an inexpensive object was stolen. Subjects either had prior knowledge of the value of the stolen article or learned of its value only after the theft. When witnesses had prior knowledge of the value of the stolen item, accurate identification of the thief was more likely. The authors concluded that the effect of perceived seriousness of the criminal act is mediated by processes that operate during, rather than after, the viewing interval: processes such as selective attention and stimulus encoding.

Regarding the actual details of the crime itself, Wells and Leippe (1981) found that the focus of attention during the crime was a critical factor. The results from eyewitnesses viewing a staged theft showed that those who accurately identified the thief averaged fewer correct answers on the peripheral details test than did eyewitnesses who identified an innocent person. Therefore, witnesses attending to the thief's characteristics processed little information about the peripheral factors. Moreover, subjects who attended to the peripheral factors had trouble identifying the thief. In a study by Malpass and Devine (1981) it was found that line-up instructions to the witness had an effect on identification. If biased instructions were given, it was implied that the witnesses were to choose someone, whereas unbiased instructions included a 'no-choice' option. The results showed that identification errors were highest under biased instructions without decreasing correct identifications.

In making the comparison between criminal situations and sporting situations, although there are many differences in the two situations, the similarities are very significant. For example, in competition the arousal level of the coach fluctuates markedly (Clifford and Hollin, 1980). Also, the sports environment differentiates between what is considered to be important and what is non-important competition. For example, Olympic events are considered more important than provincial competitions. In addition, the coach has the problem, especially in team games, of directing attention away from peripheral non-critical elements of the performance toward the more central features of performance. Finally, personal biases will always distort any subjective interpretations of observed competition or practice and will therefore render inaccurate the observational accuracy of the coach of any event (MacDonald, 1984).

Franks and Miller (1986) addressed these problems by undertaking a comparison between eyewitness to criminal situations and observations made by coaches and teachers following a sporting performance. An experiment was designed in which novice coaches were tested on their ability to observe and recall critical technical events that occurred during one half of an international soccer game. Three experimental groups received instructions either prior to or following a game. These instructions varied in the amount of information that was given to direct the observations of the coaches toward a final post-game questionnaire. The results showed that the overall probability of recalling critical events correctly for all coaches was approximately 0.42. There were no statistically significant differences between experimental groups, but there were differences in the ability of the coaches to recall certain categorized events more accurately than others. In particular, coaches in all three experimental groups recalled 'set-piece' information (corners, free kicks, throws-in, etc.) more accurately than all other categories.

The surprisingly high probability of correctly recalling information about set-pieces was thought to be due to the discontinuity that is inherent in the set-piece, i.e. the continuous nature of the game is stopped for a period of time while penalties are awarded and play is restarted in some organized format. These pauses in action may be used by the observer as some framework around which the game events can be organized. The game itself has within it organizing principles that are used by coaches. This point was made previously by Newtson (1976), who defined action that is perceived, as a change of a stimulus array.

One of the coach's main tasks is to accurately analyse and assess performance. It would seem then that this function cannot be expected to be carried out by any subjective method. Any hopes for improvement through feedback will be reduced to chance. How can this situation be rectified?

The main methods used in objectifying this process are through the use of video and/or notational analysis.

1.4 COACHING EFFECTIVENESS AND COMPUTERS

In order to examine the advances that have taken place in the area of evaluating the effectiveness of the coach, one must first examine how formal teaching effectiveness has been evaluated. Research on teaching effectiveness has been ongoing in various forms since man acknowledged the value of education. While the operational definition of teacher effectiveness has varied depending upon the context of the research, there appears to be agreement that the systematic observation of the interaction between the teacher and the student is an important ingredient in measuring this effectiveness (Siedentop, 1983). Systematic observation instruments usually consist of a number of predetermined, clearly defined categories of behaviour, as well as definite rules and procedure for their use. The focus of the instrument is directed toward a critical element in the learning process and has a sound theoretical framework upon which it is based. The usual procedure is for the recorder to observe either the teacher or student during a learning situation and code the targeted behaviours in accordance with the procedural rules of the instrument. The result is a written description of observed behavioural events supported by summary tables of frequencies, deviations, etc.

While the concept of systematic observation was developed in the education field and was initially used to collect data on teachers in the classroom setting, similar procedures have been adapted for use in a physical education setting (Dougherty, 1970; Cheffers, 1972). Since the early 1970s, numerous instruments have been developed and/or modified to focus on some aspect of teaching physical education and sport. Tharp and Gallimore (1976) were among the first to employ these techniques to collect data on coaching effectiveness, and since that time several instruments have been introduced in order to study the behavioural interaction between coaches and their athletes (Rushall, 1977; Smith, Smoll and Hunt, 1978; Langsdorf, 1979; Quarterman, 1980; Sinclair 1983; Franks *et al.*, 1986).

Franks, Johnson and Sinclair (1988) undertook the task of extending and improving upon the existing techniques and procedures of systematic observation in a sporting environment. Specific attention was directed toward the recording of coaching and athlete behaviours during team sport practices. A hierarchical model of Team Sport Practice Components was formulated (see Figure 1.2) and used as the basis upon which a triad of observation instruments were developed. These instruments collected data on the individual comments made by the coach (CAI), the technical success of athletes during practice situations (AAI) and the time management skills of the coach (ATEI).

There are several differences between the Computerized Coaching Analysis System (CCAS) and its predecessors. First, when using the CCAS the coach is required to outline the key factors of performance, the categories under which the factors will be classified, and the criteria for successful and unsuccessful performance. Some researchers have argued that knowledge of such information before the observation period may produce observer bias (Rosenthal and Jacobson, 1968) or reactivity in the coach (Smith, Smoll and Hunt, 1978). However, Franks *et al.* believed that the observer needed to know the coach's objectives before the coaching practice in order to determine whether or not the behaviour that was observed was relevant to the intended task. In addition, coaching education programmes now outline a generic model of coaching behaviour which includes the use of a coaching practice plan. Finally, it seemed likely that the coach would react more positively to any feedback process if the basis for that feedback included input from the coach.

The second notable difference between the CCAS and existing systems was that the methods used to collect data in these existing systematic observation instruments were relatively slow and inefficient. Although researchers have attempted to computerize their instruments (McKenzie and Carlson, 1984; Metzler, 1984), the majority have used a

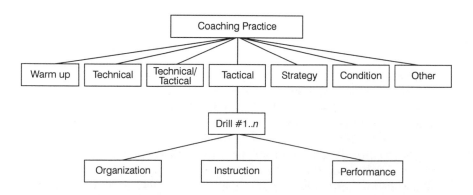

Figure 1.2 A hierarchical model of practice for a team sport.

pencil and paper method, whereby observations are coded on a recording sheet and later entered into a computer for processing. The CCAS was developed to be an on-site real-time computer driven system. A trained observer coded the coach and athlete behaviours using the keyboard of a portable (IBM-compatible) microcomputer and a touch-sensitive digitization board that interfaced with the parallel port of the computer. The area of the board being defined by a 12 inch square and an array of 14 400 switches that lay just beneath the touch-sensitive surface. A machine language subroutine was written that scanned these switches at a rate of 10 Hz. When a closed switch was found, the x,y-coordinate of this point was read into an array in order that it could be retrieved as a previously specified input event. This type of input device allowed flexibility when designing the tablet's overlay. Following the coding session, the data were then tabulated, analysed and printed to screen or hard copy. These results could then be available immediately or stored for later analysis and used to create a database of recorded behaviours.

An important feature of the CCAS is its ability to recall the audiovisual representation of the previously recorded behaviour. In order to accomplish this a computer–video interactive system was developed that augmented the previously described observation instruments. Application of this technology allowed the computer to control the functions of the VCR. Moreover, it offers a significant potential for the efficient retrieval of audiovisual images that depict previously recorded behaviours (Petty and Rosen, 1987; Franks, Nagelkerke and Goodman, 1989). The observed behaviour is recorded and stored along with the corresponding time of the event. At the same time, a video recording is made of the observation session and a computer-produced time code is dubbed onto the second audio channel of the videotape, giving the computer data and the video data a common time frame. At the commencement of the observation period the analyst can access, via the computer, not only a digital and graphical summary of behavioural data, but can also view the video scene that corresponds to one of a classified group of specified behaviours.

The purpose of a recent study (Johnson and Franks, 1991) conducted at the Centre for Sport Analysis, University of British Columbia, was to determine the reliability of data collected by observers trained in the use of the CAI of the CCAS. In addition, the validity of the instrument was also considered at all stages of it's development and testing. During the development of the CCAS, and the Model of Team Sport Practice Components on which it was based, consideration was given to content validity. A draft of the model, the CCAS categories and their definitions were presented to and discussed with a panel of observational analysis experts, members of the Coaching Association of Canada, Master Coaches and other members of the coaching fraternity. These people were asked to comment on how well the model and system described the total range of possible behaviours to be coded. Based on their comments and suggestions, revisions were made to both the model and system before the final draft was completed. Further, a follow-up questionnaire was presented to the coaches who participated as subjects in this study. The questionnaire included questions about the completeness of the model and the system as well as their perceptions on the utility of the data collected by the instrument. After having direct contact with the model and one component of the CCAS system, the CAI, all coaches suggested that they felt the model appeared complete in their minds and felt that the information collected would be useful in terms of professional development.

In summary, the use of systematic observation instruments provides researchers with a method of collecting behavioural data on both the coach and the athlete. These data can be analysed and processed in a variety of ways to provide a descriptive profile that can be used for giving both the athlete and the coach feedback about their actions. Advances in both computer and video technology can make this observation process more efficient and also provide the coach with audiovisual feedback about their interactions with athletes.

1.4.1 TRAINING THE SYSTEM USERS

In order to use these computer analysis systems in an accurate and reliable manner a structured training programme that deals with all levels of the system should be developed. Hawkins and Dotson (1975) suggested that there are at least three potential sources of error in obtaining objective, accurate data from a systematic observation instrument such as the CCAS described above. The definition of behaviour given to the observer by the experimenter may be vague, subjective or incomplete. The behaviour may be difficult to detect because of it's subtlety or complexity, because of distractions or because of other factors obstructing the observing process. Finally, the observer may be poorly trained, unmotivated or otherwise incompetent.

Training observers in the use of such analysis instruments could affect all three of these possible error sources. There are two fundamental goals of a training programme. The first one is teaching the observer the data collecting and recording techniques required by the instrument. The second and more difficult task is teaching the observer the behaviour categories and their definitions which made up the instrument. In order to be adequately trained, the observer must not only have knowledge of these categorical definitions but must understand them and be able to apply them to different behavioural situations. For this to be possible, the definitions must be unambiguous and mutually exclusive. Systematic errors that can be identified during training suggest a misinterpretation of these definitions which may be due to their ambiguity.

The training programme should train the observers to observe, i.e. where to look, how to look and what to look for? Proper training in this area may help reduce the errors of behaviour detection mentioned above. The training program should also provide some method of evaluating the observer's progress toward the goals of understanding the definitions and becoming a skilled observer. This evaluation should help provide data on the observer in terms of systematic and random errors. A high frequency of random errors may indicate incompetence or a lack of motivation on the part of the observer. In addition, such an evaluation could be used to assess the observers understanding of recording techniques.

A study by Bass (1987) suggested that a computer–video interactive training system was an effective training method in terms of training to establish an observational repertoire and maintenance of this repertoire. The training tape consisted of a number of segments of videotape about which questions were asked by the computer. The computer interacted with the VCR by reading a time code on the tape, using this time code to access predetermined tape segment locations. The observer interacted with the computer by typing in answers to the questions relating to a segment of videotape. Based on the subject's responses to these questions, the computer selected the next segment of videotape to be viewed. Incorrect responses caused the computer to review a previous segment of tape while correct responses may cause it to 'branch' to a new segment. An interactive system such as the one described would provide the means to examine the subject's data and compare it to a criterion, thus establishing the subject's progress, and identify both random and systematic errors.

1.5 SUMMARY

Coaching intervention has been based upon subjective observations of athletes. However, several recent studies have shown that such observations are not only unreliable but also inaccurate. Although the benefits of feedback and KR are well accepted, the problems of highlighting, memory and observational difficulties result in the accuracy of coaching feedback being very limited. Video analysis has been shown to benefit the most advanced athletes but care must be taken when providing this form of feedback to any other standard. On a practical level therefore, problems seem to arise for the coach when considering the use of video feedback. The major problem is that of identifying the 'critical elements' of successful athletic performance. The problem is identifying the key events to the players.

To overcome these problems analysis systems have been devised. In developing these systems it was necessary to define and identify the critical elements of performance and then devise an efficient data entry method, such that in certain situations a trained observer could record these events in real-time. When the demands of the complexity of the systems were such that real-time notation was not possible, then post-event analysis has been completed using the slow motion and replay facilities afforded by video. The benefits of using computers to record human athletic behaviour in this way can be summarized in terms of speed and efficiency, and these are ideally demonstrated in Figure 1.3.

The use of systematic observation instruments provides researchers with a method of collecting behavioural data on both the coach and the athlete. These data can be analysed and processed in a variety of ways to provide a descriptive profile that can be used for giving both the athlete and the coach feedback about their actions. Advances in both computer and video technology can make this observation process more efficient and also provide the coaches with audiovisual feedback about their interactions with athletes.

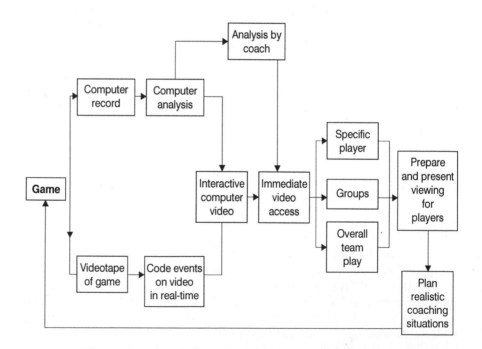

Figure 1.3 A schematic diagram representing the coaching process, utilizing some of the computer-aided analysis and feedback technology.

The use of video in notational analysis

2

Peter Treadwell and Keith Lyons, University of Wales Institute, Cardiff

2.1 INTRODUCTION

Over the last 40 years video has become a taken-for-granted aspect of our everyday lives. This chapter shares with you some examples of how video has been used in the analysis of performance in sport. For a background to such use you might like to have a look at summaries in Lyons (1988) and Franks and Maile (1991).

2.2 THE POTENTIAL OF VIDEO IN SPORT

Most readers of this chapter will have direct experience of video technology. Sports broadcasts, for example, have made increasing use of video to give audiences multiple perspectives of sporting events. Slow motion and freeze-frame images are regularly used to extend the fleeting moments of sport.

We come to expect such video support of performance in sport. If we are passive consumers of televised sport we can develop a visual and observational dependency on the images provided. It is very easy to let others observe for us. On the other hand, television can encourage us to become visually literate by enabling us to actively observe what is taking place. When considering the potential of video we ought to reflect on how we consume professional broadcast material. Domestic video equipment significantly extends this potential. With a basic VCR, we can record a sport programme and then replay it in our own time at some point after the event. This lapsed-time facility means that we can control the images made available to us by sport broadcasts. Video can become our tool.

Similarly, the development in domestic video cameras has made it increasingly possible to make personal records of sporting performance. Lyons (1988) has given an overview of the potential use of domestic video cameras for teachers and coaches in physical education, dance and sport. Video is used regularly in many schools and higher education institutions. We want to encourage the use of video by students of sport. We suggest that a video recording provides a relatively permanent, flexible resource for analysis (Dowrick, 1991).

Video is particularly helpful for coaches who seek to optimize performance. This process involves assessing and modifying performance. Hastie (1990), amongst others, has indicated how video and notational analysis contribute to this.

Many coaches have to video and analyse performance with little or no help from outside agencies. This is particularly the case in so-called 'minor sports'. At élite levels of performance, it is likely that coaches will have available video and analysis support systems. At their best, such systems are defined by the coach for her/his needs. Notational analysts who work with coaches in these applied contexts should be sensitive to the coaches' needs (Lyons, 1992).

In their links with coaches, notational analysts have to consider the relationship between quantitative methodologies and qualitative concerns. Evidence about the process of observation indicates how important notational analysis can be in adding to a coach's performance. Studies in applied psychology and sport psychology have shown that the observational skills of coaches are variable (Darst, 1983; Ellis, 1984; Franks and Miller, 1986). Factors that can influence observational accuracy include: observer state of arousal, perceived seriousness of competition, nature of observational medium (live event or videotape), the focus of attention and the 'priming' needed in this area of 'eyewitness testimony'. For examples of some of this early work in notational analysis, see Sharp (1986), Hughes (1988) and Treadwell (1988). Franks and Miller (1986) remain an original and illuminating source of information about accuracy of observation in the coaching process.

Notational analysis of video recordings can be used to enhance a coach's recall of a performance. The availability of augmented information extracted from video can inform the coaching process.

Some sports place a greater demand on observation and accuracy of recall than others. In invasion games like association football and rugby football, the coach is faced with a large number of parameters that define the sport action. There are large numbers of single events that can be quantified. These events are performed by different players, in varying playing positions and at different times during play. The sequencing of action leading up to a single event is also of importance (O'Shea, 1992; Carter 1995). In invasive games, video and notational analysis can deal with performance of individual players or with aspects of unit and team play. Video provides a permanent record of performance for repeated viewing and analysis.

2.3 EXAMPLES OF VIDEO USE IN NOTATIONAL ANALYSIS

In this section a range of studies are reviewed. Much of the published literature has focused on player performance rather than coach performance.

2.3.1 STUDIES OF PLAYING SPORT

The earliest notational analyses of sport required analysts to attend a sporting event (Messersmith and Corey, 1931; Winterbottom, 1959) or have access to films of games (Reep and Benjamin, 1968). Such work identified characteristics of performance that stimulated further research.

In association football, for example, Charles Hughes (1984), the Director of Coaching at the Football Association, used video and notational analysis to build upon Walter Winterbottom and Charles Reep's work. His research confirmed Reep and Benjamin's (1968) assertion that goals tend to be scored from passing sequences that involved a small number of passes. He suggested that strategies for attack should be adopted that maximize the use of shorter possessions rather than those that emphasis maintaining possession over a period of time.

A number of researchers set out to check the accuracy of this goal-scoring theory and used video to verify data. Russell (1987) studied passing movements in relation to strikes on goal in international matches. Bate (1988), in his work with Notts County football club, noted that 98% of goals scored by the club were scored from four or less passes and that one-third of these were set-piece plays in the attacking third of the pitch. Taylor (1988) and Herborn (1989) used a hand notation system to investigate goal attempts and 'reacher' tactics (a 'reacher' was defined by Charles Reep as a single pass from the defensive third to the attacking third of a pitch) in professional soccer. Herborn (1989), for example, compared and contrasted English first division and European international football, and found that the most successful teams mixed tactics during their games. Hughes, Robertson and Nicholson (1988) compared patterns of play of successful and unsuccessful teams in the 1986 World Cup. They concluded that successful teams gained more territorial advantage and played more possession football than the less successful sides, and forced errors from their opponents by closing down space in all areas of the pitch. Hughes and Lewis (1987) investigated whether or not successful teams use different attack ploys to unsuccessful teams. They concluded that winning teams passed the ball more when attacking, particularly out of defence, and in the final third of the pitch. Winning teams also controlled the centre field much better than losing teams.

Some researchers have focused on the physiological demands imposed in association football and have used video as the basis of time-and-motion analysis to 'obtain detailed and objective data on the movement patterns of game play and to indicate how this information can be applied to fitness training' (Mayhew and Wenger, 1985). Some of the early examples of this kind of work can be found in articles written by Brooke and Knowles (1974) and Thomas and Reilly (1976). The latter, for example, deduced from their analysis that movement patterns in soccer were predominantly aerobic in nature and that a 'high aerobic capacity is desirable for outfield soccer players'. Withers *et al.* (1978), Mayhew and Wenger (1985), Patrick and McKenna (1988) and Dufour (1992) added to this kind of research.

Video is an important resource in such research since the ability to accurately measure distance and time is critical. From the mid-1980s some departments of sport science in UK higher education institutions such as Liverpool John Moores University and University of Wales Institute, Cardiff have encouraged undergraduate students to develop small-scale time-and-motion analyses of soccer performance. Researchers in Japan have also made considerable use of video to develop this kind of analysis. Oshashi *et al.* (1988) have looked at movement speeds and distances covered by players. They digitized movement by linking video material to potentiometers. Yamanaka *et al.* (1988) extended this work to referees.

The practical objective of coaches utilizing data from such studies is for fitness training to replicate the demands of the game. Winterbottom (1959) and Wade (1967) established a tradition of analysis of soccer. They wanted to have a 'scientific' input in their everyday training and coaching so that they could give a specificity to the preparation of soccer players for competition. The development of video technology has meant that their innovative work can become even more 'scientific'. Winkler (1988, 1993), for example, has developed a sophisticated data capture system called computer-controlled dual video system (CCDVS) to evaluate individual and team performance in soccer. The potential of such systems for notational analysis is enormous.

Researchers in other sports have added to the stock of analysis material in association football. In rugby union, for example, there is a growing community of workers who are linked with senior rugby clubs and international teams. At the Centre for Notational Analysis at the University of Wales Institute, Cardiff, video recordings have been used to facilitate accurate hand notations of performance over 15 home international seasons and three World Cup cycles. Other researchers have developed systems to analyse élite rugby union performance, and these include Docherty *et al.* (1988) in Canada, Maclean (1992) in Scotland and Bouthier (1994) in France. The most recent example of video and computerized notation in rugby union is the work undertaken by Potter and Carter (1995) in relation to the Rugby World Cup 1995.

In rugby league, Larder (1988) developed a sophisticated hand notation system for use with video recordings. He concentrated on key variables linked to defence and possession. Data collected was used to give a comprehensive individual player and team report. Larder developed his system whilst the Director of Coaching for the British Amateur Rugby League Association, and it offers a prime example of a coach using objective analysis of player performance for the common good of player, team and coach. More recently, O'Hare (1995) has identified how rugby league analysts have used lapsed-time computerized notation to further their understanding of the game.

Netball is another sport that has experience of notational analysis. Although there are limited live broadcasts of netball and therefore few opportunities to record 'off-air', a small number of researchers have used video for analysis purposes. Brown (1978) noted that the coaching of netball needed to change from a reliance on subjective observations to a much more objective process. According to Embrey (1978), match analysis was adopted in netball in order to make the most of each player's potential. Some of the earliest analysis in netball produced data specific to game skills, game structure and team play. Otago (1983) analysed activity patterns of netball players. Potter (1985) developed a hand notation system to analyse live and video-recorded games. Her analysis compared the path of the ball towards the goal after the centre pass in games with that advocated in coaching textbooks. Fuller (1990) analysed the games played in the 1987 world championships in an attempt to identify performance trends capable of differentiating between winning, losing and drawing teams. Steele and Chad (1991, 1992) have added to interest in analysis in netball by comparing movement patterns in training with those in game play. More recently (Palmer, Hughes and Borrie, 1994; Longville, Allen and Hughes, 1996; Tuckwell et al., 1996; Borrie et al., 1994) continued use of post-event analysis from video has enabled detailed knowledge of playing patterns in successful netball and how coaches can then use this information with their players.

Dagget and Davies (1982) noted that there was a distinct lack of match analysis data relating to field hockey. In an early study, Miller and Edwards (1982) used video to analyse the workloads of a full-back in one game of hockey. Morris and Bell (1985) recorded games on video and performed a lapsed-time computer analysis in order to establish the effectiveness of players' passing skills. Andrews (1985) used videotape recordings of men's international hockey games to analyse attacking play in the goal circle. Hughes and Billingham (1986) conducted a detailed computer analysis from videotapes of women's hockey to investigate the hypothesis that the right side to the field is used more frequently for attacking build ups. The effect of playing surface on the patterns of play was examined in detail from video, using a computerized system, by Hughes and Cunliffe (1986). Wilson (1987a,b) conducted a detailed analysis of women's hockey in Canada and McNamara (1989) has analysed women's hockey in Wales. Beynon (1995) has used computerized analysis to investigate patterns of play at the women's 1994 World Cup.

Lyons (1988) has provided examples of how other sports have used video for analysis purposes. The growth of interest in video since that time has meant that more and more journals are publishing articles about notation and extending the number of models available to students and those involved in sports performance. We are conscious that our examples of video use have been selective and have focused on a small number of invasive team sports.

Underwood and Macheath (1977), for example, identified relatively early the possibility of using video to analyse racket sports. Since that time there has been considerable interest in the use of video to analyse performance. For a discussion of the use of hand and computerized notation in racket sports you might like to have a look at Hughes's (1994) summary.

2.3.2 STUDIES IN COACHING SPORT

Interest in coaching behaviour and coaching effectiveness has been stimulated by research in education linked to teacher effectiveness. Early studies of coaching behaviour used real-time systematic observation strategies. Tharp and Gallimore (1976), for example, report their research with the UCLA basketball coach in the 1974–75 season, when they monitored 15 practice sessions. They noted that the coach was involved in 2326 acts of teaching in the 30 h observed. This is a substantial flow of information to observe and encode as it happens.

Although Tharp and Gallimore's real-time methodology was replicated by some researchers (see Lacey and Darst, 1985) other researchers of teaching behaviour made a strategic decision to use video recordings of lessons in an attempt to deal with an equivalent flow of information in classroom contexts (Anderson and Barrette, 1978). Their methodology had an important impact on subsequent studies of coaching behaviour. Video recordings were used 'to obtain an objective and detailed description of in-class events as they occurred in their natural settings' and were then subjected to descriptive analysis (Anderson, 1978).

In the 1980s researchers at the University of British Columbia in Vancouver developed interests in coaching behaviour and coaching effectiveness and made considerable use of video. Franks and Goodman (1986), for example, tested 40 of Canada's top soccer coaches in conjunction with a group of 40 physical education students on the accurate observation of soccer videotapes. Their results suggested that the coaches were only marginally better at accurately recalling events than were the students. Recently a graduate student at the University of British Columbia (More, 1994) has drawn upon traditions of work at Vancouver to use video records of coaching performance as one vehicle for modifying coaching behaviour. More (1994) analysed video recordings of coaching sessions with a systematic observation schedule to identify verbal behaviour.

2.4 EVALUATION OF VIDEO IN NOTATIONAL ANALYSIS

Anderson and Barrette (1978), Lyons (1988), Darst *et al.* (1989) and Dowrick (1991) have all indicated the role that video can play in providing permanent records of performance for analysis purposes. Sport by its nature is fleeting and without a permanent record is consigned to personal memory and an oral tradition. In other disciplines such as music and dance, composers and choreographers have made performances amenable to repetition over time by establishing notation conventions.

Notational analyst in the 1990s have a range of choices about the uses to which video can be put. Some analysts will work in real-time with coaches and players at sporting events and provide augmented feedback without immediate access to video recordings. Other analysts will conduct their lapsed-time research in laboratory settings with the kind of technology reported by Winkler (1988, 1993). In either case video recordings provide a valuable means of establishing and checking intra- and inter-observer reliability (Van der Mars, 1989).

Central to the whole process of notational analysis is the question of an audience for such material. British television viewers are now experiencing a range of information as they watch sport. Just as we became consumers of action replay, we are now becoming consumers of match facts. What decisions have television producers made about such information? We are engaged at the Centre for Notational Analysis (University of Wales Institute, Cardiff) in a range of projects with coaches and with students. At each stage we try to clarify the relationship between the advancement of knowledge and the needs identified by a coach or governing body of sport. We firmly believe that it is our task to make notational analysis comprehensible and non-threatening. We think video is an important tool in this process.

Video and notational analysis offer augmented information. Whilst there appear to be equivocal research findings in relation to the role of video in motor skill acquisition (Lyons, 1988), there are signs that video is an important motivational support for players and coaches (Hastie, 1990; Templin and Vernacchia, 1995). Those analysis systems that allow for positive focusing on performance excellence and constructive criticism linked to error detection appear particularly important. These systems allow for a macro-analysis of performance and the micro-analysis of game elements or actions.

Video enables researchers and sports performers to share an understanding of performance. It takes a considerable amount of patience and skill to empower researchers, coaches and players to use notational analysis. Edited video material can embody the analysis so that viewing can encourage dialogue about quantitative information and qualitative analysis. At its best video becomes a transparent medium for performance enhancement. As such it is a medium that captures performance and also captivates its audience.

2.5 CONCLUSION

Video is an important tool for analysis. High-quality video equipment and video images are making fine grain analysis increasingly possible. Video gives us a chance to record, observe, reflect and check performance accurately.

Developments in digital, non-linear and interactive video offer a fascinating challenge to notational analysts. Although some might prefer ultimately to work closely with players and coaches, and provide an immediate feedback on performance, video will continue to enhance the quality of reflective practice in the art of notational analysis.

Sports analysis 3

The aim of this chapter is to provide an insight into how different sports can be broken down into a series of decisions represented by a limited number of actions and their possible outcomes. These logical progressions provide the inherent structure within each sport. The construction of flowcharts of different sports is examined, together with the definition of key events in these respective sports. The next step is to design a data collection and data processing system, so anyone interested in designing a notation system should read this chapter first.

3.1 INTRODUCTION

Before discussing the work and research done in the field of notational analysis, including both manual and computerized systems, it is necessary to explore methods of applying analysis to sport in general. As stated in previous chapters, the very essence of coaching athletes is to instigate an observable change in behaviour. Methods of analysis used to measure these changes form the central focus of the remaining sections of this chapter. Objective performance measures should serve as the basis for future planning in any coaching process (see Figure 1.3). While it is clear that both the quantification of performance and the assessment of qualitative aspects of performance are required, it would seem from the current research in these fields (see Sections 2.2 and 2.3), that the former has been largely ignored and the latter has many inherent weaknesses. This section, therefore, focuses on measures of performance that can be collected in order to analyse quantitatively the performance of an athletic event. First, analysis systems will be discussed with a view to applying them generally to either team sports or individual sports. In later chapters these systems are then extended into data recording systems. Current research work, both pure and applied, is reviewed and assessed. Finally, the recent extension of these systems by the development of fast and inexpensive microcomputers will form the nucleus of the final sections of the book.

3.2 CREATING FLOWCHARTS

The information that is available during a game is diverse and extensive. Continuous action and a dynamic environment make objective data collection difficult. Any quantitative analysis must therefore be structured. As there are so many ways in which to collect information about any sport, there are two very important points that should be considered:

1. Consult with the best technical expert (i.e. coach) of the game to be analysed.
2. The potential use of the information should guide how the system will be designed, i.e. make sure that what is required from the analysis system has been completely determined before starting anything else.

The first step is to create a 'flowchart' or logical structure of the game itself. This means defining the possible actions in the game and linking these actions with the possible outcomes, thus describing the sequential path the game can take. This is more easily explained by example. In a team sport such as field hockey, Franks and Goodman (1984) described the game very simply by a two-state model. Either 'our' team has possession or the opposing team has possession of the ball. This would be the top of what Franks and Goodman termed 'the hierarchy'. They then proposed that the next level of questions in the hierarchy would be:

1. Where on the field did our team gain and lose possession?
2. Can these areas be easily identified? (e.g. field divided into six areas)
3. Who on the team gained or lost possession?
4. How was possession gained and lost? (e.g. was it from a tackle, an interception, foul, etc.)

These questions can be included in the hierarchical structure as indicated in Figure 3.1 [For those interested in reading around the subject further, Franks, Wilberg and Fishburne (1982) developed a series of detailed and more complex structures in which they modelled the decision-making processes of athletes engaged in team games. This work is very interesting from a modelling point of view, but as it approaches the problem from a perceptual point of view on behalf of the player, rather than an analytical view from the coach, it is not directly applicable here. However, it does provide a basis for a more thorough understanding of how to build up hierarchical structures.]

The questions posed in Figure 3.1 can yield extremely useful information, although this level of analysis is obviously very simple. It is best to anticipate the form in which you wish to look at your data. Simple

Figure 3.1 Hierarchical structure of a model for representing events that take place in a team game such as field hockey, soccer, basketball, water polo, etc.

tabulated records are often the easiest to produce and are easily translated to pictorial representations which are always easier to assimilate. More detailed analyses might be concerned with the techniques individuals used during performance. It might also include physiological and psychological parameters that are mapped along a time axis during the performance. No matter how simple or complicated your intended analysis, always start as simply as possible and gradually add other actions and their outcomes bit by bit (in computing terminology this would be termed the addition of more 'sub-routines').

Franks and Goodman (1984) go on to suggest a simple series of steps or tasks in the evaluation of performance. The first one is based upon the above analysis and states:

TASK 1: Describe your sport from a general level to a specific focus.

The next step outlined by Franks and Goodman is fundamental in forming any evaluative analysis system:

TASK 2: Prioritize key factors of performance.

The final step in the process being:

TASK 3: Devise a recording method that is efficient and easy to learn.

The first two steps are discussed further with more examples in this chapter; the third task is given separate consideration in Chapter 5.

Consider our simple analysis of the team sport above (Figure 3.1). This can be made more sophisticated by considering in more detail the possible actions and their respective outcomes (Figure 3.2). These actions and outcomes can then be incorporated into a model for the events taking place in this team game, which happens to be soccer, but which could easily be transposed to any team sport. This is shown in Figure 3.3.

The natural sequential logic of the game can be followed. As possession is gained by one of the players, a number of choices of actions are presented to the player. The choice, and the outcome of the action, determines whether this side retains possession, scores a goal, gives away a free kick, etc. Inevitably this system can be made more sophisticated still; that is always possible with any system. For example, the dribble, run, tackle, foul, etc., have not been included nor have any actions

Action	Outcome	Effect on possession
Pass	Good	Retained
	Bad	Lost
Shot	Wide	Lost
	High	Lost
	Blocked	Retained or Lost
	Saved	Lost
	Goal	Lost
Cross	Good	Retained
	Bad	Lost
Corner Kick	Good	Retained
	Bad	Lost
Goal Kick	Good	Retained
	Bad	Lost
Throw-in	Good	Retained
	Bad	Lost
Goalkeeper's Throw	Good	Retained
	Bad	Lost
Goalkeeper's Kick	Good	Retained
	Bad	Lost

Free Kick – Pass, Shot, etc., and their subsequent routines

Penalty – Shot (subsequent routines)

Figure 3.2 Some actions, and their respective outcomes, for soccer.

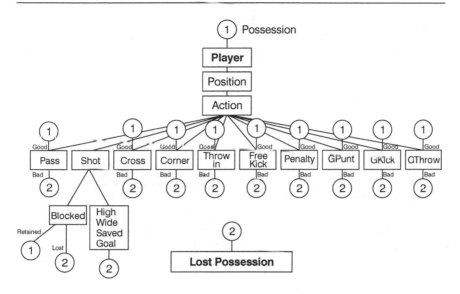

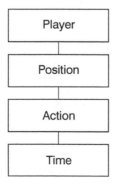

Figure 3.3   Simple shematic flowchart of soccer.

when not in possession. The difficult decision to make in designing this type of model is knowing when the limitations of the model are acceptable within the terms of reference of the desired data.

The core elements, i.e. 'Player', 'Position', 'Action', in Figure 3.4 can be seen to be fundamental to analysis systems. If 'Time' is also included then this would represent the most complex of systems. These elements are rarely included in all systems, e.g. if we were analysing the attacking patterns of a hockey team, we would not need to record the players'

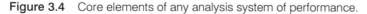

Figure 3.4   Core elements of any analysis system of performance.

identities, only the position on the pitch, the action and any outcomes (if any). If we were examining the workrate of a player then all we would be recording would be the position, the action (stand, walk, jog, run, etc.) and possibly the time. These basic elements form the heart of any analysis of a sport.

Consider the game of squash as another example. This is a field invasive individual racket sport. Other than the definition of the playing area, the logic of this game could as easily be applied to tennis or to badminton, which are non-field invasive. The system in Figure 3.5 shows the simple logic needed to record and analyse the key elements of the performance. To include the scoring system would require considerable additions to this flowchart. The basis of the 'English' scoring, a similar system is used in badminton, is that the server receives a point if he/she wins the rally. If the non-server 'handout' wins the rally, he/she does not receive a point. The winner of the rally serves for the start of the next rally. This simple logic to the game of squash is complicated a little by the concept of 'lets' and 'strokes'. A 'let' is when one player impedes the other in the process of his/her shot. This results in the rally being played again, no change in score, same server. A 'stroke' is given against a

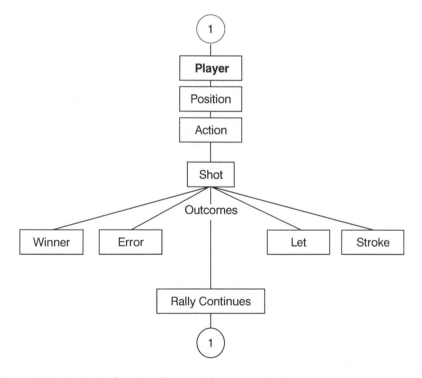

Figure 3.5 A simple flowchart for squash.

player when he/she prevents the opponent from hitting the front wall with a direct shot or prevents a winner. (The concept is a little more complicated than this, as all squash players will testify, but this explanation should suffice for non-combatants.) So a 'stroke' given against a player is equivalent to the player conceding an error.

Creating the model for the logic of the sequence of the shot production and respective positions is relatively straight forward (see Figure 3.4). If the shot is a winner then that player serves the next rally. Whoever hits an error, or receives a 'stroke' adjudged against him/her, does not serve the next rally. The 'let' ball decision results in the rally starting again. If none of these conditions apply then the ball is still in play and the other player strikes his/her shot from the notated court position. In most simple systems for racket sports, analysts will start with a 'winner/error' analysis – recording the type of shots that were winners or errors and where on the court they were played.

One way of incorporating the logic of the scoring, and who serves, into the model of the action, is to keep the definition of the server and non-server throughout the rally. This helps clarify whether the score is increased at the end of the rally or not, depending upon who won. The selection of actions or, in this case, shots, to be inserted into these models, as in the previous examples, is determined by the detail of complexity required by the data collection. Sanderson and Way (1979) used a relatively complex menu of shots, which included:

straight drive	cross-court drive
straight drop	cross-court drop
volley drive	volley cross drive
volley drop	volley cross drop
boast	volley boast
lob	cross-court lob
others	

Included in 'others' were infrequent shots such as cross-angles, corkscrew lobs, skid boasts, back wall boasts, shots behind the player's back, etc. Perhaps this selection of shots does not look too complex at first sight, but consider these facts. Sanderson and Way divided the court into 28 cells for definition of position. In the course of one match they would record in the region of 4500 items of information. Processing this data would take another 40 person-hours of work. In addition, the learning time to use the system 'in-match' was 5–8 h. This was a complex system despite its apparent simplicity and it produced the data that its designers required. However, it is only too easy to gather too much data – be sure that your system gathers only the data needed. The recording system is discussed in detail in Chapter 5.

Franks and Goodman (1986), working with David Hart and John MacMaster, both of the Canadian Water Polo Association, developed a flow diagram of water polo. The design was attack based, whereby the events, the player responsible, and the reason, are recorded. By using this flow diagram, a computer program was constructed so that the whole history of the game was stored and produced for analysis. This system is further discussed later in Chapter 5 and also in Chapter 6.

3.3 LEVELS OF ANALYSIS – THE TEAM, SUBSIDIARY UNITS AND INDIVIDUALS

Although there are many facets of the team's performance that could be described, there are only a limited set of priority elements that serve a useful function with a view to improving performance. In deciding upon which information is useful, Franks, Goodman and Miller (1983b) suggested that the coach should be guided by three elements:

1. Coaching philosophy
2. Primary objectives of the game
3. Database of past games.

For example, if a game objective has roots in the principle of possession then the important questions to be answered should relate to possession (i.e. total number of possessions, where on the playing surface possession was lost and won, who was responsible for winning and losing possession, etc.). Coaching philosophy may also dictate certain defensive or offensive strategies to implement at critical time periods during a game. If this is the case, then the analysis should be directed toward objective counts of defensive or offensive behaviours during these periods of play. It should be noted that Franks *et al.* contend that:

> The most important of these three elements is the formation of a database of past games. With such a database it is possible to formulate a predictive model.

If one knew how, where and when goals or points were scored in past games, a probabilistic model could be constructed to aid future training and performance. Technical and tactical training could then be directed toward the high probability events. Coaching could then be directed at gradually modelling a team to more fully fitting a winning profile.

After all of the significant game-related questions have been defined by the technical expert it is necessary to decide upon the level of analysis that is needed. Figure 3.6 illustrates a primary level of team analysis. The example extends the soccer model already used but it must again be emphasized that this can be equally be applied to other team games. Four areas are considered for information gathering: possession, passing, shooting and set-pieces. However, within each of these categories more detail is available. For example, when a shot is taken, this analysis should not only reveal if the shot was on or off target, but also, if it was on target, was it saved or was it a goal? Further information about the off-target shooting could also be gathered – was it high, wide or high and wide? This type of information is extremely important and should greatly influence subsequent coaching practices.

Franks, Goodman and Miller (1983b) stated, 'The information gained from set-pieces (i.e. corner kicks, throw-ins and free-kicks) should be relative to some prescribed definition of success or failure.' Coaches should have expectations of performance at set-pieces in a game such as soccer. Other games will have similar structured phases where similar definitions of performance should be met, e.g. American football, yardage on a running play; field hockey, percentage of short corners converted to goals; rugby league, number of tackles made by specific positions, etc. The definition of performance in each case will depend upon the per-

SOCCER EXAMPLE

1. POSSESSION INFORMATION
   (a) Total Possessions
   (b) Where possessions were won and lost:
       Defending 1/3, Mid-field 1/3, Attacking 1/3

2. PASSING INFORMATION
   (a) Square passes
   (b) Back passes
   (c) Forward passes
   (d) Consecutive passes

3. SHOOTING INFORMATION
   (a) Opportunity
   (b) On target
   (c) Off target
   (d) Blocked
   (e) Shooting angle

4. SET PIECE INFORMATION
   (a) Corner kick
   (b) Free kick
   (c) Throw in

Figure 3.6   Primary level game analysis – team (Franks, Goodman and Miller, 1983b).

sonal philosophy of the coach in relation to her/his sport. These expectations should be made clear to the players and should be practised. For example, a free kick that is awarded in the defending third of the field should be delivered in less than three moves to the attacking third of the field, whereas a free kick that is awarded in the attacking third of the field should result in a strike on goal in less than three moves. If these expectations are not met then the set-piece is registered as a failure. Franks, Goodman and Miller (1983b) go on to say,

> It is important to note that these definitions of success and failure should be continually upgraded to correspond to the level of performance and realistic expectations of the coach. If the definitions are unrealistic then the evaluation will not be sensitive to the performance changes.

A detailed analysis of an individual player is illustrated in Figure 3.7. It would take a very detailed and comprehensive recording system, involving a battery of experts, to gather the data for this sort of analysis. Franks *et al.* have, however, provided a very complete example of the way to go about defining the type of data required for an individual analysis. The player has two distinct categories of performance that can be evaluated: on-the-ball and off-the-ball behaviour. These behaviours could be recorded in a cumulative fashion, e.g. number of defensive recovery runs, or given a success/failure rating, e.g. 20 successful square short passes and 10 unsuccessful short passes gives a success/failure ratio of 2:1. The area of the field in which events occur could, and should, be included in these computations to give the necessary spatial dimensions to the analysis. The division of the area of the pitch is again subject to the detail required; a simple division of the pitch into six equal areas would give a definition of the attacking, mid-field and defending one-third's of the pitch. Other studies have used finer definition overall, and then a finer definition yet again in the penalty area (Church and Hughes, 1986; Hughes, Kitchen and Horobin, 1996), so that these areas of specific interest have a finer degree of detail to them. Finally, further data relative to physiological requirements can be accessed in methods of measuring heart rate and blood lactates during and/or after game action. These measures can be correlated to technical data and then inferences can be made about the complete performance of individuals within a team game.

The way of applying these analyses, demonstrated in this example, should be applied to units in a team as well as the whole team or individuals. The efficiency of attacking, mid-field or defensive groups of players within a team can be assessed. This is one objective way of selecting the best combinations of players within the tactical sub-groupings within a team, and monitoring their continued performance.

For sports, such as tennis, golf, martial arts, etc., individual levels of analysis can be applied, as those shown in Figure 3.7.

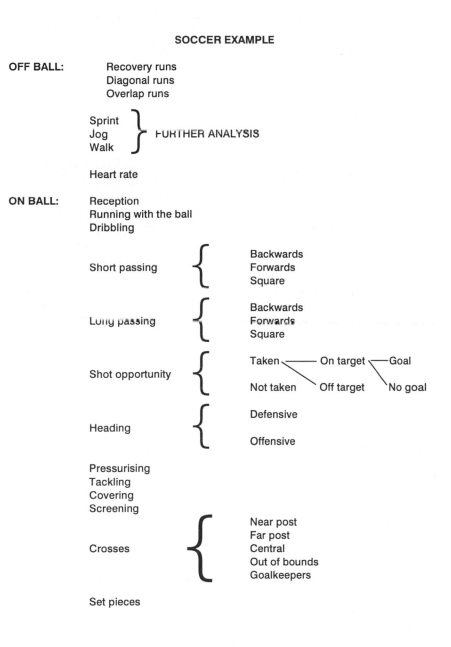

SOCCER EXAMPLE

OFF BALL: Recovery runs
Diagonal runs
Overlap runs

Sprint
Jog   } FURTHER ANALYSIS
Walk

Heart rate

ON BALL: Reception
Running with the ball
Dribbling

Short passing   {   Backwards
Forwards
Square

Long passing   {   Backwards
Forwards
Square

Shot opportunity   {   Taken — On target — Goal
Not taken   Off target   No goal

Heading   {   Defensive
Offensive

Pressurising
Tackling
Covering
Screening

Crosses   {   Near post
Far post
Central
Out of bounds
Goalkeepers

Set pieces

Figure 3.7   Individual analysis (Franks, Goodman and Miller, 1983b).

3.4 SUMMARY

Logical analysis of the form and function of the events taking place in a sport is necessary before any analysis can take place. Franks and Goodman (1986) outlined three steps in forming any analysis system:

TASK 1: Describe your sport from a general level to a specific focus.

TASK 2: Prioritize key factors of performance.

TASK 3: Devise a recording method that is efficient and easy to learn.

By elucidating tasks 1 and 2, the creation of a notation system becomes an easy and logical progression. Practising these logical definitions is not difficult but it is a skill that becomes easier and easier with practise.

The more complex the sport, e.g. team games like soccer or American football, then the more care that must be taken in deciding exactly what is required of the system. Which units of the team, or individuals, are to be analysed, which actions and events have the most relevance, etc.

The next step in analysis logic is to decide the level at which the analysis will take place. If it is a team game, then what units of the team are going to be analysed? Or are individuals to be monitored? Or the whole team? This type of decision does not apply in individual sports, but the level or degree of detail of output must be decided – and it is vital that these decisions are made early in the analytical process.

Notational analysis – a review of the literature

4

4.1 INTRODUCTION

The aim of this section is to offer as much information about notation systems as possible. The chapter is written in the form of a literature review of the research work already published in this field. Although this is written for, and by, sports scientists, it is hoped that anyone with an interest in this rapidly growing area of practice and research will find it equally interesting and rewarding.

It is not possible to trace the work of all those coaches and sports scientists who have contributed in one way or another to notational analysis. A large number of these innovative people did not see the point of publishing the work that they did, regarding it as merely part of their job, and consequently cannot receive the just acclaim that they deserve here in this compilation. There is no doubt that all the published workers mentioned within the following chapter could cite five or six other 'unsung' innovators who either introduced them into the field or gave them help and advice along the way.

The review is aimed at being as comprehensive as possible but, being aware that inevitably some published work will be missed, it is structured to follow the main developments in notational analysis. After tracing a historical perspective of the roots of notation, the application of these systems to sport are then developed. These early systems were all hand notation systems; their emerging sophistication is followed until the advent of computerized notation. Although the emphasis is given to the main research developments in both hand and computerized notational systems, where possible the innovations of new systems and any significant data outputs within specific sports are also assessed.

4.2 HISTORICAL PERSPECTIVE

General, rudimentary and unsophisticated forms of notation have existed for centuries. Hutchinson (1970) cited evidence indicative of the fact that for at least five centuries attempts had been made to devise and develop a system of movement notation.

Further, the Egyptians, thousands of years ago, made use of hieroglyphs to read dance, and the Romans employed a primitive method of notation for recording salutatory gestures. Research shows that the earliest recorded form of music notation was conceived in the 11th century (Hutchinson, 1970; Thornton, 1971), although it did not become established as a uniform system until the 18th century.

Historical texts give substantial evidence pointing to the emergence of a crude form of dance notation much later, in about the 15th century. Thornton (1971) stated that the early attempts at movement notation may well have 'kept step' with the development of dance in society and as a consequence the early systems were essentially designed to record particular movement patterns as opposed to movement in general.

It becomes apparent, then, that dance notation actually constituted the 'starting base' for the development of a general movement notation system. Arguably the greatest development in dance notation was the emergence of the system referred to as 'Labanotation' or 'Kinetography-Laban', so-called after its creator, Rudolph Laban, in 1948. Laban highlighted three fundamental problems encountered in the formulation of any movement notation system:

1. Recording complicated movement accurately.
2. Recording this movement in economical and legible form.
3. Keeping abreast with continual innovations in movement.

It was these three fundamental problems that left dance in a state of flux, incapable of steady growth, for centuries (Hutchinson, 1970). As already mentioned, the development of Labanotation represented a major factor in the evolution of notation – Knust (1979) said:

> Kinetography-Laban, or Labanotation is the most widely used of all movement notation systems.

The next 'step' in the development of movement notation came in 1947 with the conception of another form of dance notation, Choreology, published in 1956, by Jean and Rudolph Benesh. In this form of notation, five staves formed the base or matrix for the human figure, i.e.

Top of head

Top of shoulder

Waist

Knees

Floor

All notation was completed on a series of these five-line grids with a complex vocabulary of lines and symbols.

The major underlying disadvantage of both the Benesh and Laban methods of notation in terms of sport is that they are both primarily utilized for the recording of patterns of movement rather than its quantification. Similarly, Eshkol (1958) and, later, Curl (1966) attempted to develop a system of movement notation based entirely on the mathematical description of movement in terms of the degrees of a circle in a positive or negative direction. However, as with the systems of Labanotation and Choreology, this system did not allow the description of movement in terms familiar to sport or everyday life. As Brooke and Knowles (1974) stated:

> The Benesh and Laban methods of notation are more suitable for recording expressive movement and articulate skills than for gross motor activity of major team games.

Movement notation systems, developed primarily in the field of expressive movement, gradually diversified into game analysis, specifically sport. However, ensuing research proved severely limited both in variety and detail, as reported by Sanderson (1977):

> The majority of little-published research that there is in game analysis is concerned with basketball and soccer – and at a fairly global and unsophisticated level.

There are a number of texts that contain sections devoted to research in notational analysis. The best of these are copies of proceedings of conferences on football (two) and racket sports respectively (Reilly et al., 1988, 1993; Reilly, Hughes and Lees, 1995). There is also a book, *Science of Soccer*, again edited by Reilly (1996), which is a compendium of contributions by different sports scientists on the application of their own specialisms to soccer. There are three chapters in this book that are based on notational analysis. Finally, there are the proceedings of the three world conferences on notational analysis of sport. The presentations of the first two conferences are compiled in one book, *Notational Analysis of Sport I & II* (Hughes, 1996), and the first section has a number of keynote speakers who present a varied but enlightened overview of different aspects of notational analysis. Croucher (1996) presents a lucid and clear analysis of the way in which notational analysis can be used in a practical and real setting. To complement this practical presentation, Winkler (1996a,b) introduces all the problems associated with computer analysis of a sport, using his experiences with German soccer as a source of practical examples. An overview of computerized analysis of sport was presented by Hughes (1996a), but the section in this book supersedes this.

From a philosophical point of view, Treadwell (1996) presents an educational aspect to the potential uses of notational analysis. Lyons (1996) completed what must be the first historical piece of research in notational analysis and delivered a fascinating snapshot of the work and life of Lloyd Messersmith, one of the earliest pioneers of notation in sport, also clearing up some of the misconceptions about his research. The final text, the proceedings of the third conference on notation, are at present being edited and processed (Hughes, 1997).

4.3 THE DEVELOPMENT OF SPORT-SPECIFIC NOTATION SYSTEMS (HAND NOTATION)

Probably one of the first attempts to devise a notation system specifically for sport analysis was that of Messersmith and Bucher (1939), who attempted to notate distance covered by specific basketball players during a match.

Notation systems were commercially available for American football play-analysis as early as 1966 (Purdy, 1977), and the Washington Redskins were using one of the first in 1968 (Witzel, cited by Purdy, 1977). Interestingly, American football is the only sport that has as part of its rules a ban on the use of computerized notation systems in the stadium. How this could be enforced is not clear; however, all clubs that have been contacted have been very helpful. All claim to use a similar hand notation system, the results of which are transferred to computer after the match. Clubs exchange data just as they exchange videos on opponents. Because of the competitive nature of this, and other 'big money' sports, little actual detailed information was not available.

Although some sports have little notational research published, this does not mean that systems do not exist or are not used in these disciplines. For purposes of clarity and reference the following section has been sub-divided into specific sports, even though in some areas there is not a great deal of information to report.

4.3.1 TENNIS

The first publication of a comprehensive racket sport notation was not until 1973, when Downey developed a detailed system which allowed the comprehensive notation of lawn tennis matches. Detail in this particular system was so intricate that not only did it permit notation of such variables as shots used, positions, etc., but it catered for the type of spin used in a particular shot. The Downey notation system has served as a useful base for the development of systems for use in other racket sports, specifically badminton and squash.

4.3.2 SQUASH

Several systems have been developed for the notation of squash, the most prominent being that by Sanderson and Way (1977). Most of the different squash notation systems possess many basic similarities. The Sanderson and Way method made use of illustrative symbols to notate 17 different strokes, as well as incorporating court plans for recording accurate positional information. The major emphasis of this system was on the gathering of information concerning 'play patterns' as well as the comprehensive collection of descriptive match data. Sanderson felt that 'suggestive' symbols were better than codes, being easier for the operator to learn and remember. These were used on a series of court representations, one court per activity, so that the player, action and position of the action were all notated. In addition, outcomes of rallies were also recorded, together with the score and the initials of the server. The position was specified using an acetate overlay with the courts divided into 28 cells. The system took an estimated 5–8 h of use and practise before an operator was sufficiently skillful to record a full match actually during the game. Processing the data could take as long as 40 h of further work. Sanderson (1984) used this system to gather a database and show that squash players play in the same patterns, winning or losing, despite the supposed coaching standard of '. . . if you are losing, change your tactics'. It would seem that the majority of players are unable to change the patterns in which they play.

Most of the data that Sanderson and Way presented was in the form of frequency distributions of shots with respect to position on the court. This was then a problem of presenting data in three dimensions – two for the court and one for the value of the frequency of the shots. Three-dimensional graphics at that time were very difficult to present in such a way that no data were lost or that was easily visualized by those viewing the data. Sanderson overcame this problem by using longitudinal and lateral summations. Not only were the patterns of rally-ending shots examined in detail, but also those shots $(N - 1)$ that preceded the end shot and the shots that preceded those $(N - 2)$. In this way the rally ending patterns of play were analysed. The major pitfall inherent in this system, as with all long-hand systems, was the time taken to learn the system and the sheer volume of raw data generated, requiring so much time to process it.

4.3.3 SOCCER

A recent publication, *Science and Soccer* (Reilly, 1996), contains three chapters relating to match analysis and presents a sound source of background reading for the application of this discipline to soccer.

(a) Patterns of play

Reep and Benjamin (1968) collected data from 3213 matches between 1953 and 1968. These matches included 9175 goals, the passes leading to these goals, how possession was gained and the position of these actions were all recorded. It was found that 80% of goals resulted from a sequence of three passes or less. Fifty percent of all goals came from possession gained in the final attacking quarter.

Bate (1988) explored aspects of chance in football and its relation to tactics and strategy in the light of the results presented by Reep and Benjamin (1968) and data from unpublished research collected by Hughes in 1987. Bate claimed that goals are not scored unless the attacking team gets the ball and one, or more, attacker into the attacking third of the field. The greater the number of possessions a team has the greater chance it has of entering the attacking third of the field, therefore creating more chances to score. The higher the number of passes per possession, the lower will be: the total number of match possessions, the total number of entries into the attacking third and the total chances of shooting at goal. Thus Bate rejected the concept of possession football and favoured a more direct strategy. He concluded that to increase the number of scoring opportunities a team should:

1. Play the ball forward as often as possible.
2. Reduce the square and back passes to a minimum.
3. Increase the number of forward passes and forward runs with the ball of 40 yards or more.
4. Play the ball into space as often as possible.

Pollard, Reep and Hartley (1988) used Reep and Benjamin's (1968) method of notation in order to quantitatively assess determinants and consequences of different styles of play. It was suggested that elaborate styles relied upon multi-pass sequences of possession, and that direct styles of play significantly relied on long forward passes and long goal clearances. In addition it was found that there was no relation between the degree of elaborate style and the use of width. Pollard, Reep and Hartley concluded that it was important for the coach to build up a style profile of each opponent for future analysis by using this type of quantitative assessment of playing style.

A hand notation system developed by Ali (1986) recorded 13 basic factors of the game: dribbling, short pass, long pass, goal, off-side, shot on target, ball intercepted by goal keeper, header on target, header off target, intercepted short pass, intercepted long pass, shot off target and the position of the restarts. The system attempted to ascertain whether there were specific and identifiable patterns of attack, and how successful each pattern was in influencing the result of the match. It thus considered only sequences in the attacking half of the field; these patterns were recorded on the prepared pitch diagram in graphic form. The data was entered into a computer in terms of x,y-co-ordinates on the pitch diagram and compared in relation to pattern and constituent. The final action of each type of pattern was analysed to determine its influence on the game. Ali found that attacking patterns that proceeded along the length of the wing were more successful than those through the centre, the most likely result of a long pass is off-side and that set-plays involving a great number of passes increased the likelihood of a goal.

Ali (1992) went on to analyse patterns of play of an international soccer team by considering five matches played by Scotland during 1986–88. He identified five types of attacking patterns of play, each of which represented large numbers of attacks. Nine different types of final action were also defined and the analysis showed that there were significant relationships between final actions and patterns of play. Ali claimed that the large number of attacks for each pattern overcame the low number of matches analysed, citing numbers in the mid to high 40s; however, with nine possible final actions, this leaves the ratio of frequency of attack to final action to be about 5:1. This would seem low for statistical significance.

Harris and Reilly (1988) considered attacking success in relation to space and team strategy, by concentrating mainly upon space in relation to the defence and overall success of an attacking sequence. This was a considerable departure from many of the systems previously mentioned, which have tended to disseminate each sequence into discrete actions. Harris and Reilly provided a variable index describing the ratio of attackers to defenders in particular instances, while simultaneously assessing the space between a defender and an attacker in possession of the ball. The variance of these were analysed in relation to attacking success, where a successful attack resulted in a goal, an intermediate attack resulted in a non-scoring shot on goal and an unsuccessful attack resulted in an attack ending without a shot. The results showed that successful attacks tended to involve a positive creation of space, where an attacker passes a defender; an unsuccessful attack generally involved a negative use of space, which enabled the defence to provide sufficient depth and concentration. This would seem to support Bates' (1988) conclusions concerning square and backward passing which involves slowing an attacking sequence in terms of direction.

Hughes, in a personal communication with Bates (1988), conducted an analysis of international soccer in the 1980s. It was found that 80% of goals scored at all levels of international soccer were scored from movements involving four or less passes and that 50–60% of all movements leading to shots on goal originated in the attacking third of the field.

Lanham (1993), who has worked for a number of top British soccer clubs as an analyst, presented an interesting analysis of some of the data that he had accumulated over the previous decade. He proposed that there was a near constant figure, with a variation of about 10%, for the number of possessions required, at all levels, to score a goal. This 'magic' figure is 182. Lanham found that successful teams scored goals in less possessions than the average 182 and their opponents took a proportionate amount more than this figure to score against them.

Olsen (1996), who was the coach to the Norwegian team, discussed the need for closer links between the 'academic' and the 'practical', and he cited this as a key reason for Norway's success in international football in recent years. Their aim behind doing the analysis was:

1. To measure the team's effectiveness through counting scoring opportunities.
2. To measure the types of attacks and their efficiency.
3. To gain more knowledge of the match syntax in general.
4. To have a quantitative and qualitative analysis of each player.

It was particularly refreshing to appreciate the views of Olsen, coming as they did from someone who was not just a theoretician, and in that the data and information were from such a practical and applied source.

Rico and Bangsbo (1996), in designing their notation system for soccer, clearly delineated their operational definitions – an excellent example of how to utilize a well designed system. They used examples of the Danish soccer team in the European Championship (1992) to demonstrate the analyses. Potter (1996a) also presented a system for notation of soccer and presented a database of the 1994 World Cup (all 52 matches). The validity tests in this paper are sound and very clearly explained, and the data presented in such a way that it is hoped that other researchers might follow Potter's example.

(b) Movement analysis

Brooke and Knowles (1974) conducted a study into the description of methods and procedures for the recording and subsequent analysis of field movement behaviour in soccer, and to consequently establish the reliability of that method. Shorthand symbols were utilized to represent variables and parameters to be measured. Validation of the system was never clear and some of the data has to be questioned. Reilly and Thomas (1976) recorded and analysed the intensity and extent of discrete activities during match play in field soccer. They combined the use of hand notation with the use of an audio tape recorder, to analyse in detail the movements of English first division soccer players. They were able to specify work-rates of the different positions, distances covered in a game and the percentage time of each position in each of the different ambulatory classifications. The work of Reilly has continually added to this base of data, enabling him to clearly define specific physiological demands not just in soccer, but in all the football codes (Reilly, 1992). This piece of work by Reilly and Thomas has become a standard against which other similar research projects can compare their results and procedures.

A very detailed analysis of the movement patterns of the outfield positions of Australian professional soccer players was completed by Withers *et al.* (1982). They classified players into four categories: fullbacks, central defenders, midfield and forwards ($n = 5$). Players were videotaped whilst playing. At the end of the match they were informed that they were the subject and were then required to 'calibrate' the different classifications of motion. The subject was videotaped, whilst covering the centre circle, as follows from a walking start of 3–5 m: walking, jogging, striding, sprinting, moving sideways, walking backwards and jogging backwards. The average stride length was then calculated for each of these types of locomotion. The data produced by Withers *et al.* agreed to a great extent with that of Reilly and Thomas (1976). Both studies showed that players spend 98% of the match without the ball and were in agreement in most of the rest of the data, the only difference being that the English first division players (Reilly and Thomas) were stationary a great deal more (143 s) than the Australian players (45 s). Withers *et al.* went on to link their very detailed data analysis with training methods specific to the game and position.

4.3.4 WRESTLING

Ichiguchi, with a variety of different sets of colleagues (1977, 1978a–c, 1979, 1981a,b), developed a detailed system for notating wrestling and then went on, with different sets of co-workers, to apply this system at a series of competitions. His detailed analysis of these competitions enabled a data analysis of a high degree of complexity. They were able to detail such parameters as the mean scorings in the bouts, probabilities of winning once the first score was made, the types of activity that won bouts and the successful techniques employed in winning.

4.3.5 VOLLEYBALL

A method for recording team statistics in volleyball was devised by Byra and Scott (1983) at Dalhousie University, Nova Scotia. The system was designed to record only your own team and needed a 'quick, accurate and efficient' statistician to operate it. It was recommended that the same operator should be used from match to match and that he/she must be able to analyse the statistics for immediate feedback to the coach during the match. In some situations the authors felt that it would be most efficient to use two statisticians. Compilation of the data after the match required only 20–25 min. Byra and Scott introduced another system for analysing the play of your opponents in volleyball. This system was based upon six main items that the authors felt should be monitored by a coach when 'scouting' the opposition. These were: starting line-ups, individual spiking tendencies, setter tendencies, individual service reception strengths and weaknesses, and team service reception patterns.

4.3.6 NETBALL

Otago completed a study on netball players that utilized the same techniques as Withers *et al.*, detailed above. Amongst the conclusions drawn in this piece of work were the following:

1. Players in the same position demonstrate different activity patterns depending upon the tactics of their team and/or opponents.
2. Each position has a unique activity pattern.
3. Centres spend the highest mean time active during a game.
4. Defensive players spend the highest percentage of time shuffling.
5. The anaerobic alactic energy system is the dominant energy source during a netball game.

Because the data was collected and presented in a different way to the above study on soccer, it is difficult to draw comparisons, although it would seem that netball players sprint more than soccer players.

Miller and Winter (1984) used the same techniques of video analysis to analyse not only the specific movement patterns unique to the different positions in netball, but combined this with an analysis of the accuracy of passing when players are subjected to varying degrees of pressure. Not only were they able to define specific training routines for the different positions, but they went on to make strong recommendations about the need for better preparation for competition. The practice drills need to be more specific to the game and include progressively increased pressure, even including physical contact (which is illegal in netball). They went on to recommend that the role of the sports psychologist at major tournaments should be extended to include the post-match game analysis studies.

An analysis of the statistics of netball shooting for 12 highly skilled shooters selected from eight grade A netball teams competing in Western Australia was completed by Elliott and Smith (1983). Using a squad of data recorders, the performance of these shooters was recorded throughout a whole season. The procedures and analysis forms for the notation were designed on the basis of recommendations by Embrey (1978) and Barham (1980). They produced a comprehensive analysis of the percentage accuracy of this standard of player, also breaking down the analysis with respect to distance from the hoop.

4.3.7 FIELD HOCKEY

A study by Miller and Edwards (1983), using almost exactly the same technique as Withers *et al.*, but only for the analysis of one match, showed that the field hockey player studied spent 47 min 10 s walking (66.4%), 10 min 52 s running (15.3%), 1 min 16 s sprinting (1.8%) and 11 min 42 s standing (16.5%).

Andrews (1985) developed a system of notation specifically for the analysis of attacking circle play in field hockey. The system contained a substantial degree of detail, although major disadvantages existed in that the notation was merely concerned with a particular area of the game as opposed to encompassing the game as a whole; it was a long-hand method and as such was susceptible to pitfalls inherent in all such systems.

4.3.8 RUGBY UNION

Rugby union presents unique problems for analysis with its set-piece moves, the 'scrum' and the 'line-out', and also the activity ensuing from a tackle in either 'rucks' or 'mauls'. Lyons (1988) has gathered data by hand on the Home International Championship for a period of ten years and has created a sound database. From this database he claimed to predict the actions, e.g. the number of scrums, lineouts, passes, kicks, penalties, etc., in the England–Wales match in the 1986–87 season to within three passes and two kicks.

Treadwell (1992) presented a summary of the work completed at Cardiff by the team working there, demonstrating that game models were clearly tenable for rugby union regardless of weather, selection, refereeing or even coaching style. Over 40 different action variables were defined and data collection was completed live using hand notation. This was validated using a computerized system to analyse matches from video, post-event. Data from the Five Nations championships over four years were presented to confirm the hypothesis that the game of rugby union provides a rhythm for prediction of certain variables.

Du Toit *et al.* (1989) made a time, movement and skill analysis for rugby union at senior club level in South Africa in 1987. Three video cameras were used. One followed the match, one followed a forward and one followed a back in each of 12 matches. Their methodology provided the possibility to compare between positions and over a period of time and take into account the game situation. Their results included:

1. The length of an average match was 88 min 37 s.
2. 77% of each playing periods were below 20 s.
3. Average play to rest ratio for forwards was 14:22 and backs was 12:24
4. Scrums lasted 5 s; lineouts 4 s, loose play situations 6 s.
5. Forwards moved 3730 m; backs 3900 m.
6. Average of 39 scrums, 45 lineouts, 49 loose-play situations.
7. Average of 35 tackles, 24 running skills, 169 handling skills, 82 hand kicks.

They cited research by Coupon in the early 1970s that showed that actual playing time in a game of rugby was 27 min, but found that many other research papers had different figures for many of the aforementioned variables. There is a need when comparing time-and-motion studies to consider whether every researcher's definition of each activity is the same. For instance, Grehaigne, Bouthier and David (1996) used the following measurements: stop (0 m/s), walk (0–2 m/s), jog (2–4 m/s), cruise (4–6 m/s) and sprint (greater than 6 m/s).

Research into movement analysis and definition of fitness profiles is of value to rugby union coaches, players and others but it does have its limitations, and there is a need for some other important aspects to be considered. For any fitness or training norms to be taken from such studies, there is a need to ensure that:

1. A specific player/position is tracked for the entire match and for a series of matches. This will then give a global figure which will also have accounted for environmental factors such as weather and pitch conditions, importance of the match and personal attitude of the player.
2. The nature of the game is accounted for. The work-rates of the player may vary from position to position according to whether the game is fast and fluid or whether they are on the winning or losing side.

Carter (1996) did combine quantitative and qualitative information in a time-and-motion analysis and heart rate monitoring of a back-row forward. The results showed that the requirements for playing in each of the three back-row positions did vary. The qualitative recording of game incidents and training methods did add another dimension to the research. A clear analysis of the performance of England (Potter, 1996b), as an example of one of the international teams in the Five Nations tournament (1992–1994), demonstrated the power of notational analysis in a team sport, but this type of research might benefit from a directed hypothesis rather than just reporting data.

One of the first analyses of officials in a sport (Hughes and Hill, 1996) demonstrated the difficulties that rugby union has with its complex laws, in particular in the line-outs. This type of analysis is surely the way forward for the training and development of professional officials in all the professional team sports.

4.3.9 COACH ANALYSIS

A system that was not for the analysis of competitive performance, but rather the analysis of the performance of a successful coach, was developed by Dodds and Rife (1985). A winning collegiate hockey coach was observed across 17 practice sessions through one complete competitive season. A category system for event recording verbal and non-verbal behaviours delivered to the team and the 16 individual players, produced descriptive-analytic information about relative behaviour frequencies for offence and defense, starters and non-starters, and field players and goalies. Players and coach rank ordered each team member for perceived amounts of coach attention during the season, and the coach was interviewed at the end of the season. Players and coach perceptions were more closely correlated with each other than either perception correlated with observed data. Most frequently used behaviour categories included 'praise', 'instruction', 'criticism/cue' and 'alert' (management). The authors felt that at the time they were taking an initial step toward providing a predictive model for winning coaches. It is interesting to compare this optimism with the findings of Franks, Johnson and Sinclair (1988) with their computerized systems for analysing coaching behaviour.

4.3.10 GAELIC FOOTBALL

The rules of Gaelic football were changed in 1990 in an attempt to increase the ball-in-play time and hence make the game more attractive – a scenario repeated more than once in a number of sports. The rule changes related to side-line kicks, which under the new rules were to be taken from the hand, free kicks and goal kicks. The aims of a study by Doggart *et al.* (1993) were to analyse the time saved by the rule changes and the specific aspects of play which contributed to the changes in playing time. Hand notation was used, post-event from video, measuring the stoppage times due to free kicks, side-lines and goal kicks. It was found that there was a small increase in the playing time (2%) and this was concentrated on the side-lines rather than the free kicks. It was also recommended that further work could be completed to explore ways of improving the game by reducing time lost. A fact that might be repeated for other sports.

4.3.11 SUMMARY

Hand notation systems are in general very accurate but they do have some disadvantages. The more sophisticated systems involve considerable learning time. In addition, the amount of data that these systems produce can involve many hours of work in processing them into forms of output that are meaningful to the coach, athlete or sports scientist. Even in a simple game like squash the amount of data produced by the Sanderson–Way system of notation required 40 person-hours of work to process one match.

The introduction of computerized notation systems has enabled these two problems, in particular the data processing, to be tackled in a positive way. Used in real-time analysis or in post-event analysis in conjunction with video recordings, they enable immediate, easy access to data. They also enable the sports scientist to present the data in graphical forms more easily understood by the coach and athlete. The increasing sophistication and reducing cost of video systems has greatly enhanced the whole area of post-event feedback, from playback with subjective analysis by a coach to detailed objective analysis by means of notation systems.

4.4 COMPUTERIZED NOTATION

Using computers does introduce extra problems of which the system users and programmers must be aware. Increases in error possibilities are enhanced by either operator errors or hardware and software errors. The former type of error is when the system user unintentionally enters incorrect data, e.g. presses the wrong key on the keyboard. Any system is subject to perception error where the observer misunderstands an event or incorrectly fixes a position but the computer–operator interface can result in the operator thinking the correct data is being entered when it is not. This is particularly so in real-time analysis when the data must be entered quickly.

Hardware and software errors are introduced by the machinery itself, or the programs of instructions controlling the operation of the computer. Careful programming can eradicate this latter problem.

To minimize both of these types of problems, careful validation of computerized notation systems must be carried out. Results from both the computerized system and a hand system should be compared, and the accuracy of the computerized system quantitatively assessed.

Computers have only recently impinged on the concept of notation analysis. Franks (1983) maintained that this form of technology is likely to enhance manipulation and presentation due to improved efficiency. This postulation is supported by the work of Hughes (1984, 1985).

Four major purposes of notation have been delineated:

1. Analysis of movement.
2. Tactical evaluation.

3. Technical evaluation.
4. Statistical compilation.

Many of the traditional systems outlined above are concerned with the statistical analysis of events which previously had to be recorded by hand. The advent of on-line computer facilities overcame this problem, since the game could then be digitally represented, first via data collection directly onto the computer and then later documented via the response to queries pertaining to the game (Franks, Goodman and Miller, 1983a). The major advantage of this method of data collection is that the game is represented in its entirely and stored in ROM or on disk. A database is therefore initiated and is a powerful tool once manipulated.

Team sports have the potential to benefit immensely from the development of computerized notation. Purdy (1980) suggested that the sophisticated data manipulation procedures that were available would aid the coach in his efforts to ameliorate performance.

The information derived from this type of computerized system can be used for several purposes as suggested by Franks, Goodman and Miller (1983a):

1. Immediate feedback.
2. Development of a database.
3. Indication of areas requiring improvement.
4. Evaluation.
5. As a mechanism for selective searching through a video recording of the game.

All of the above functions are of paramount importance to the coaching process, the initial *raison d'être* of notational analysis. The development of a database is a crucial element, since it is sometimes possible, if the database is large enough, to formulate predictive models as an aid to the analysis of different sports, subsequently enhancing future training and performance.

4.4.1 SOCCER

One of the major developments in computerized notation has been the development of a mini-system devised by Franks (1983). Franks configured a keyboard on a mini-computer to resemble the layout of a soccer field and designed a program which yielded frequency tallies of various features of play. The path of the ball during the game was followed, so off-ball incidents were considered extraneous. A video was time-locked into the system so that relevant sections of the match could be replayed visually alongside the computer analysis.

Evaluation is an essential component of sport (Wilkinson, 1970) because it provides the coach with a means of establishing norms from the model based on the 'post mortem' in order to fulfil selection and scouting needs. An essential prerequisite of evaluation is that it must be carried out as objectively as possible. Franks *et al.* (1983, p. 77) maintained that:

> If it can be measured – it is fact, if it cannot be measured – it remains opinion', also applies to the coaching arena.

One of the major conclusions related to previously noted observations (Hughes, 1973) concerning the number of passes leading to a goal. It was suggested as a result of the analysis, that it would be extremely beneficial to performance if coaches could advise players to keep the number of passes in sequence down to three or less. This application of the research could be improved and a more thorough analysis of the parameters is required to enhance the result. Minimal consideration was given to the number of games to be notated prior to the establishment of a recognized system of play. This is an important point, since any fluctuation in the patterns and profile will affect the deduced consequences, particularly with reference to the match outcome. Teams may also vary their system and pattern of play according to opponents, although these factors are not considered. Furthermore, the existence of patterns of play peculiar to individual players was not illustrated. It is in this area that the study by Church and Hughes (1986) concentrated, in an attempt to investigate the presence of patterns of play in a soccer team and whether any reasons can be found to explain the results.

Church and Hughes developed a computerized notation system for analysing soccer matches using an alternative type of keyboard, called a concept keyboard. This is a touch-sensitive pad that can be programmed to accept input into the computer. This permitted pitch representation to be graphically accurate and action and player keys to be specific and labelled. This considerably reduced the learning time of the system, and made the data input quicker and more accurate. The system enabled an analysis of patterns of play on a team and player level, and with respect to match outcome. An analysis of six matches played by Liverpool during the 1985–86 season resulted in a number of conclusions, the most important of which were:

1. A greater number of passes were attempted when losing than when winning.
2. Possession was lost more often when losing.
3. A greater number of shots were taken when losing than when winning.

Hughes, Robertson and Nicholson (1988) used the same concept keyboard and hardware system developed by Church and Hughes (1986), but with modified software, to analyse the 1986 World Cup finals. Patterns of play of successful teams, those teams that reached the semifinals, were compared with those of unsuccessful teams, i.e. teams that were eliminated at the end of the first rounds. A summary of the main observations is as follows:

1. Successful teams played significantly more touches of the ball per possession than unsuccessful teams.
2. The unsuccessful teams ran with the ball and dribbled the ball in their own defensive area in different patterns to the successful teams. The latter played up the middle in their own half, the former used the wings more.
3. This pattern was also reflected in the passing of the ball. The successful teams approached the final sixth of the pitch by playing predominantly in the central areas while the unsuccessful teams played significantly more to the wings.
4. Unsuccessful teams lost possession of the ball significantly more in the final one-sixth of the playing area, both in attack and defence.

Hughes and Lewis (1987) extended this work, analysing attacking plays only, to examine whether such unsuccessful teams use different attacking patterns to successful teams. An attack was defined as any move or sequence of moves that culminated, successfully or otherwise, in an attempt on goal. A total of 37 individual action variables and 18 different pitch divisions were employed in the data collection program. The data analysis program employed chi-square test of independence to compare the frequency counts of each action available, with respect to position on the pitch, between successful and unsuccessful teams.

It was concluded that successful teams passed the ball more than unsuccessful teams when attacking, particularly out of defence and in the final attacking end of the pitch. As in the previous work by Hughes *et al.*, the successful teams used the centre of the pitch significantly more than unsuccessful teams. Further differences demonstrated that successful and unsuccessful teams used patterns of play that vary significantly in attack. Implications were drawn with respect to the optimization of training and preparation for success in élite soccer match-play.

Partridge and Franks (1989a,b) produced a detailed analysis of the crossing opportunities from the 1986 World Cup. They carefully defined how they interpreted a cross and gathered data on the following aspects of crosses:

1. Build up.
2. Area of build up.

3. Area from which the cross was taken.
4. Type of cross.
5. Player positions and movements.
6. Specific result of the cross.
7. General result, if the opportunity to cross was not taken.

Fifty of the fifty two games of the competition were analysed from videotape, using specifically designed software on an IBM XT microcomputer that enabled each piece of information relating to crossing opportunities to be recorded and stored. The program recorded the time at which all actions took place during the match, for extracting visual examples post analysis, in addition to the usual descriptive detail about the matches, i.e. venue, teams, etc. A second program was written to transform and down load this data into dBASE III+. This database was then queried to reveal selected results. The authors summarized their results by considering, what they termed, 'key factors'. These were as follows:

1. Take the opportunity to cross the ball if (a) a target player can contact the cross, (b) you have the chance to play the ball behind defenders and eliminate the goalkeeper.
2. The cross should be played (a) first time, where possible, (b) behind defenders, (c) past the near post, (d) without loft and hang time.
3. Target players should be in position to contact the cross by (a) individual moves to get goal side of the marking defender, (b) being as direct as possible, (c) not running past the near post to contact the ball, (d) always making an attempt to contact the ball.
4. Supporting players should position themselves to (a) seal off the top of the penalty area, (b) seal off the backpost area (not allow any ball to go through the backpost area).
5. Crosses should not be taken from areas close to the corner flag. Instead, the crosser should dribble toward the goal and either win a corner or get into the penalty area and cross to a particular player.

In conclusion the authors related their results to the design of practices to aid players' understanding of their roles in the successful performance of crossing in soccer.

The work of Reilly and Thomas (1976) and Withers *et al.* (1982) established criterion data for the analysis of physiological output in any sport, but in particular soccer. Mayhew and Wenger (1985) used the principal ideas behind these works and calculated the time spent by three professional soccer players in different match-play activities by analysing videotapes using a specially designed computer program. The results indicated that soccer is predominantly an aerobic activity, with only 12% of game time spent in activities that would primarily stress the anaerobic energy pathways. The mean time of 4.4 s for such high-intensity exercise led the authors to conclude that the alactacid energy supply system was the anaerobic system of primary importance. The intermittent nature of soccer was partly described, and suggestions for the design of soccer-specific training programmes were offered. The work did not extend in any way the previous efforts of Withers *et al.* (1982) or Reilly and Thomas (1976), whose purpose was to relate such work-rate profiles to the physiological fitness levels of players.

Dufour (1993) presented an analysis, using computer-assisted video feedback and a specific algorithm for the statistics, of an evaluation of player and team performance in three fields: physical, technical and tactical. He demonstrated the ability of his computerized systems to provide accurate analysis and feedback for coaches on their players and teams. Yamanaka, Hughes and Lott (1993), using an updated version of the systems used by Hughes, Robertson and Nicholson (1988), demonstrated the ethnic differences in international soccer by analysing the 1990 World Cup. They defined four groups: British Isles, European, South American and Developing nations, and by analysing the respective patterns of play in matches with respect to pitch position were able to conclude on the different playing styles of these international groups. They also presented data in a case study of Cameroon, who had had such a successful World Cup, comparing their data to that of the other groups to examine the way in which they had developed as a footballing nation. Jinshan *et al.* (1993) completed an analysis of the goals scored and the techniques used in this World Cup, and compared these with those scored in the 1986 World Cup. They found few differences between the two competitions. Partridge *et al.* used a digitization pad similar to that used by Hughes *et al.* (1988) and used this sophisticated system to compare the World Cup with the World Collegiate Championships. They found significant levels of differences in the skill levels of the two sets of players, particularly in dribbling and passing, and made positive suggestions to coaches at the collegiate level.

The work of Gerisch and Reichelt (1993) used graphical representation of their data to enable easier understanding by the coach and players. Their analyses concentrated on the one-on-one confrontations in a match, representing them in a graph with a time base, so that the development of the match could be traced. Their system could also present a similar time-based analysis of other variables, inter-linking them with video so that the need of providing simple and accurate feedback to the players was attractively achieved.

Winkler (1993) presented a comprehensive, objective and precise diagnosis of a player's performance in training and match-play using a computer-controlled dual video system. His system used computer-controlled assessment systems to assess physical fitness factors in training. In addition he used two video cameras, interlinked by computer, to enable a total view of the playing surface area. This, in turn, enabled analysis of all the players in a team throughout the whole match, on and off the ball – something that not many systems have been able to produce.

A sophisticated analysis of the definition of playing space in which players perform (Grehaigne, Bouthier and David, 1996) introduced new ideas and directions for research in soccer. A more practical approach by Tiryaki *et al.* (1996) demonstrated how analysis can help some sides achieve unexpected results – this research team had worked with the Turkish team that surprised Switzerland and qualified for the 1996 European Championship finals. Another practical example of the uses of notational analysis as a form of feedback, Partridge and Franks (1996) researched the actual effect of feedback on performance. Although limited by the number of subjects, the research demonstrated that the feedback did produce beneficial changes in nearly all the subjects, and that the best aspect of the feedback was the change in attitude of the players in thinking about and analysing their own performances.

4.4.2 SQUASH

Hughes (1983) modified the method of Sanderson and Way so that the hand-notated data could be processed on a mainframe computer. The manual method was modified so that a match could be notated live at courtside using a microcomputer. Because of difficulties with the speed of the game and the storage capacity only one player was notated. Hughes established a considerable database on different standards of squash players and reviewed his work on squash in 1986. He examined and compared the differences in patterns of play between recreational players, country players and nationally ranked players, using the computerized notational analysis system he had developed (Hughes, 1984). The method involved the digitization of all the shots and court positions, and these were entered via the QWERTY keyboard.

A detailed analysis of the frequency distribution of shots showed that the recreational players were not accurate enough to sustain a tactical plan, being erratic with both their straight drives and their cross-court drives. They played more short shots and although they hit more winners they also hit more errors.

The county players played a simple tactical game generally, keeping the ball deep and predominantly on the backhand, the weaker side of most players. They hit significantly more winners with straight drives. Their short game, consisting of boasts, drops and rally-drops, although significantly less accurate than the nationally ranked players', was significantly more accurate than the recreational players'.

The nationally ranked players, because of their far greater fitness, covering ability and better technique, employed the more complex tactics, using an 'all-court' game. Finally, the serves of the county players and the recreational players, because of shorter rallies, assumed greater importance than the serves of the ranked players.

In an unusual but very interesting piece of sports analysis, Alexander *et al.* (1988) used the mathematical theory of probability to analyse and model the game of squash. Mathematical modelling can describe the main features of a game such as squash and can reveal strategical patterns to the player. They suggested that squash is an example of a Markov chain mathematical structure, i.e. a series of discrete events each having associated probability functions:

The probability that A wins a rally when serving is P_a
The probability that A wins a rally when receiving is Q_a

The probability that B wins a rally when serving is $P_b = 1 - Q_a$
The probability that B wins a rally when receiving is $Q_b = 1 - P_a$

If two opponents are of the same standing then $P_a, P_b, Q_a, Q_b = 0.5$

The probability that A wins a point when serving is the sum of each winning sequence of rallies:

$P_a = 1/2 + 1/2^3 + 1/2^5 + 1/2^7 + \ldots = 2/3$ (geometric series)

P_a wins 9–0 $= (2/3)^9 = 0.026$

If A is stronger player with $P_a = 2/3$ and $Q_a = 3/5$ then:

Probability that A wins when serving is 5/6; when receiving is 1/2.
Probability of A being in a serving state is 3/4.

The probability of winning a game is the sum of all the probabilities of each possible score, i.e. sum of p (9–0), p (9–1) ... p (9–8), p (10–9). The model does ignore such things as off-days, fatigue, etc. By presenting all these associated probabilities Alexander *et al.* were able to compute the potential benefits of winning the toss, so as to serve first – a surprisingly large advantage. Also they were able to recommend strategies for players having to choose how to 'set' the game, when the score reaches 8–8, depending on the respective skill and fitness levels.

In an attempt to circumvent the problems posed by presenting frequency distributions on two-dimensional representations of the playing area, Hughes and McGarry (1988) developed a system that updated the Hughes (1984) system, using a concept keyboard for input and using an Acorn BBC microcomputer. They specifically tackled the problem of three-dimensional graphical output of the data from a squash match. Their system enabled the presentation of the frequency distributions in colour three-dimensional histograms, with the capability of rotation. Comparative presentations of data were also possible. It is interesting to compare this form of presentation with that of Sanderson, who did not have the facility of computers, and the present-day analysis systems that are integrated into their respective graphics and database systems.

Hughes, Franks and Nagelkerke (1989) were interested in analysing the motions of athletes of any sport, without having to resort to the long and arduous job of cinemategraphic analysis nor the semi-qualitative methods associated with notational methods, used live or from video. They attempted to combine the best of both systems without the faults of either. They designed a tracking system that enabled the use of the immediacy of video, and, by using mixed images on the same VDU screen, accurate measurements of the velocities and accelerations of the players, usually associated with film analysis. A 'Power Pad' was used to gather positional data along with the time base. The playing area representation on the 'Power Pad' was videoed and its image mixed with that of the subject tape. Careful alignment of the images of the two 'playing areas' enabled the subject and the tracking stylus on the bit pad to be both viewed at the same time, and an accurate tracing of the movements of the player onto the simulated playing area in real-time. A careful validation of the system showed its accuracy and the short learning time required by operators.

Hughes and Franks (1991) utilized this system and applied it to squash, comparing the motions of players of differing standards. They presented comparative profiles for four different standards of players, spanning from club players to the world élite. The profiles consisted of analyses of distance travelled, velocities and accelerations during rallies. The work provides reference data against which physiological studies of squash play can be compared. In addition the distance travelled during rallies by both recreational and regular club players was surprisingly short, the mean distance being approximately 12 m for both top club players and recreational players. Hughes and Franks were able to present suggestions about specific training drills for the sport. Their system could also compare the individual profile of a player to those of his peer group, so giving a direct expression of his relative fitness – as an example they chose to analyse some of the reasons why Jahangir Khan has dominated squash for so long. This profile was of the 1989, and seven times, World Champion, compared to that of the top six in the world (data which included his own profile). The data clearly showed the vast physical advantage that he has over the best athletes in the world at this sport.

An unusual application of computerized notation that used a concept keyboard connected to an IBM computer was that by Tillin (1990), who notated the levels of aggression by female players at Wimbledon. Each shot was given a score from a scale of aggression, determined by pace, placement and from where the ball was taken. The scale was from '1' to '7', '1' being for a totally defensive soft shot, '7' being for an all-out, attacking shot for the line from an attacking position. Aggression was then correlated with the game and match scores to examine whether the successful players were more or less aggressive on the critical points in a game, or in the critical games of a set. She found that generally players were less aggressive on the critical stages of the match, but that on critical points the player who was losing would be more attacking. Play was found to be progressively more aggressive as each set continued.

A recent innovation in attempting to solve the problems of data entry was the utilization of a new language, Visual BASIC, which enables a graphical user interface, i.e. the operator enters data by moving an arrow round the screen using the 'mouse' and clicking to enter a selected item. All IBM-compatible systems can run these software packages. This language was used to write a system for squash, which was used by Brown and Hughes (1995) to examine the effectiveness of quantitative feedback to squash players. Whilst this system of data entry will not be as quick as the concept keyboard, when used by a fully trained and experienced operator, it is again very easy to use, attractive to the eye and the extra hardware requirements are nil. It was used by Hughes and Knight (1995) to examine the differences in the game of squash when played under 'point-per-rally' scoring as opposed to the more traditional English scoring. The former had been introduced to most senior international tournaments because it was believed to promote more 'attacking' play, shorter rallies and hence make the game more attractive. It was found that the rallies were slightly longer on average, not significantly so, that there were more winners and the same errors – this being attributed to the lower height of the 'tin' under these new rules.

A similar system was used by Hughes and Clarke (1995) to analyse the differences in the playing patterns of players at Wimbledon, on grass, to those of players at the Australian Open, on a synthetic surface. They found very significant differences between the two surfaces, particularly with the ball in play time. This averaged about 10% for the synthetic surface (14 min in an average match of just over 2 h) whilst it was as low as 5% on grass (7 min in an average match of just over 2 h). This work, that of Hughes and Knight (1995) and some analyses of squash tournaments using tennis scoring (Hughes, 1994) prompted Hughes (1995a) to analyse and recommend a new scoring system in squash to try to make the game more attractive. Hughes recognized the need to shorten the cycles of play leading to 'critical' points in squash – currently it takes about 15–20 min to reach a game-ball – by having more, shorter games, more critical points will arise, and this will raise the levels of excitement and crowd interest. Badminton has the same problems with its scoring systems and the ensuing activity cycles.

McGarry and Franks (1994) created a stochastic model of championship squash match-play which inferred prospective from previous performance through forecasting shot response and associated outcome from the preceding shot. The results were restricted because it was found that players produced the same patterns of responses against the same opponent ($P > 0.25$) but an inconsistent response was found when competing against different opponents ($P < 0.25$). This contradicts earlier work by Sanderson (1983) who found that squash players played in the same patterns against different opponents, whether winning or losing, but this may well be a function of the finer degree to which McGarry and Franks were measuring the responses of the players. However, these results led to further analysis by these authors (1995) of behavioural response to a preceding athletic event and they again found the same results. They confirmed that sport analysis can reliably assume a prescriptive application in preparing for future athletic competition, but only if consistent behavioural data can be established. The traditional planning of match strategies from a priori sport information (scouting) against the same opponent would otherwise seem to be an expedient and necessary constraint. A review of work completed in the computerized analysis of racket sports (Hughes, 1995b), together with a number of papers in match analysis of racket sports, is included in *Science of Racket Sports* (Reilly, Hughes and Lees, 1995).

4.4.3 FIELD HOCKEY

Franks, Wilson and Goodman (1987) developed an analysis program using the Apple IIe computer. The analyst viewed the game from a central and elevated position and recorded the flow of play. During half time and after the game the sequential data was stored (some 2000 events) on disc and a menu-driven analysis program was accessed. The analysis selection was made and the results were computed and printed either on the screen or hard copy.

The key factors of performance were identified as: goals scored and conceded; shots taken and the results of such shots; possession of the ball and where possession was lost or gained; types and number of passes made; success or failure at set plays, including free hits, side-line hits, penalty corners and corners; and information relating to the goalkeeper's performance. The field hockey analyst formerly used the computer keyboard as a representation of the field to enter the data. However, after extensive preliminary experiments, it was decided to use a 'Power Pad' to ease the data entry.

Hughes and Cunliffe (1986) observed the England ladies hockey team to study the effect of different surfaces on the patterns of play in field hockey, and to provide feedback on performance to the England coaching staff. This consisted of the patterns in which the team was playing and also individual player profiles, i.e. analyses of all actions by each individual, to whom she passed and where, from whom each received passes, tackles, free hits, etc. The data were entered via the QWERTY keyboard. It was concluded that tactics adopted on artificial turf differ from tactics applied on grass. The rolling resistance on artificial surfaces is less than that on grass; an artificial surface is also more uniform so that the ball rolls more evenly. Both these factors were thought to be the major reasons that players on artificial surfaces ran with the ball more than on grass and that there were more touches per possession in play on artificial surfaces.

The printed feedback provided for the coaches was modified to meet the coaches' own perceived requirements. These requirements inevitably changed each time they received analyses of matches, so the data processing software had to be continually modified. This would seem to be a natural and inevitable part of this feedback process.

Hughes and Billingham (1986) developed another system for field hockey that analysed patterns in passing sequences among team members. All data were entered via a digitization pad in the specific order of player number, pitch position and action variable. The system was applied to analyse six women's International hockey teams, with match data for the analysis provided in the form of pre-recorded videotapes. Results showed that the successful teams made significantly greater use of the right-hand side of the pitch, forced more short corners and were tackled in possession significantly fewer times, than the non-successful teams. Significantly more successful shots were taken from the left-hand side of the shooting circle for all teams, although successful teams took a significantly greater number of shots at goal than non-successful teams. The significance of the former is linked with the successful teams attacking significantly more on the right wing from where crosses would enable players on the left side of the circle greater shooting opportunities.

4.4.4 WATER POLO

Working with David Hart, Technical Director, and John MacMaster, Executive Director, Canadian Water Polo Association, Franks and Goodman (1986b) defined a flow diagram of water polo. It was attack-based, whereby the events, the player responsible, and the reason (e.g. pick) are recorded. By using the flow diagram to enter the information (in this particular case, a Radio Shack model 100 portable computer) a complete history of the game was produced. This 'script' of the game could then be reviewed by the coach or players, either alone or in concert with a videotape.

A complete game analysis was also provided with respect to almost all the details of the game. For instance, for any player, it could be determined how many shots he took, how many goals were scored, how often and why he either gained or lost an advantage over an opponent, etc. The summary of the area of the pool in which shots were taken and goals were scored, and the area of the net can also be provided. By compiling the analysis over a number of games, useful patterns of action emerged.

4.4.5 FENCING

The speed of this sport required Elliott (cited by Franks and Goodman, 1986) to examine the overall structure of combat rather than the specific techniques being used. Fortunately, the rules in fencing strictly govern the nature of offensive and defensive actions and these were interpreted as the data input and were viewed as superior alternatives. These improvements in data entry will be manifest in the ease with which analysts recorded the information, and added to the precision and validity of the acquired data. A database of past international games was collected and from this database several key aspects of successful performance have been formulated. In addition, training programs are being developed that will assist coaches in the use of such an analysis system.

4.4.6 WRESTLING

The system developed by Gary Gardiner (cited by Franks and Goodman, 1986) for wrestling, used the Pascal language and was based on an Apple IIe microcomputer. This system allowed for the collection of individual data, such as type of move (e.g. single-leg dive), the time during the bout that the move was made and where it occurred on the mat. The results of each move are also coded and stored on diskette.

An extensive database is being compiled using world championship and Olympic finals of every weight class. The type of information that could be made available from such a database relates both to the monitoring of Canada's athletes and to the scouting of the anticipated opponents. Detailed analysis of most favoured moves, their success and failure rates, and moves that opponents have trouble countering, can all be accessed with relative ease and counter-offensive action employed. Therefore, Gardiner described wrestling in terms of who takes the initiative in a given exchange, where the exchange takes place in the field and the opponents involved in the exchange. Specific techniques used and targets hit were recorded only when a point was scored. By following the 'syntax' of the fight, it was possible to record live-action play. Taking this idea one step further, basic success and failure information collected on specific athletes could be applied to the structure of decisions and actions in simulated combat. Thus, various tactical plans were tested for their effect on the outcome.

4.4.7 ICE HOCKEY

A detailed and complex system for ice hockey was developed at the School of Kinesiology, Simon Fraser University by Goodman and Franks (1994). This system utilized two 'Power Pads', touch-sensitive keyboards, very similar to the concept keyboards described above. Because the rate of change of substitutes is so high in ice hockey, one of these pads was used solely to keep track of who was on the ice at any particular time. The other was used for recording the game actions in the usual way. Both pads were connected to a laptop IBM-compatible PC and the matches were notated live. At the moment the system is being used by a number of the top professional NHL ice hockey teams, on a commercial basis.

4.4.8 BASKETBALL

Hughes and Feery (1986) worked on a system to notate basketball matches. The aim of the study was a develop and validate computerized systems that recorded and analysed in-event occurrences of basketball in respect to the position, the action and which member of the team being analysed, performed the action. A BBC B+ microcomputer, memory capacity 64 K, was used but because of the amount of data collected, the software systems had to be sub-divided into separate programs. A concept keyboard, a touch-sensitive pad consisting of 128 cells, was used as an ancillary keyboard to input the information about player, action and position.

The major system, was used to record all relevant data using a 10 × 5 cell full court positional analysis. The second system, for shot analysis, was used to record shot data in respect of four defensive options using an 8 × 8 cell half court positional analysis. The statistics obtained from the computerized system and a long-hand notational analysis validated the system at the $p < 0.01$ level.

The scoring patterns were found to be dependent upon the defence being played but the patterns were also different depending upon the type of game, i.e. American, English National League or European. The three-point line had no effect on the shooting pattern in America; there were observable differences in England, but these were also non-significant.

It was felt that the systems could be improved by the inclusion of the outcome of the action, the pressure on an action, in particular shots, and possibly increasing the detail of the positional analysis.

4.4.9 SAILING

A very complex piece of work on the analysis of tactics in inland dinghy racing was completed in 1986 by Hughes and Nicholson.

In dinghy racing some uncertainty exists as to whether the racing speed of boats or the tactical ability of helms is the dominant parameter in determining skill levels. An understanding of this would greatly aid coaching techniques in the sport.

A video-based computerized notation system was developed which allowed the position of boars to be recorded throughout a race, within an accuracy of 12 m. Twelve helms were split into three ability groups – Expert, Intermediate and Beginners – based on the sailing handicapping system. Eight races were notated and a significant difference in mean group velocity was found for races 1–4 between Expert and Beginner ($p < 0.001$), and for races 5–8 between Expert and Intermediate ($p < 0.05$).

The software, developed on a BBC B+ microcomputer, was used to digitize and analyse the video data. A plastic overlay with a grid marked on it was placed over the video screen. A similar grid was generated by a small program on the BBC B+ and output to the monitor. The digitization consisted of moving a cursor around the grid on the computer screen till it matched the point to be digitized on the video screen. Each boat and two bank stations were digitized at a point in time chosen by the operator; the time, number of boats in frame, individual boat name and screen co-ordinates were stored. The relative screen co-ordinates were converted to real co-ordinates and used in the triangulation to find the boat position. The positions and distances travelled through the points taken were numerically displayed and graphically represented. A number of subsidiary programs were necessary for setting up, data files and correcting digitization errors.

4.4.10 RUGBY UNION

Rugby union presents slightly different problems for analysis, with its set-piece moves, the scrum and the line-out, and also the ensuing action after a tackle: either rucks or mauls. Treadwell (1987) developed software that utilizes the concept keyboard to analyse rugby union. Hughes and Williams (1987) developed software using a similar system of hardware (*cf.*

previous work on soccer). The system was designed to notate the matches post-event using videotapes. Four computer programs were written. The data collection program was constructed with the help of an international coach, who helped define the most important variables to be recorded. The other three programs analysed the data and provided the output. Once again the concept keyboard was used to help gather the data. The pressing of the sub-routine keys, i.e. 'scrum', 'lineout', 'ruck' or 'maul', caused the software to direct the input back to the QWERTY keyboard where additional data was entered, such as: the order in which players arrived (ruck or maul), quality of ball (scrum, ruck or maul), etc.

The developed system was used to notate five matches from the Home International Series over the past two years, involving all the participating nations. A comparison was made for each match between the two playing sides and then the results were collated and analysed statistically for differences in the patterns of play between the French, Scottish and Irish compared to the English and Welsh sides.

No significant differences were found between the patterns of play for successful and unsuccessful teams, although a number of differences were found between the patterns of play of the three nations compared to the other two ($p < 0.05$). France, Scotland and Ireland have played, for the last two seasons, in different patterns to England and Wales.

Docherty et al. (1988) analysed 27 players during matches to assess the time spent in the various activities of the game. Computerized notation of the frequency and total, mean and percentage times of six activities was undertaken. The players selected were either centres or props; eight players were tracked by four cameras in 5 min intervals for a minimum of 40 min per match. The players spent:

1. 47% of the time walking and jogging.
2. 6% of the time running and sprinting.
3. 9% of the time tackling and competing for the ball.
4. 38% of the time standing.
5. Centres sprinted for 3% of the time, the props for less than 1% of the time.
6. Players spend 85% of the match in low-intensity activity.

The system of Hughes and Williams (1987) was upgraded and transferred to IBM software architecture and used to investigate the effects of the rule changes in rugby union in the 1991–92 season. It was found that the ball in play time actually decreased, and the only other significant changes were to the rucks and mauls. These systems were also used to investigate the 1991 World Cup (Hughes and White, 1996; Stanhope and Hughes, 1996), comprehensive analyses of the way in which points were scored, the way the successful and unsuccessful teams used their respective threequarters and forwards. This whole analysis of this tournament also places all these data onto a database, which will be invaluable as it will enable longitudinal comparisons across tournaments to be made.

Hughes, Kitchen and Horobin (1996) used some of this data as a comparative norm with which to compare similar analyses of women's international rugby matches taken from the Five Nations championship. These data showed very clearly the result of the stark physiological differences between male and female rugby players in the comparative figures in distances gained from kicks and yardage gained, in all positions, in running with the ball. There were also indications that the women's game is still in the early stages of technical development and further studies should be repeated in years to come to help the coaches remain aware of the shortcomings.

4.4.11 AMERICAN FOOTBALL

A computerized notation system for American football was developed by Hughes and Charlish (1987) using a DEC-20 mainframe computer. The amount of data being collected precluded the use of a microcomputer. The data was collected using the QWERTY keyboard, all relevant variables being assigned a certain coding and positioning in the play. The structure of the analysis allowed information to be collected on:

1. The position of the play.
2. Offensive and defensive formations prior to the snap of the ball.
3. The action and result of the play.

The notation was performed post-event using videotapes of television games.

The system was validated by comparing the computerized results of one whole match with data recorded by hand, using slow motion replays to ensure accuracy. There was no significant difference between the two sets of results ($p < 0.01$).

An analysis of 329 offensive plays produced results that showed no significant difference in the patterns of play of winning and losing offences. However, the results revealed trends that further analysis would confirm the existence of differing patterns. The analysis also showed that from plays which started within 10–20 yards of the defence's end zone, a significantly higher proportion ($p < 0.005$) of passing plays resulted in touchdowns compared to running plays.

4.4.12 CRICKET

Cricket has traditionally been a statistically orientated sport, the complexity of the scoring book is testimony to this fact. Consequently, both players and coaches have always been amenable to the introduction of methods of refining this collection, and processing, of data, which cannot be said of a number of other sports. A number of different manual systems exist. In 1987, Croucher introduced his system called 'Cricket-Stat', which would seem , from the literature, to be a commercial product. It combines a manual notation system with an IBM computer to process the results. This involves notating a match onto special recording sheets and then transferring this data to the computer. Croucher claims that the notation can, 'with a little practice, be easily done by one person'. He also claims that although the software is 'user-friendly', the data entry will take some time, depending upon the skill and speed of the user. He goes on to point out that the output includes over 50 pages of tables per innings, which means over 200 pages of tables for a four-innings match. After pointing out that the interpretation of the output must be completed by the user, Croucher claims that not only will the system make it 'easier to devise game strategies' but 'Cricket-Stat' will make players consider more carefully how they play the game. It would seem that the system could transpose a one-day match into a five-day study, with so much detail and data.

4.4.13 VOLLEYBALL

Quantitative analysis of performance in volleyball is not a new concept, but Eom (1988) included an extra degree of sophistication in his system by designing a quantitative assessment of the degree of difficulty of the skill required for the action being notated. Several studies have already attempted to collect objective data for volleyball (Baacke, 1982; Penner, 1987), but, as in most notation studies, when an action or skill was being notated, no account was taken of the quality of the skill performance that preceded it. In addition, these skills were treated in the same manner, disregarding whether they occurred in an attack process or in a counter-attack process.

A sample of 164 games from the 3rd FIVB Korean Cup (1987) was taped for analysis. A computer interactive recording system was used to store and analyse the data in sequential form. A five-point numerical rating system, developed by Eom (1987), was used to quantify the playing actions. Stochastic analysis using a Markov model (first- and second-order) was applied to detect the sequential dependencies of the events in each process. The data, represented in the form of a transition matrix, was analysed using a chi-square test to investigate whether a skill that occurred at time $(t + 1)$ or time $(t + 2)$ is dependent upon a skill occurring at time t. Further analyses were conducted to compare a transitional matrix in the attack process with that in the counter-attack process and among the quick, medium and high attack.

Initial work with this system has shown the following results:

1. The transition probability matrices were not equivalent for the attack process and the counter-attack process. For the attack process, success was more dependent upon the preceding events (i.e. 0.81 between the serve reception and the set, and 0.83 between the set and spike).
2. For both attack and counterattack processes, the second-order transition probabilities were highly significant. That is, spike success was strongly dependent upon the quality of the pass, 0.79 and 0.73, respectively.
3. Among the types of spike, success in the quick and medium attack were highly dependent upon the quality of the set, 0.87 and 0.92, respectively.

Handford and Smith (1996) described the development and application of a systematic approach to performance analysis. They went about the problem of designing a computer-based system and carefully explained how the software was put together and also the detailed analytical systems associated with the data collection They used the World Student Games in Sheffield (1991) to establish reliability and validity of their systems, and also as a way of involving the coaches in the system's development in a practical way. They produced satisfactory intra- and inter-observer reliability tests, fundamental to any sound system.

4.4.14 AUSTRALIAN RULES FOOTBALL

Patrick and McKenna (1988) developed a system for the computerized analysis of Australian rules football which they called the CABER system, a mnemonic for 'Capture and Analysis of Behavioural Events in Real-time'. Data recording consisted of entering quantitative and qualitative information about the game. The quantitative data included all the actions in the game such as ball possessions and disposals, team events, and defensive and offensive actions. The qualitative data included adjectival qualifiers such as the quality (good, poor), pressure (uncontested, contested) and the location (wings, back pocket). Two operators were required to use the system, one verbalizing the actions, the other entering the data on a special 'football keyboard'. The system could be used for analysis of single player analysis, systematic breach of the rules and the defensive pressure placed on the possessions of the opposition. The authors were unable to differentiate between successful and unsuccessful teams on the basis of a simple summation of match statistics, stating that a complex interaction of many variables affects the outcome of the game. They are currently working on this interaction, which may have importance not only in Australian rules football but also Gaelic football.

McKenna *et al.* (1988) completed a computer–video analysis of activity patterns in Australian Rules Football. Four Victorian Football League players were videotaped over a complete game. The activity of each player was classified according to: (1) movement type and (2) game-related activities. Movement types used were the same as earlier reported (Mayhew and Wenger, 1985), comprising stationary, walk, jog and high-intensity run. The game related activities were comprised of all ball contacts, body contacts (including tackles and bumps), and physical efforts such as jumps, dives and fall over/get up. The action was then further sub-divided into high-intensity and low-intensity activities.

A computer–video system was used in the analysis. Analysis was conducted from a videotape replay, although the authors stated that real-time analysis was possible. The authors claimed high reliability was found between repeated notations of the same section of match ($r \geq 0.92$ for the total time and $r \geq 0.83$ for the number of occurrences of each activity), although the latter figure would seem to be rather low.

The players analysed, who all played as 'rovers' in Australian Rules Football, spent 94% of their time in low-intensity activities. The mean duration of high-intensity activities was 2.7 s, with 65% of all high-intensity efforts less than 4.0 s and 80% less than 6.0 s. McKenna *et al.* compared their data with that for Australian soccer players (Withers *et al.*, 1982) and English soccer players (Reilly and Thomas, 1976). The physiological implications of their results were discussed with a view to making recommendations for the specific training needs of the sport.

4.4.15 COMPUTERIZED COACHING ANALYSIS SYSTEM (CCAS)

This system, developed by Franks, Johnson and Sinclair (1988), was a natural extension of the work done by Franks *et al.* (1986). It is based upon the model of team sport practice components. Although researchers have attempted to computerize their coaching assessment instruments (McKenzie and Carlson, 1984; Metzler, 1984), the majority use a pencil and paper method to record observations, and then transfer them later to the computer for processing. The CCAS was developed to be an on-site real-time computer driven system. It consisted of three interactive computer programs that structure the acquisition, immediate analysis and storage of pertinent observable behaviours displayed by coaches and athletes during a typical coaching practice. A trained observer codes the coach and athlete behaviours using the keyboard of a portable (IBM-compatible) microcomputer and a touch-sensitive digitization board (a 'Power Pad') that interfaces with the parallel port of the computer.

At present this system has been tested with two team sports. Initial pilot tests were carried out with the Canadian Soccer Association's

Coaching education program. A comprehensive series of experiments (Johnson, 1987) was then carried out to determine the intra- and inter-observer reliability ratings while using the system to analyse coaching and athlete behaviour in a basketball practice. In addition a training program was implemented that used computer interactive video technology. This training program was found to be reliable (greater than 80% intra- and inter-observer agreement on all categories of all instruments) and the training program could produce observers with this level of expertise in approximately 4 h. Further experiments are currently being conducted using various team sports to test the system's generalizability.

Franks (1992) presented an integrated view of how computerized analysis systems can help in the education of the coach. First, through the use of computer-aided instructional packages the coach can gain knowledge about how individual athletes acquire and control skilled actions. Secondly, Franks offered the computer–video interactive system as a way in which coaches can learn about analysis of competitive performance. Finally, he presented the coach analysis systems as a way for coaches to gain objective information about their interaction with their athletes during coaching and training sessions.

4.4.16 COMPUTER-CONTROLLED VIDEO

One of the most exciting and potentially significant outgrowths of computerized sport analysis is the recent advent of interactive video technology. The ability of computers to control the video image has now made it possible to enhance existing sport specific analytical procedures. An inexpensive IBM-based system was described by Franks, Nagelkerke and Goodman (1989). The system operates in conjunction with an IBM XT (or compatible) and requires a circuit board to be resident within the computer. The system was designed to interact with a VCR that has a 34-pin remote control outlet (some Sony and Panasonic AG and NV series). The interaction between the computer and the VCR was outlined as well the technical details of the circuit boards. In addition, several software programs were given that demonstrate the control features of the circuit board.

Franks and Nagelkerke (1988) developed such a system for the team sport of field hockey. The analysis system, described by Franks and Goodman (1986), required a trained analyst to input, via a digitization pad, the game related data into a microcomputer. Following the field hockey game, a menu-driven analysis program allowed the analyst to query the sequentially stored time–data pairs. Because of the historical nature of these game related sequences of action, it was possible to perform both post-event and pre-event analysis on the data. That is to say, questions relating to what led up to a particular event or what followed a particular event could now be asked. In addition to presenting the sports analyst with digital and graphical data of team performance, the computer was also programmed to control and edit the videotape action of the game action.

The interactive video–computer program accessed the times of all specific events such as goals, shots, set plays, etc., from the stored database. Then, from a menu of these events, the analyst could choose to view any or all of these events within one specific category. The computer was programmed to control the video such that it found the time of the event on the video and then played back that excerpt of game action. It was also possible to review the same excerpt with an extended 'lead in' or 'trail' time around that chosen event. This system is at present being tested and used by the Canadian national women's hockey team.

The system has recently been modified for use to analyse and provide feedback for ice hockey and soccer. A number of professional ice hockey clubs are currently using it, as well as the national Canadian team. The soccer system has only recently become available, and at the time of writing there are no examples of its application.

4.4.17 SUMMARY

To summarize the developments in computerized notational analysis, one can trace the innovative steps used in overcoming the two main problems of dealing with computers – data input and data output.

The initial difficulty in using a computer is entering information. The traditional method is using the QWERTY keyboard. However, unless the operator possesses considerable skills, this can be a lengthy and boring task. Assigning codes to the different actions, positions or players that have some meaning to the operator can make the key entry easier. The next step is to assign areas of the keyboard to represent areas of the pitch, numbers for the players and another section of the keyboard for the actions (see Hughes and Cunliffe, 1986). An alternative to this approach to his problem is to use a specifically designed keyboard (Franks *et al.*, 1983; Alderson and McKinnon, 1985), that has key entry designed ergonomically to meet the particular needs of the sport under analysis.

The major innovation, however, in this area, that eased considerably the problems of data entry both in terms of skill requirements and learning time, was the introduction of the digitization pad. In Britain most workers have utilized the 'concept keyboard' (Hughes and Feery, 1986; Sharp, 1986; Treadwell, 1988) whilst in Canada, Ian Franks, at his Centre for Sport Analysis at University of British Columbia, Vancouver, has utilized another pad that has the trade name 'Power Pad' (Franks *et al.*,

1986). These are programmable, touch-sensitive, pads, over which one can place an overlay that has a graphic representation of the pitch and aptly labelled keypad areas for the actions and the players. This considerably reduces the skill required for fast data entry and the learning time required to gain this level of skill.

Another highlight, that is still awaited, is the introduction of voice entry of data into the computer Although Taylor and Hughes (1988) were severely limited by the amounts of funding for their research, they were still able to demonstrate that this type of system can and will be used by the computer 'non-expert'. Although systems are expensive at the moment, computer technology is an environment of rapidly decreasing costs, even as the technology races ahead, so one can expect that this will be the next big step forward in the use of computers, in general, and sports systems in particular.

Notational analysis, whilst having been the platform for considerable research, has its foundations in practical applications in sport. In these situations, it is imperative that the output is as immediate as possible, and, perhaps more important, clear, concise and to the point. Consequently, the second strand of innovation that one can trace through the development of different systems is that of better output.

The first systems produced tables and tables of data, incorporated with statistical significance tests, that sport scientists had difficulty in interpreting; pity the coach or the athlete attempting to adopt these systems. Some researchers attempted to tackle the problem (Sanderson and Way, 1977), but not everyone would agree that this type of presentation was any easier to understand than the tables of data. Representations of frequency distributions across graphics of the playing area (Hughes, Kitchen and Horobin, 1986), traces of the path of the ball prior to a shot or a goal (Hughes and Cunliffe, 1986; Franks and Nagelkerke, 1989) and similar ploys have made the output of some systems far more attractive and easier to understand. The system developed by Hughes and McGarry specifically tackled this problem and produced some three-dimensional colour graphics that presented the data in a compact form, very easy to assimilate. Finally, the computer-controlled video, interactive systems (Franks, Nagelkerke and Goodman, 1989) present the users of analysis systems the potential of immediate analysis combined with the visual presentation of the feedback of the action.

4.5 THE FUTURE OF NOTATIONAL ANALYSIS

In terms of technological development, notational analysis will undoubtedly move as rapidly as the developments in computer technology and video technology as we approach the 21st century. There are two developments that will almost certainly happen over the next few years. The first will be the development of 'all-purpose', generic software. Work in some centres has almost reached this point now. Another technological advance that will make computerized notation more easily handled by the non-specialist will be the introduction of 'voice-over' methods of data entry. Taylor and Hughes (1988) have demonstrated that this is possible now, but relatively expensive at present day prices. These are expected to drop rapidly over the next couple of years and voice interaction should therefore be a natural extension of any computing hardware system.

The integration of both these technological developments with computerized video feedback will enable both detailed objective analysis of competition and the immediate presentation of the most important elements of play. Computerized systems on sale now enable the analysis, selection, compilation and re-presentation of any game on video to be processed in a matter of seconds. The coach can then use this facility as a visual aid to support the detailed analysis. Franks (1988) devised a more detailed model of the feedback process that could be possible with this type of technology.

As these systems are used more and more, and larger databases are created, a clearer understanding of each sport will follow. The mathematical approach, typified by Eom (1988) and McGarry and Franks (1994, 1995), will make these systems more and more accurate in their predictions. At the moment the main functions of the systems are analysis, diagnosis and feedback – few sports have gathered enough data to allow prediction of optimum tactics in set situations. Where large databases have been collected (e.g. soccer and squash) models of the games have been created and this has enabled predictive assertions of winning tactics. This has led to some controversy, particularly in soccer, due to the lack of understanding of the statistics involved and their range of application. Nevertheless, the function of the systems could well change, particularly as the financial rewards in certain sports are providing such large incentives for success. The following glimpse (Franks, 1996b) into future integrated match analyses should help illustrate this point:

> The analysis from the match has been established and after reviewing a brief summary of the game statistics the coaching staff are concerned that late in the game crosses from the right side of the team's attack were being delivered behind the defenders and close to the opposing team's goalkeeper. The result being that the front strikers were not able to contact the ball despite making the correct approach runs (information also gained from the match summary). The coaching staff call for videodisc (immediate recovery) excerpts of each crossing opportunity from the right side of the field in the last 15 min of play. Along with this visual information, the computer retrieves other on-line information that is presented in the

inset of the large projected video image. This information relates to the physiological condition of the player(s) under review leading up to the crossing opportunity. In addition a three-dimensional analysis of the crossing technique is presented as each cross is viewed. One player had been responsible for these crosses. Upon advice from the consulting exercise physiologist the coaching staff have concerns about the telemetered respiration and heart rate of the player. A time–motion analysis of the player's movements in the second half of the game is called for, as well as a profile of the player's fitness level and physiotherapy report prior to the game. These are also retrieved from the same videodisc. After considering the information the coaching staff record their recommendations for team and individual improvement and move on to the next problem provided by a comparison of the predicted data and real data. A computer program running in the background is busy compiling instances of good performance (successful crosses) and poor performance that will make up an educational modelling program for the individual player to view. Also the expert system of coaching practice is being queried about the most appropriate practice for remedial treatment of crossing in this specific setting. An individual fitness programme is prescribed when another expert system is queried. The final question that is asked of the mathematical model is 'given these changes are implemented, what is the likelihood that the number of crosses in the final 15 min from the right side of the field will be more successful against our next opponent and what is their expected effect on match outcome?

All aspects of the above scenario are either in place or are under investigation in notational analysis laboratories throughout the world.

Technological advances aside, the real future of notational analysis lies in the growing awareness by coaches, athletes and sports scientists of its potential applications to all sports. Whether the most sophisticated and expensive of systems is being used, or a simple pen and paper analysis, as long as either system produces accurate results that are easy to understand, then coaches, athletes and sports scientists will increase their insights into sport performance.

How to develop a notation system

5

5.1 INTRODUCTION

The aim of this chapter is to enable you to be able to develop your own hand notation system. No matter how simple or complicated you wish to make it – the same underlying principles apply. If you are hoping to develop a computerized system, the same logical process must be followed, so this section is a vital part of that developmental process too. To gain the most benefit from this chapter, Chapters 3 and 4 should have also been read.

5.2 DATA COLLECTION SYSTEMS

FIRST STEP: You must decide what you want from your system before you design the system.

This does sound a little odd but the reason for this lies in the fact that notation systems provide masses of data. Unless you have a crystal clear idea about what data you wish to collect, then you will find that your system will collect confusing, and sometimes irrelevant, information. Keep in mind the old adage about not seeing the wood for the trees. Time spent working on what form(s) your output might take can save a great deal of frustration later. Most importantly, it also simplifies the job of defining input. Having once decided what you want, the process of designing your data collection system is simple and straightforward. Often the most difficult part is making sense from the mass of data – this is true for all analysis systems. Here too, it pays to plan ahead.

Before collecting any data, decide how it is going to be presented. If you are going to use statistics to process the data, know exactly which statistical techniques are to be applied.

This will be discussed in more detail later in Sections 5.4 and 5.5.

The simplest way of starting is to consider a basic example. A field hockey coach may wish to have more information about the shooting patterns, or lack of them, for her/his team. Consequently this coach will need an output from this system consisting of:

1. Position of the pass preceding the shot (the assist).
2. Player who made the pass.
3. Type of pass.
4. Position from which the shot was taken.
5. Which player made the shot.
6. Outcome of the shot, i.e. goal, save, block, miss (wide), miss (high), corner, etc.

(If field hockey is not a game with which you are familiar, this method will as easily apply to any field-invasive team sport such as basketball, soccer, water polo, lacrosse, etc.)

The data needed to be notated in this example is relatively simple. The next step is to assign notation symbols for each of the above variables. First divide the pitch into segments or cells and give each one a code – this could be either a number or a letter, but there are usually advantages in using specifically one or the other. Deciding upon how the playing surface should be divided is not always as simple as it might appear. Using small cells does enable fine definition of the positions at which actions take place, but the more cells you have the more data you have to collect in order to have significant numbers of actions in each cell. If in doubt, err on the side of simplicity – the most influential research on soccer was done with the pitch divided into three, i.e. the defending third, the middle third and the attacking third. The hockey pitch in Figure 5.1(a) is at the other extreme of definition with a large number of position cells.

As position, player, action, etc., are notated it is often useful to have the codes entered in the system alternating from letter to number to letter. This makes interpretation of the data much simpler. Any saving that can be made in the number of items entered, can also mean a large saving in time – often the difference in being able to notate 'in match' or not. It is easy to identify players by their shirt number (if they have one of course), but if there are more than nine in a team or squad then you have to note two digits instead of one. Some systems in the past have employed letters for the players '10' and '11'. In Figure 5.1(a), letters have been used to differentiate between respective areas of the pitch rather than numbers. The significance of this is that, for each of the areas above, there is only a single item of information required to be written down, irrespective of which area. This may sound trivial, but when systems can be recording thousands of items of data, each small saving in design at the developmental stage will increase the effectiveness of the system many times over.

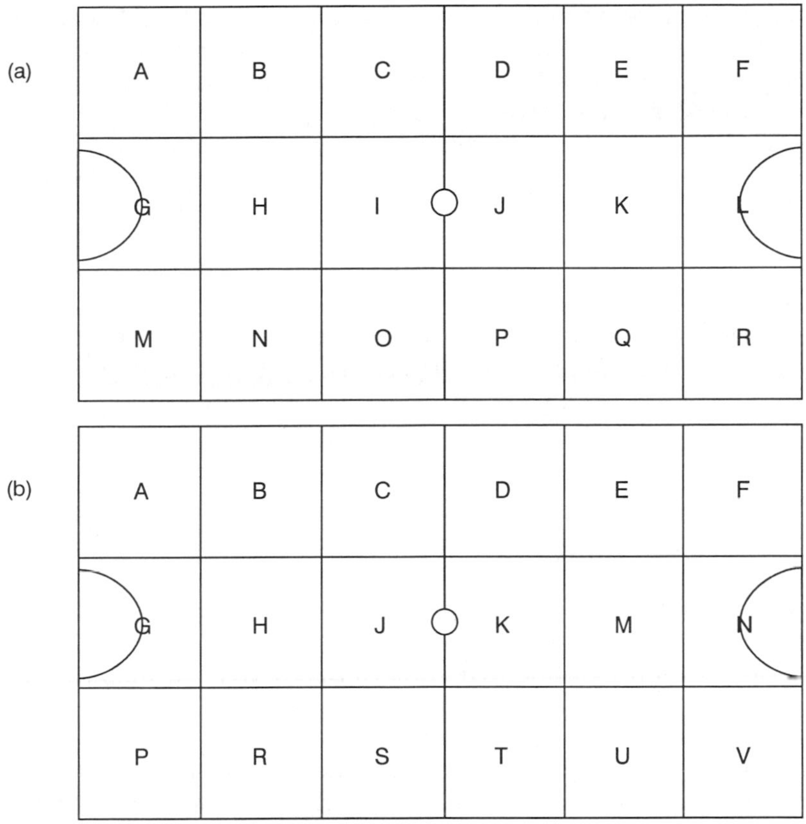

Figure 5.1(a) A schematic representation of the playing area in field hockey divided for notation. **(b)** A schematic representation of the playing area in field hockey divided for notation, with selective coding.

So let us assume that the coach has decided to use letters for pitch cell divisions and numbers for the players of the team. Does the coding of position cells above seem a reasonable layout? A number of potential problems present themselves. The use of letters 'I', 'L' and 'O' could present some translational problems later. Most notation is done at speed. 'I' and 'L' can easily be confused both with each other and the number '1', and of course the letters 'O' and 'Q' with zero '0'.

The main problem now with the above representation of the playing area is one of definition. Will these pitch divisions give the coach sufficient information on the significant areas of the pitch from which his team are shooting well or poorly? It would seem unlikely. In this situation previous researchers have used unequal divisions of the playing areas, making the definition finer in the areas of most interest. In this example this will be around the goal. There are a number of ways of doing this. Figure 5.2 is one simple way, using a representation of just half the playing area – this does, however, negate the possibility of notating shots at goal from the player's own half.

Another way of doing this would be to use arcs from the goal as shown in Figure 5.3. This has been used in a number of systems, both in basketball and soccer, to good effect. In both games there is an optimum area from which to shoot, which is more easily defined in this way.

For our example let us assume that the coach is using the area representation shown in Figure 5.2 and that players are identified by their shirt numbers. The two actions that we are notating are the pass and the shot. There are four different types of pass that our coach has defined:

Flick	F
Push	P
Arial	A
Hit	H

Now we only have to decide on the possible outcomes of the other action variable, the shot, and we have a notation system. The coach has decided at this stage not to differentiate between types of shot, so it is the outcome of the shots that need coding. As we are writing letter and then number as we notate position and player, let us use a letter code for the action outcome. A number of systems involve specifically invented symbols but, for the sake of keeping this example simple, let

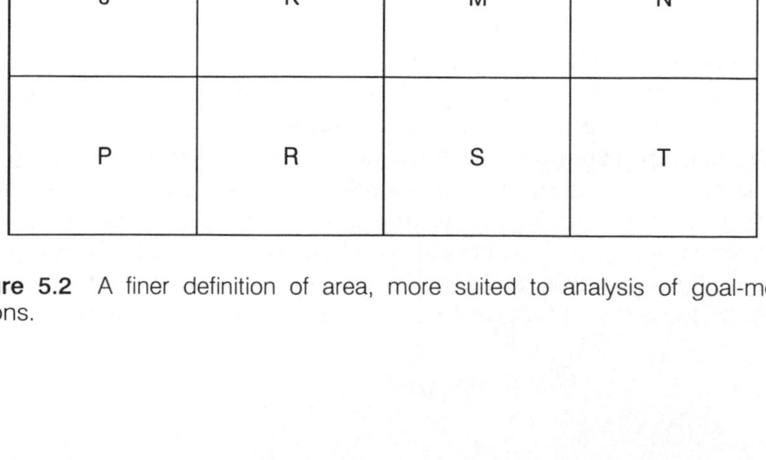

Figure 5.2 A finer definition of area, more suited to analysis of goal-mouth actions.

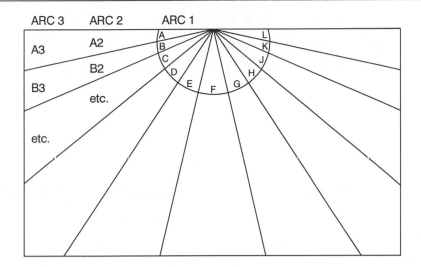

Figure 5.3   An alternative way of dividing the shooting area.

us stick to recognized numeric and alphanumeric symbols. A simple code would be:

GOAL	G
Saved	S
Wide	W
High	H
Blocked	B
Rebound	R

The coach is now able to start notating a match. An example of the type of data obtained is shown in Figure 5.4.

In this way the coach, or any other operator, can record the position from which the shot was made, who made it and the outcome. Because of the way that the data have been entered, a number, a letter, another number and a separate line for each shot, interpretation of the data is relatively easy.

Remember that the codes chosen here in this example were chosen for simplicity, a number of systems utilize invented symbols that represent actions or outcomes. This is a decision that can only be made by the individual designing the system. Use whatever you are most comfortable and familiar with. Above all keep it as simple and as easy as possible.

		Notation system			
Position	Player	Pass (Assist)	Position	Player	Shot Outcome
H	7	P	D	9	S
M	6	F	F	9	B
K	11	P	E	7	W
G	10	P	A	8	G
H	7	P	D	9	B
etc.	etc.	etc.	etc.	etc.	etc.

Figure 5.4   Example of data from a simple example of assist and shot analysis in hockey.

The only problem facing the coach now is processing the data. First, enough data will need to be collected to make it significant, then the distribution of the shots and their assists, with respect to players or position, together with their outcome, can be explored. This form of data processing is very important in most forms of analysis and feedback. Data analysis is a difficult part of notational analysis, a separate section is devoted to it later in this chapter.

The figure above makes it easy to record the data, there is less chance of becoming confused and it is easier to interpret the data once recorded. It also makes it easier for someone else to understand the data collection system; should that be desirable. Decide who is likely to use your system; if it is only for your own use, only spend as much time 'dressing it up' as is necessary.

Always remember that when other people either use your system or are presented with the data from your system, they will tend to judge the whole system by its appearance.

5.3 DATA COLLECTION SYSTEMS IN GENERAL

What can we learn in general terms about notational analysis from our example? In the most general form of notation the following parameters are being recorded:

1. Position.
2. Player.
3. Action – and the subsequent outcome(s).
4. Time.

This is the most general situation possible in any match analysis; in most notation systems only two or three of these variables will be necessary.

In individual sports, such as squash, tennis or gymnastics, the notation of which player is involved becomes easier. In team sports it becomes more difficult, depending upon the analysis and the form of the output. In certain situations, perhaps where the movements of one particular player are being recorded, it will be unnecessary to record that player because the notation is only about the one performer. The time variable is not used as frequently as the other variables in notation systems, it increases the complexity considerably, but there are some analyses which will require it. Analyses where velocities, accelerations and/or rates of work are the desired output from the data will use a time base. Reilly and Thomas (1976) completed what can be regarded now as a classical study of motion analysis in soccer, by using a combination of hand notation, with stop watches and audio tape recorders. Position and action are nearly always involved in notation systems, although there are examples of systems not using one or other of these two. In summary then, most systems will use two or three of the above variables – there are very few instances where it is necessary to use all four.

In our example we recorded position, player and then the outcome of the action (shot). The beginning and end of each sequence were indicated by using a new line for each event.

Position. The way in which the position was defined in the example was as good a way as any in going about recording positional data. The needs of the system often dictate the definition required within the system. Obviously the finer the definition the more accurate the information; however, the finer the definition the more data will need to be collected to make it significant. Be careful not to submerge yourself in too much data or too much data collection – notation is not an end in itself, the end product has to justify the time spent on it. Notating position is always a compromise between accuracy and having manageable data.

Player. Recording which player executed the action cannot be very different in more sophisticated systems. In individual sports the system may only be notating one player at a time, so differentiation will not be necessary.

Action. What made our example a relatively simple one was that we were considering only two actions – the assist and the shot. But even so, the system still required four different types of pass (assist) and five possible outcomes of the shot to be notated. These again could have been more complicated since it may be useful to know whether possession was regained after the save or the block. Consider then the complexity of the situation when defining all the possible actions, and their respective outcomes, in a game such as soccer or hockey or basketball. It is this logical and structured analysis, coupled with a clear idea of the salient information that is required from the game, that forms the nucleus of any notation system. A sound system, that will produce consistent and meaningful data, must be based on a careful analysis of the sport to be notated. It is most important to be able to understand the logic of the game structure of the sport under study – a separate section is devoted to sport analysis (see Section 3.2).

Before considering a few more examples, a few notes to remember:

1. *You must have a clear idea what information you want from the system.*

2. *Make the data collection and the data processing as simple as possible to start with. Build the complexity of your system in easy stages, adding on to what you know works and to what you can handle.*

3. *Test your system on a small part of a match or event using video. In this way you can practise and improve your notation skills, and also find out how accurate you are. Then practise some more – after that my advice is to practise some more. There is nothing worse than notating for half an hour, getting in a muddle and then realizing you have made a mess of the whole thing (always after you have promised a detailed analysis to someone important).*

4. *Having tested the system, does it collect the data you wanted? It is easy to be carried away with the design stage, adding on little bits here and collecting a little more information there, until the whole structure has assumed gargantuan proportions and does not fulfil the original aims defined at the start.*

5. *The more complex your system, the longer it will take to learn. In addition the amount of output increases immensely, which means considerably more work processing the data. For example, the notation system developed by Sanderson and Way (1979) involved 5–8 h learning time and also required 40 h of work to process the data of a single match.*

   Remember: KEEP IT SIMPLE.

   You can always add to your system and build up its complexity as you grow in experience, confidence and speed.

5.4 EXAMPLES

5.4.1 A CRICKET NOTATION SYSTEM

Cricket is a game that has used notational analysis of one form or another for a long time. The main analyses and scoring systems only incorporate data on the batsmen's run-gathering and bowlers' wicket-taking performances. There are a number of sophisticated systems that record very detailed data for player analysis; this example is a simple way of obtaining more detailed information about a player's performance – a complete understanding of cricket is not necessary to be able to follow the logic involved in setting up the system. By analysing a batsman's performance in more detail, her/his strengths and weaknesses become apparent, either for rescheduling her/his training and practising or for the opponents to reshape their tactics when playing against her/him.

In this simple example, which could easily be modified for rounders or baseball, it has been decided that the position of the player is not important. The data to be recorded are the player, the action and the outcome.

In cricket batsmen play off either the front foot or the rear foot, which leads to two sets of symbols to represent the possible strokes made by the batsman. The following symbols were invented:

Front foot strokes

Forward defensive	F\
Straight drive	FSD
Off drive	FOD
Cover drive	FCD
Square drive	FSQD
On drive	FOND
Leg glance	FG

(For non-aficionados of this strange and wonderful game, the terms 'off', 'cover', 'square' and 'on' refer to areas of the pitch. The term 'leg glance' means playing the ball off the legs with a glancing shot, for a right hander the ball will travel in the direction of 7 o'clock if the batsman is facing noon.)

Back foot strokes

Backward defensive	B\
Square cut	BSQC
Cover drive	BCD
Off drive	BOD
Pull shot	BP
Hook shot	BH
Leg glance	BG

(The 'pull', 'hook' and 'cut' are different techniques of striking the ball; the important point here, for the sake of understanding the principles behind the example, is to recognize to which area the ball has been directed.)

The number of runs scored by the batsmen is shown at the end of the sequence. For example:

BCD3

shows that the batsman scored three runs playing the cover drive of the back foot.

Additional symbols are:

0   The batsman played the ball, but scored no runs.

M   The batsman played at the ball, but missed.

L   The batsman left the ball.

E   The batsman edged the ball (he did not hit it with the full face of the bat).

5.4.2 EXAMPLES OF ANALYSIS OF CRICKET DATA

Batsman: *BOYCOTT*	Score: *27 (not out)*
Number of balls played:	*47*
Number of times played and missed:	*1*
Most frequent shot:	*Forward defensive – 14*
Number of scoring shots:	*13*
Most frequent scoring shot:	*Square cut – 5*
Shot which scored the most runs in total:	*Square cut – 10*
Shot which scored the second most runs in total:	*Square drive – 9*
Percentage front foot strokes:	*60%*
Percentage back foot strokes:	*40%*
Percentage of runs scored on the onside:	*22%*
Percentage of runs scored on the offside:	*78%*

Batsman: *MOXON*	Score: *21*
Number of balls played:	*25*
Number of times played and missed:	*5*
Most frequent shot:	*Backward defensive – 6*
Number of scoring shots:	*10*
Most frequent scoring shot:	*Cover drive – 3*
Shot which scored the most runs in total:	*Cover and straight drive, Leg glance, Back defensive – 4*
Shot which scored the second most runs in total:	*As above – 4*
Percentage front foot strokes:	*61%*
Percentage back foot strokes:	*39%*
Percentage of runs scored on the onside:	*23.5%*
Percentage of runs scored on the offside:	*76.5%*

Batsman: *BLAKEY*	Score: *41*
Number of balls played:	*29*
Number of times played and missed:	*1*
Most frequent shot:	*Forward defensive – 6*
Number of scoring shots:	*13*
Most frequent scoring shot:	*Pull shot/hook – 5*
Shot which scored the most runs in total:	*Hook shot – 14*
Shot which scored the second most runs in total:	*Pull shot – 9*
Percentage front foot strokes:	*46%*
Percentage back foot strokes:	*54%*
Percentage of runs scored on the onside:	*100%*
Percentage of runs scored on the offside:	*0%*

This system, although quite simple, does provide batsmen, or opposing bowlers, with very pertinent details about their most frequent shots, most effective shots and least effective shots. For example, a good tactic for a team fielding against batsman Blakey would be to put the majority of their fielders on the legside, leaving perhaps two or three of their best catchers on the offside, to tempt him to play that side. First, this would cut down the run rate on the leg-side, but he would be bound to try to play on the offside, his weaker side, where hopefully he might make a mistake, perhaps giving a catching opportunity. A similar analysis could be completed for the bowlers, showing their weaknesses and strengths. Because cricket is such a slow game, this type of analysis can easily be done in-match and the results processed during the game, enabling better tactical evaluations of the game situation. Keeping the data, i.e. building up a database, enables planned practices specific to opponents before they are played and a clear understanding by all the players in the team of the tactics to be employed in beating those opponents.

This data could be further detailed by drawing an overview of the directions in which the scoring shots were made. This type of analysis has been used extensively in cricket, detailing where batsmen are most, and least, successful. This is very useful information in placing field settings against these batsmen and planning the tactics of the direction of the bowlers' aim.

There are many ways in which this data could be examined in more detail, becoming more and more specific. The question that must always be answered before proceeding to the next level of analysis is, 'will the information provided by this further analysis be worth the time spent in processing it?'. It is very easy to become involved in analysis for the sake of analysis – questions such as 'will the players find it of use?' or ' does the coach need this much information?', could help to keep your work in perspective.

5.5 GENERAL STEPS IN ANALYSIS

There are a number of steps in analysis that this cricket example highlights very well.

1. *Always start with general overview, or summary data, of the main variables, actions and outcomes that were notated.*
2. *Where there are large differences in sets of data, or discrepancies to expected levels of performance, then perform a more detailed analysis of the data, attempting to show areas or events that explain or contrast these data.*

In this example of the cricket match, the analyses of the performances of the batsmen show one or two interesting pieces of information. For example, Blakey scored runs on only one side of the pitch, Moxon played and missed the ball five times as opposed to the other batsmen's once, Boycott's 'score per ball-faced' was much lower than the other two batsmen. Each set of data asks another question in turn. Analysing the patterns of the bowlers and linking these to the batsmen's' data, would certainly go a long way to answering these questions.

3. *Before going on to another analysis of this data, perhaps proceeding to a finer level of definition, always refer back to the general overview, in case there is another problem that merits further analysis first.*

In examining the data for Blakey above, it would be tempting to immediately complete a chart of the direction in which all his shots were hit. However, in examining the overall data it would seem that perhaps the most productive way ahead would be to analyse the patterns of the bowlers. This could explain this anomaly, as well as providing further descriptive data about the relative performances of the other batsmen with respect to the particular bowlers involved. It will also give a detailed analysis of the bowlers' performance, which could be presented in much the same way as the data of the batsmen.

4. *Be very critical of the time to be spent on any analysis; be sure it is worth the effort. Do not smother important facts with a multitude of other data – keep the analysis simple.*
5. *Be aware of to whom the data will be presented – this may limit the level of analysis to which you may proceed; it will certainly limit the way in which you can present your data. If 10% of your presented information is not understood, the players and/or coaches will reject 100% of your analysis.*

Remember – your whole system will be judged on its output.

Is it clear?

Is it well laid out?

Can the presentation be simplified?

Compare the following ways of presenting the same data.

Presentation 1

Batsman: Blakey Score:41

Number of balls played:29

Number of times played and missed:1

Most frequent shot:Forward defensive 6

Number of scoring shots:13

Most frequent scoring shot:Pull shot/hook 5

Shot which scored the most runs in total:Hook shot 14

Shot which scored the second most runs in total:Pull Shot 9

Percentage front foot strokes:46%

Percentage back foot strokes:54%

Percentage of runs scored on the onside:100%

Percentage of runs scored on the offside:0%

Note how much more difficult it is to extract meaningful information from the data. Compare this with the presentation used in the text.

Presentation 2

Batsman: *BLAKEY*	Score: *41*
Number of balls played:	*29*
Number of times played and missed:	*1*
Most frequent shot:	*Forward defensive – 6*
Number of scoring shots:	*13*
Most frequent scoring shot:	*Pull shot/Hook – 5*
Shot which scored the most runs in total:	*Hook shot – 14*
Shot which scored the second most runs in total:	*Pull shot – 9*
Percentage front foot strokes:	*46%*
Percentage back foot strokes:	*54%*
Percentage of runs scored on the onside:	*100%*
Percentage of runs scored on the offside:	*0%*

Presentation 3

Batsman: *BLAKEY*		Score: 41
Number of balls played:		29
Number of times played and missed:		1
Most frequent shot:	*Forward defensive*	6
Number of scoring shots:		13
Most frequent scoring shot:	*Pull shot/Hook*	5
Shot which scored the most runs in total	*Hook shot*	14
Shot which scored the second most runs in total	*Pull shot*	9
Percentage front foot strokes:		46%
Percentage back foot strokes:		54%
Percentage of runs scored on the onside:		100%
Percentage of runs scored on the offside:		0%

However, this presentation can be improved and made more easy to interpret. Consider the third presentation of the same data above. There are probably a number of ways in which this presentation could be improved. This is inevitable – production of output, and its interpretation, is very much a matter of individual perception. Try to keep it as simple as possible – always remember your output will seem easy and obvious to you, because you have been handling this data for some time (2–3 weeks is not unusual). Think of the person who is seeing it for the first time. The use of colours in the text always helps definition of important data. Of course, wherever possible, graphs, figures, histograms and pie-charts should be used. Your system will usually be designed to meet the specific needs or demands of the coaches, players or work involved, but it is even more important that your output, and its format, should be specifically tailored to your clientele. **As you gather more and more detailed data, this part of the notation task becomes correspondingly more difficult.**

5.6 DIFFERENT FORMS OF DATA

There are a limited number of forms in which the data occurs. The easiest way of building ideas of how data can be presented is to familiarize yourself completely with all the other types of data presentation already in use in the field of notational analysis. A great deal of imagination has already been applied to this part of the analysis problem, but even so this is still the area least developed. Although some recent research does tackle these problems of feedback directly (Franks and Nagelkerke, 1988; Hughes and McGarry, 1989), most work has struggled to keep pace with the technological advances of computerized graphics and/or interactive video.

One of the main reasons for gathering data, forming a database, is for purposes of comparison. To test whether a comparison of performances is significantly different, and not just a chance occurrence, statistical methods are used. Statistics will not only indicate whether sets of data are different or not, but will also determine how much data has to be collected before the comparisons can be made. If you are unfamiliar with the use of these type of procedures, consult with an expert; help can usually be found at the nearest College or University. If you are going to use statistics on your data:

Decide upon your statistical methods at the design stage of your system.

The different forms in which data can fall are discussed below. The titles by which these will be referred are not standard and are defined in each section.

5.6.1 GENERAL OR SUMMARY DATA

This tends to be in the form of totals of variables, usually actions, for a team or an individual. Handling this form of data is usually done by tables, although occasion may permit the use of graphs or figures of some kind. The usual statistical test for significant differences with this form of data is a paired *t*-test. Examples of these data are shown below in Tables 5.1, 5.2 and 5.3 (squash data, Hughes, 1986; soccer data, Partridge and Franks, 1989a,b).

Table 5.1 A comparison of descriptive match data for different levels of competitive players (Hughes, 1986).

	Recreational players	County players	Nationally ranked players
Mean no. of shots per match	686	830	1651
Mean no. of rallies per match	113.2	94.6	89.2
Mean no. of shots per rally	6.03	8.80	18.48
Mean no. of winning shots per match	28.55	22.4	19.83
Mean no. of errors per match	26.0	21.1	16.83
Winner/error ratio	1.096	1.07	1.18

Table 5.2 Comparison of nationally ranked players to county players – shot patterns that have differences in frequency ($P <$ 0.05) (Hughes, 1986).

Analysis		Chi-square	
Shot	Pattern	Longitudinal Presentation	Lateral Presentation
1. drive	total distribution	9.52*	6.93
2. cross-court drives	"	1.68	3.64
3. cross-court volley (short)	"	9.75*	8.26*
4. cross-court volley (long)	"	3.76	4.02
5. boast	errors	10.02*	4.43
6. drop shot		2.49	5.00
7. cross-court volley (short)		5.20	5.60
8. drives	winners	5.62	5.61
9. boasts	(n–1) to winner (by opponent)	6.10	2.44
10. cross-court	(n–1) to winner (by opponent)	4.21	4.21
11. cross-court	(n–2) shot to an error	4.21	4.20
12. services	(n–2) shot to an error	5.15	2.86
13. services	shot to be a winner	4.23	4.19

All data listed have difference levels of $P < 0.05$ unless *$P < 0.01$.

5.6.2 FREQUENCY DISTRIBUTIONS

Output design begins to become a little more difficult with the problems posed by enabling a clear understanding of the presentation of frequency distributions. Two-dimensional distributions are not difficult. A graph, a histogram, etc., will demonstrate clearly any important data. See, for example, Figures 5.5 and 5.6, which show the distribution of an action variable, the shot, with another variable, the players. Both demonstrate the main point of the data – that certain players are not shooting as often as others.

The presentation becomes more difficult once more variables become involved, or the distribution across a playing area is examined. The playing area is usually a two-dimensional space, or regarded as such, so a frequency distribution of an action with respect to position will require three dimensions: one for the variable, another two for the playing area. A number of ways of tackling this problem have been attempted. The straightforward approach is of the type shown in Figures 5.7 and 5.8,

Table 5.3   Shooting data from the 1990 World Cup for soccer (Partridge and Franks, 1990).

	Group 'A'				Group 'B'		
	Argentina	Italy	Bulgaria	S. Korea	Mexico	Paraguay	Belgium	Iraq
Total opportunities	53	48	43	48	36	46	42	39
Taken	38	32	30	40	31	40	36	33
Not taken	15	16	13	8	5	6	6	6
Off-target	16	13	10	17	11	22	12	20
Off-target of shots taken	42%	41%	33%	42.5%	35.5%	55%	60%	61%
Blocked	7	7	12	12	4	5	2	5
Of shots taken blocked	18%	21.5%	40%	30%	13%	12.5%	3%	15%
Goals	6	5	2	4	3	4	3	1

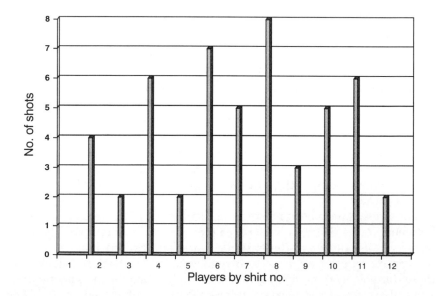

Figure 5.5   Example of the distribution of the frequency of shots per player.

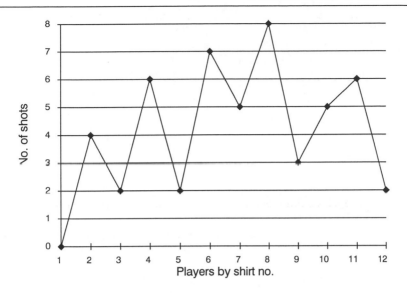

Figure 5.6 A different way of presenting the same data of the distribution of the frequency of shots per player.

which is data taken from a field hockey match (Hughes and Cunliffe, 1986). The value of the variable is inserted in the corresponding area of the pitch representation. This is, in effect, little more than a table of data but it does relate to how the frequency of the action variable is distributed across the playing area. Ideally, to gain a clear pictorial impression of the distribution of the action variable with respect to its position on the playing area, a three-dimensional graphic display should be used.

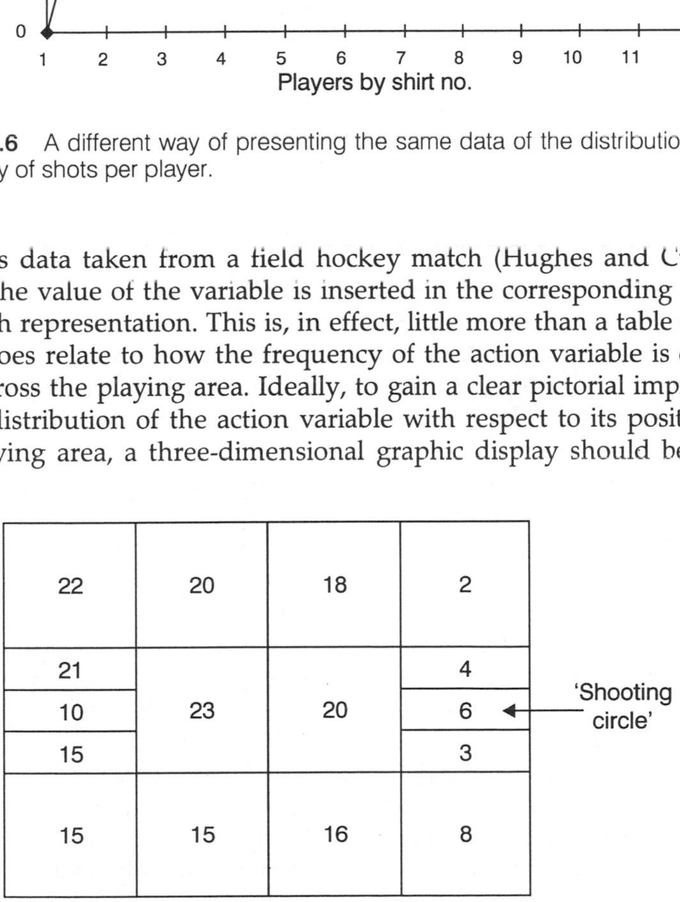

22	20	18	2
21			4
10	23	20	6
15			3
15	15	16	8

'Shooting circle'

Figure 5.7 Example of a frequency distribution of actions (number of passes, runs, etc., in each area of the pitch) in a field hockey match (Hughes and Cunliffe, 1986).

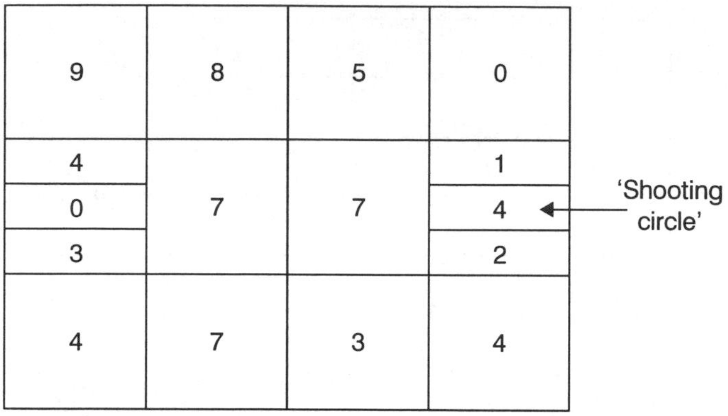

9	8	5	0
4			1
0	7	7	4
3			2
4	7	3	4

'Shooting circle' ← (pointing to the '4' cell)

Figure 5.8   Example of a frequency distribution of errors (number of errors made in each area of the pitch) in a field hockey match (Hughes and Cunliffe, 1986).

This should make the data easier to understand, as long as the presentation is good enough. It does have two associated problems, however. First, the creation of clear and understandable three-dimensional graphics is very difficult. Secondly, this degree of difficulty is considerably increased when one considers that any low frequency data occurring 'behind' high frequency data will be hidden.

Sanderson and Way (1979) tackled this problem in an ingenious way by using what they termed longitudinal and latitudinal summations across the playing surface, in their case a squash court. For example, the distribution of shots shown in Figure 5.9 was summed across the court cell by cell (a lateral summation) to give the longitudinal profile of shots. Similarly, the distribution of shots was summed along the length of the court (a longitudinal summation) to yield a lateral profile of shots. In this way a presentation of two graphs enabled a two-dimensional representation of the three-dimensional distribution of shots across the playing surface. Hughes (1986) adopted this form of presentation in his work on squash, but this was mainly for purposes of comparison of his data to that of Sanderson. Whilst some people had no problems handling this spatial transposition, it was found that a large number of coaches and athletes found it very confusing. Consequently, Hughes and McGarry (1989) went on to seek a solution to this form of data presentation using computer graphics. Nowadays most databases and spreadsheets have three-dimensional graphics integrated so that a similar form of presentation is possible without all the hard work that these researchers had to undergo. The important point is, and will always remain, that the presentation of the data should be as simple and as clear as possible.

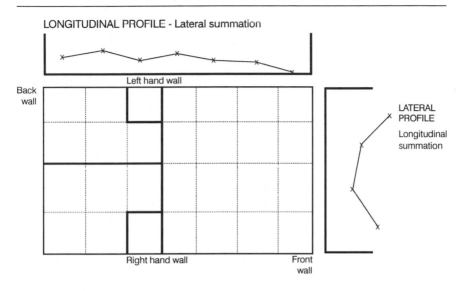

Figure 5.9   Representation of three-dimensional data distribution using two two-dimensional graphs (Sanderson and Way, 1979).

5.6.3 SEQUENTIALLY DEPENDENT DATA

In sequentially dependent data the sequence forms a set pattern with respect to position player or, most frequently, time. An example of this type of data might be the passing patterns of the ball in producing 'tries' in rugby union. Comparing two international sides, such as France and England in 1988, would produce very different approaches in their route to scoring 'tries'. France, at this time, were a very fluid running side that could pass and run with the ball anywhere on the field of play. England, at this time, were a very stilted side tactically, preferring to kick, either under instructions from their coaches or from fear of making an error, and very rarely running with the ball despite possessing some of the best three-quarters at the time. To compare sets of this type of data correlation methods would be used to test for significance.

Presenting this form of data again benefits from a pictorial approach. Figure 5.10 shows the paths of passes, runs and dribbles shots taken in field hockey (Hughes and Cunliffe, 1986). This is a very simple graphic picture, of what would otherwise be tabular data, but nonetheless effective.

Reilly and Thomas (1976) developed a notation system that combined hand notation and dictation into a portable audio tape recorder. They used the system to study work rates of players in the game of association football (soccer). They would follow the movement patterns of an individual player, recording ambulatory motions (i.e. standing, walking,

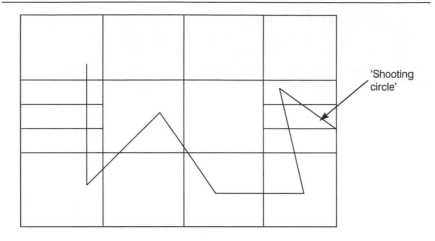

Figure 5.10 Example of sequential data – path to a shot on goal in field hockey (Hughes and Cunliffe, 1986).

trotting, running, sprinting), the position on the field of these motions and the time span involved. This enabled them to calculate distances travelled and the overall work-rate of different positions in the team.

5.7 SUMMARY

Summarizing the main points of this chapter is difficult, but in the interest of brevity remember these guidelines in developing and using a notation system.

- Make sure the you have a clear idea of what it is you are trying to analyse before you start. If possible you should also know what your output is going to be and the form it will take. Being able to do this, of course, requires a great deal of experience of notation within that particular sport. This is not possible, but the more planning done beforehand, the more fruitless hours saved.

- Keep the data collection system as simple as possible for as long as possible. If it does need to become more complex then add an extra routine at a time. Before adding another make sure that the new system works fully.

- If you are going to use statistics to test your data, for significant differences, etc., then again be sure of the procedures that you are going to use before you start collecting the data. Most statistical tests will require minimum amounts of data, so this will determine how many matches, etc., you must notate.

- If your data is to be presented to others, as is usually the case, take great care to fit the format and style of presentation to the people to whom you are attempting to communicate. Always remember that, because you have been wrestling with this type of data for some time now, what seems simple and obvious to you can be very confusing to others. If in doubt, always err on the side of simplicity.

Examples of notation systems

6

6.1 INTRODUCTION

The best way to appreciate the intricacies of notational analysis is to examine systems for the sport(s) in which you are interested or sports that are similar. Presented here are a number of examples of different systems for different sports. They have been devised by students of notational analysis and are therefore of differing levels of complexity and sophistication – but there are always lessons to be learnt even from the simplest of systems. The explanations and analyses are completed by beginners at notational analysis; coaches of these sports should not, therefore, be irritated by some of the simplistic levels of analysis for the respective sports. The encouraging aspects of these examples is the amount of information that the systems provide – even the simplest of these. Examples 6.2.1–6.2.6 are for individual sports, while examples 6.3.1–6.3.9 are for team games.

6.2 INDIVIDUAL SPORTS

6.2.1 A NOTATION SYSTEM FOR TENNIS

This system, for the notation and analysis of data for tennis, was designed to gather basic information on winners and errors. The court was divided up into sections as shown in Figure 6.1. Six sections were chosen in order to keep the recording of position and its subsequent analysis as simple as possible. A singles match was to be notated which reduced the court size, removing the need for the tram-lines and simplifying the system.

Symbols were allocated for the basic shots to be recorded, as follows:

S	serve
F	backhand drive
V	forehand volley

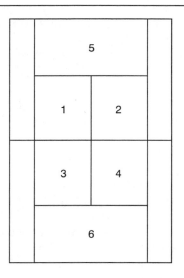

Figure 6.1   Division of the court into six cells for analysis of tennis.

V	backhand volley
L	forehand lob
L	backhand lob
Sm	smash

Having established shot symbols, it was then necessary to devise 'result of shot' symbols, i.e. whether the shot was a winner, or whether a mistake was made. These were as follows:

- A dot ('.') following a shot symbol indicates that the shot was played into the net.
- An arrow (→) following a shot symbol indicates that the ball was played out of court.
- A shot symbol followed by 'W' indicates that the shot was either an outright winner or that the opponent's shot following this one was a mistake.
- A single line indicates the end of a point.
- A double line indicates the end of a game.
- A triple line indicates the end of a set.

For the actual notation purposes, the construction of simple columns was used – one vertical column for each player. The play was notated by alternating from each column as the shots were played until the conclusion of the point. A single line was then drawn across both columns and the winning player's last shot ringed. An example of a game notated using this system is shown in Figure 6.2(a and b).

Description of point

Smith served the ball wide and Jones returned the serve with a forehand that landed short. Smith moved in to play a deep cross-court backhand, causing Jones to play a defensive backhand lob. This lob was not a good one and Smith has the chance to smash the ball, but he hit the ball out of court. Jones won the point and the score was 0–15.

The match chosen for analysis was the 1989 Ladies Wimbledon Final between Steffi Graf and Martina Navratilova. This selection was made because it incorporated a wide variety of shots while at the same time displaying constructive rallies to analyse, but did not continue for too long, as is the case with some women's matches, making notation strenuous.

Also the choice of a grass court surface would produce an exciting game without creating very short rallies as displayed in a men's game,

(a)

	Smith	Jones
	S4	F2
	B6	L5
	Sm→	

(b)

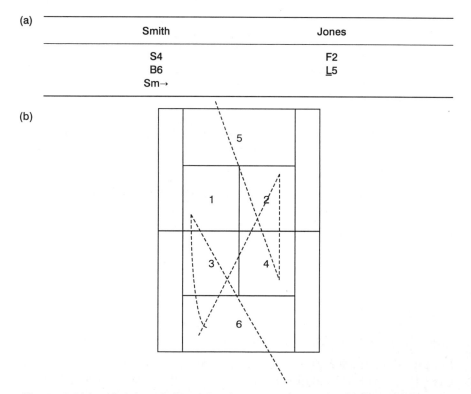

Figure 6.2(a) Notation of data using the system for tennis. **(b)** Schematic representation of data used in example in (a).

with one player hitting a fast serve that results in either a mistake or an outright winner from his opponent.

The aim of the notation was to devise a system that was simple enough to notate a match live without the use of video cameras. Therefore, although this match was viewed from video, it was notated continuously without pausing or rewinding the tape. An example of part of the notation is shown in Figure 6.3.

Results

A simple analysis of the data from this match is presented; more information could have been obtained from the data given more time.

Wimbledon Ladies Final 1989				
Steffi Graf v Martina Navratilova				
First Set (Graf won, 6–2)				
STEFFI	MARTINA		STEFFI	MARTINA
	S4			S3
D2	V3		B.	
F1 W	V→			S4
	S3		B.	
B2	V4			S3
B2 W			B→	
	S4		1–0	
F5	V4		S1	D→
F2	V3 W		S3	B5
	S3		F6	F2
B.			F6	B5
	S4		F4 W	
B2 W	V.		S4 W	
	S3		S3	F5
F5	V6 W		F4	B5
	S4		L	Sm2 W
F5	L6 W		S4	B.
XF→			1–1	
	S3			S1
F1	V4		F3 W	
F2 W			etc.	
	S4→			
	S3 W			
B.				

Figure 6.3 Example of the tennis data gathering system.

STEFFI GRAF

Mistakes   NET = 1 FOREHAND
                         4 BACKHANDS

                OUT = 2 FOREHANDS
                         3 BACKHANDS
                         2 BACKHAND LOBS

Outright Winners =   5 FOREHANDS
                         4 BACKHANDS
                         1 SERVE
                         1 LOB

Points Lost:

Unforced Errors	Navratilova Winners
12	12

MARTINA NAVRATILOVA

Mistakes   NET = 3 FOREHANDS
                         5 BACKHANDS
                         4 VOLLEYS
                         1 DOUBLE FAULT

                OUT = 4 FOREHANDS
                         4 BACKHANDS
                         1 VOLLEY

Outright Winners =   1 FOREHAND
                         8 VOLLEYS
                         2 SMASHES
                         1 SERVE

Points Lost:

Unforced Errors	Graf Winners
23	11

Summary of results

If a performance indicator is defined as:

    Tennis ratio = Number of Errors/Number of Winners

    GRAF tennis ratio   =   12/11 (or nearly 1:1)

    NAVRATILOVA tennis ratio   =   23/12 (or nearly 2:1)

Discussion and conclusions

Analysis of the results showed that in this particular match, the loser, i.e. Martina Navratilova, had a ratio of nearly 2:1 for unforced errors to winners. The players analysed were of the highest playing standard currently competing and therefore avoided playing unforced errors wherever possible. Also, the fast grass court made rallies shorter than usual with many more winners played, in contrast to the 'waiting game' played on slow clay courts. Another reason for Navratilova's results could be related to the nature of her game. She plays a high powered attacking game aiming to control play from the net position as soon as possible. Consequently her mistakes occurred in trying to get to that position but once there, very few unforced errors occurred and points were won by outright volley winners or by passing shots played by Graf.

6.2.2 A NOTATION SYSTEM FOR BOXING

First, the types of punches have to be identified, together with other behaviour variables considered to be important in defining a boxing match. These were considered to be:

i)   Jabs.
ii)   Hooks.
iii)   Upper cuts.
iv)   Misses (complete).
v)   Front body punches.
vi)   Side body punches.
vii)   Holding.
viii) Hit guard (partial miss).
ix)   Foul punching.
x)   Ducking.
xiv)   On ropes.
xv)   Knock down.
xvi)   Knock out.
xvii) Technical KO.
xviii) Points decision.

As it can be seen, there are numerous actions which constitute:

- Offensive information.
- Defensive information.
- Positional information.
- Fight outcome.

These provided too many variables to notate using a hand system as many or all could be occurring simultaneously. It is suggested that, if both boxers are to be notated, only offensive actions and specific key features could be recorded. These could be identified as:

- Jabs.
- Misses.
- Knock downs.
- Hooks.
- Body shots.
- Uppercuts.
- Holding.

The system was now progressed to separating these factors into left and right sides depending on which side the punch was thrown from. (Knock downs remained universal as the final punch would be recorded.) The symbol denoting the jab aims to represent the jab itself, i.e. a straight punch. Hence the symbol used was a straight line. The dash was placed either side depending on where it was thrown from, the left or right. This reasoning was then followed for the construction of the other symbols. Thus the notation shown in Table 6.1 was devised

Table 6.1   Symbols used in the data gathering system for boxing.

Left	Right	Punch
-]	[-	jab
(	)	hook
UL	UR	upper cut
m	m	miss
B	B	body punch
<	>	holding
v	v	knock down

For example, a boxer while holding his opponent with his left arm produces an uppercut which misses with his right; it would be notated as:

<URm

A chart (see Table 6.2) was then devised to record a fight on which the punches of each boxer could be notated in sequential order.

This format of a vertical linear layout remains common in hand systems as it enables quickly translated and stored records. One line of the chart corresponds to one punch from each boxer. In situations where punches were thrown simultaneously, both were recorded on the same line to indicate they occurred within the time space of one punch.

It was decided that certain characteristics of a fight which might ease the notation task were as follows:

Table 6.2 Example data from the Tyson versus Bruno fight (1989) using the data gathering system for boxing.

Tyson	Bruno	Tyson	Bruno	Tyson	Bruno
-]			<		<URm
	-]		<UR		<URm
(	)		<UR		<URm
)			<)m		<)m
	)		<UR		)
	)		<)	-]	
	)		<)m	(	
(			<)		<UR
BUR	<)		)		<UR
	<)		<)		<UR
(		(	<)	(m	
-]			<)		<(
)		-]			)m
(m		)			-]
URm					-]
	V		<>	(	
(	<		UR	)m	
	<		)		-]
	)		-]	(m	
		)			
<)	<)		<)		-]
<)	<)		<)	)m	
	(		<)		)
)		(	<)	(	

1. A heavyweight match in which the 'punch rate' is considerably slower than lower weight categories.
2. A fight which is relatively short in duration, so massive amounts of raw data are not produced.

The chosen match was Mike Tyson versus Frank Bruno, held in 1989 at the Hilton International, Las Vegas. This was a five-round fight between two heavyweight boxers.

Notating the fight involved first watching the fight through completely, to get a 'feeling' of punch speed and of any anomalies which may exist in their boxing style. Then, the fight was notated using the pause function on the video and, at instances when numerous punches were thrown within a very short period, a frame by frame analysis was used. The raw data was then collated by frequency tallies (see Figures 6.4 and 6.5). Summary totals could then be calculated and represented graphically (see results).

Results

From the results we can see that Bruno threw 55% of the punches;

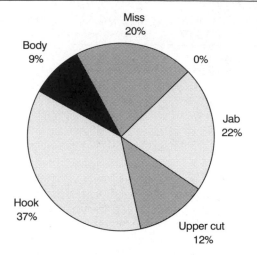

Figure 6.4 Distribution of the types of punches thrown by Tyson in the Bruno–Tyson match (1989).

however, if these are broken down round by round, we see that in the first three rounds he threw more than Tyson, and in rounds 4 and 5 Tyson threw more than Bruno (Table 6.3). This suggests that he was tiring and was failing to counter-punch. So the fight was essentially lost in rounds 4 and 5.

Both boxers had almost identical punch compositions (see Table 6.4), with Bruno missing 1% more than Tyson. However, during the fight

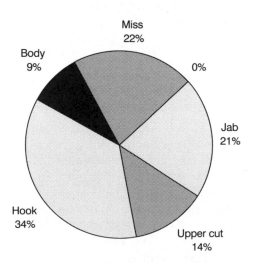

Figure 6.5 Distribution of the types of punches thrown by Bruno in the Bruno–Tyson match (1989).

Table 6.3 The round-by-round distribution
for punches thrown by Mike Tyson and
Frank Bruno (1989).

Round	Tyson	Bruno
Round 1	45	63
Round 2	42	67
Round 3	40	75
Round 4	58	52
Round 5	63	42

Bruno was cautioned for holding. This is illustrated by Table 6.5, which
shows the percentage of punches made while holding. Bruno made 41%
of his punches while holding, compared with Tyson's 4%. This is probably a reflection of Bruno trying to punch 'inside' Tyson, i.e. by staying
close you have less chance of being knocked out with one punch, which
is characteristic of Tyson's fights. This was therefore intentional and
probably not due to fatigue alone.

Bruno has a reputation for his jabs, which intimidate his opponents.
In the first three rounds his jabbing more than doubled those of Tyson
(see Table 6.6). However, from then on the number of his jabs decreased
dramatically and Tyson's increased. The final round contained roughly
the same number of jabs thrown by each opponent. This was probably
due to Bruno having only the strength to produce jabs, and Tyson trying
to finish the fight off with hooks and uppercuts, which are more powerful punches. All the statistics tend to suggest that the fight was won in
rounds 4 and 5. See Figure 6.6.

Conclusions

1. This simple system does enable the notation of a boxing match by a
   post-event analysis of video. While acknowledging that the results
   describe the basic techniques employed by a boxer during a match,

Table 6.4 The percentage analysis of the
actions of each of the two boxers.

Action	Tyson	Bruno
Miss	23	24
Jab	26	28
Hook	26	21
Body	15	17
Uppercuts	10	8

Table 6.5   The number of punches thrown while holding.

Tyson	Bruno
8	89

one must recognize that the notation in itself was very simplified and somewhat crude, and did not address many essential aspects of a fight, i.e. positional information, defensive information, and subjective measures of power and accuracy (which may require the knowledge of a skilled coach).

2. Considering the speed of boxing matches, it was almost impossible to notate a fight live. The use of video and playback was therefore essential.

However, some very simple and basic information clearly maps the progress of the fight and gives a quantitative analysis of the progress of the two boxers during the bout.

Table 6.6   The number of jabs thrown in each round.

Round	Tyson	Bruno
Round 1	5	9
Round 2	8	21
Round 3	8	20
Round 4	15	7
Round 5	6	5
Total	42	62

6.2.3 A NOTATION SYSTEM FOR SQUASH

The development of this system charts how the ideas of using this form of hand notation system are modified by the practical use of the system. In research this would be called a series of pilot studies; in more common parlance, the system was being refined by a process of trial and error (based on sound ideas, of course).

This particular notation system was designed to investigate the importance of the serve and service return in squash. Research has shown that in the shorter rallies of county players and recreational players, the serve, and conversely the return of serve, assumes a greater significance in relation to the outcome of the rally (Hughes, 1985). If substantiated, this could radically improve most players' levels

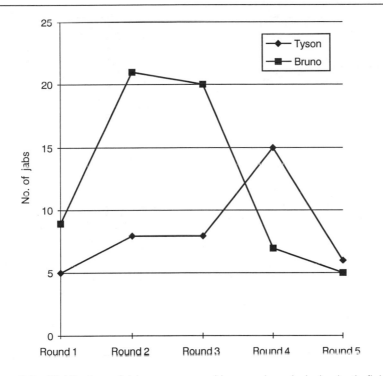

Figure 6.6 Distribution of jabs on a round-by-round analysis by both fighters (Bruno–Tyson, 1989).

of performance, as at this time most players tend to have the attitude that the serve is merely a means of starting the rally unlike tennis, where the game recognizes the potential of the serve to immediately place their opponent under pressure.

The first step in developing a full service-and-return notational analysis system was to concentrate firstly on the service alone.

Method A

1. The service area on a squash court was divided into sections and allocated with a code (Figure 6.7)
2. A recording sheet was designed (Table 6.7). The sheet contains various columns, play is recorded from left to right and top to bottom. This continues until all the columns are completed.
   (i)   Information of the players, venue, ability, etc., is recorded.
   (ii) The score and players initials are entered.
   (iii) The codes corresponding to the appropriate sections in which the ball lands were ringed.

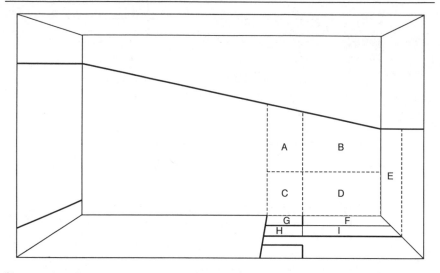

Figure 6.7 Schematic diagram showing the court divisions for notating the serve in squash.

(iv) The type of serve was also ringed.
   L = lob
   D = drive
   B = angled/boast
(v) If the serve was a fault or a winner, the column was ticked.

The system was used to notate a game; this highlighted several flaws which were then corrected and the method A refined.

Table 6.7 Recording sheet for the first attempt at a system for notating the serve in squash.

Player	Area of court where serve landed	Serve type	Fault	Winner
	A B C D E F G H	L D B		
	A B C D E F G H	L D B		
	A B C D E F G H	L D B		
	A B C D E F G H	L D B		
	A B C D E F G H	L D B		
	A B C D E F G H	L D B		
	A B C D E F G H	L D B		
	A B C D E F G H	L D B		
	A B C D E F G H	L D B		
	etc.	etc.		

Method B

1. This time the service area was divided into fewer coded sections. This made the notation of service position easier (Figure 6.8).
2. The recording sheet (Table 6.8) was further developed.
   (i) The column for notating the position of the serve was made simpler by allowing the analyst to write the codes themselves. This also allowed the order that the ball hit the walls and floor to be indicated, which is important.
   (ii) Another problem highlighted by method A was when a ball was volleyed without landing in any section. The volley return was notated in the method B recording sheet by a small letter representing the area over which the ball was volleyed, e.g. d ^ ball volleyed in section D.

The next step in the development of the notation systems was to construct a method to analyse the service return.

Method C

1. The recording sheet (Table 6.9) was modified again to incorporate the type of service return. The sheet was now used in the following way.
   (i) The server's initials were recorded (this in effect recorded who was receiving).
   (ii) Each type of shot that could be played as a return of serve was allocated a code:

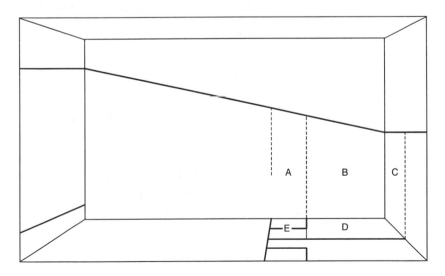

Figure 6.8   Schematic diagram showing the modified court divisions for notating the serve in squash.

Table 6.8 Recording sheet for the second attempt at a system for notating the serve in squash.

Player	Area of court where serve landed	Serve type	Fault	Winner
		L D B		
		L D B		
		L D B		
		L D B		
		L D B		
		L D B		
		L D B		
		L D B		
		L D B		
	etc.	etc.		

D = drive
L = lob
X = cross-court
F = forehand
B = backhand
V = volley
A = reverse angle
The type of return is built up using these codes, e.g. a backhand cross-court volley = BXV

(iii) A winner is indicated by the symbol 'W', a fault by 'F'.

Method D

This system was yet again modified and improved on. It was decided that the information on the type of return did not provide enough information. Thus, a system was developed to indicate the position of the return as well as type of return.

1. A sheet with a diagram of a squash court was used to identify the code where the service return landed (Figure 6.9).
2. The codes for the type of service return were modified from Method A. They were simplified to:

V = volley
D = drive
L = lob
B = boast

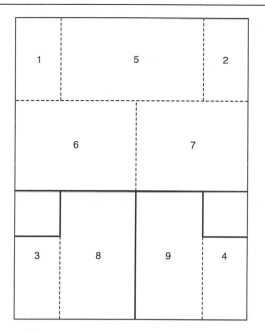

Figure 6.9 Schematic diagram showing the division of the court to identify the area where the return of serve landed.

Dp = drop
a = Reverse angle
3. A winner is represented by the symbol 'W'. An error is represented by the symbol 'E'.
4. The score was also indicated on the sheet.

These codes, together with the previous ideas produced the final notation sheet shown in Table 6.10. The initial aim was to develop a notation system that would analyse both serve and service return simultaneously. The repetition of using these similar, but improving, systems is a common way of refining a notation system. This final method was then used to notate two games of a local club standard, live. The finals of the 1989 British Open were also notated using video post-event.

Results

The notational analysis can be used to demonstrate the type of results which can be obtained and hence highlight the particular conclusions which can be reached.

From just a brief analysis of the results, it would suggest that the original hypothesis that the serve is more important to players of a lower standard is

Table 6.9 Recording sheet for a system for notating the serve and service return in squash.

Server	Area where serve landed	Serve type	Fault/win	Return type	Fault/win
		L D B			
		L D B			
		L D B			
		L D B			
		L D B			
		L D B			
		L D B			
		L D B			
		L D B			
	etc.	etc.			

supported. For example, in a match between Rodney Martin and Jahangir Khan, Martin consistently returned serve to a good length, yet still lost game 5 very easily; this would not be so with a club standard game. Another point was that in both open finals (in the games notated) no direct winners from serve or return were achieved; this compared with several in the local club match.

If further data was obtained using this method, such hypotheses could be substantiated more firmly. These results could be used to

Table 6.10 Recording sheet for a system for notating the serve, the service return and the position where the return landed in squash.

Server	Area serve landed	Serve type	Fault/win	Return type	Area of return	Fault/win	Score
		L D B					
		L D B					
		L D B					
		L D B					
		L D B					
		L D B					
		L D B					
		L D B					
		L D B					
	etc.	etc.					

analyse a specific player's weak points, e.g. volley return. The various patterns and relationships produced by the data could thus be vital to a player/coach to improve performance. An example of such patterns from the data was that for Martine Le Moignan. Her return of serve would appear important in her game with Susan Devoy:

'Her' forehand straight drive return produced only one winning rally out of five, also the backhand cross-court which was attempted four times produced no winners; however, all her backhand drives won the rally.

Conclusions

The system worked well and was capable of achieving the aims originally defined. The ideal aspect of this example, although somewhat belaboured, was the way that it demonstrated how a system can be improved step by step, and how important it is to try out your system before attempting to put it into practical use.

6.3 TEAM SPORTS

6.3.1 A NOTATION SYSTEM FOR BASKETBALL

The schematic representation of a basketball court, in Figure 6.10, shows the court position used in the notation. In basketball a team squad consists of ten team members, five on the court at any one time. For the pur-

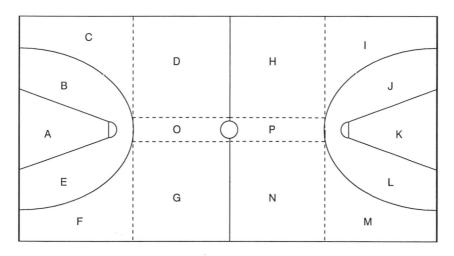

Figure 6.10 Schematic representation of the basketball court in order to define positions cells for a data gathering system.

pose of this notation the players were assigned numbers in the range from 4 to 14 (1, 2 and 3 were not used to avoid confusion with the letters I, Z and B), although some teams, and all American ones, often use numbers like 33, 42, etc.

The actions under consideration in this hand notation and the symbols used to represent them are listed as follows:

Actions	Symbol		
Tip off	TO		
Dribble	D		
Drive	V		
Shot	S	B/M	(basket good – B)
Lay up	L	B/M	(basket missed – M)
Rebound	R		
Pass	P		
Fastbreak	F		
Foul	FL	time)	
Free Throws	FT	time)	The time the action occurred
Turnover	T	time)	should be recorded
Substitution	SB	time)	
Out of court	0	time)	
Sideline ball	SL		
Base line ball	BL		

These symbols, together with the player number and his position on the court, are written down in columns in a table in the following manner.

> **6   G   P**

i.e. Player No. 6, in position cell G, passed the ball.

The following is an explanation of the events notated in Table 6.11.

Line	Comments
1	The tip off was won by No. 6 who passed.
2	No. 7 received the ball in H and dribbled
3	to I where the ball was passed
4	to No. 13 in K who shot and missed.

5   Team B: No. 4 rebounded in K
6   dribbled from K
7   to L where the ball was passed
8   to 13 in N who was fouled by No. 5.
9   No. 13 took a side line ball in N passing
10   to No. 10 in N who dribbled
11   to O where the ball was passed
12   Turnover – after 2 min 59 s
13   No. 6 intercepted the ball in C and passed
14   to No. 13 in I who scored a lay-up.
15   The running score is 2–0, time 3 min 1 s
16   Base line ball in K is passed by No. 4,
17   the ball goes out of court in I.
18   Substitution: No. 6 comes on for No. 4.
19   Side line ball in I is passed by No. 6.

Conclusion and discussion

A coach or analyst can use this very simple notation system to gather performance data of individual players or the whole team. It can be used to analyse from which side of the court the most successful attacks come;

Table 6.11   A demonstration of how the notation system works.

Team A	Time	Team B
TO 6 P		
H 7 D		
I 7 P		
K 13 S M		
		K 4 R
		K 4 D
		L 4 P
	2:20	N 13 FL (5)
		SL-N 13 P
		N 10 P
	2:59	T
C 6 P		
I 13 L B	3:01	
2-0		
		BL-K 4 P
		I O
	3:05	SB-4/6
		SL-I 6 P
	etc.	

what success rate the team and individuals achieve at rebounds (do they win more than they lose?); how successful they are in the majority of freethrows; is there any increase in success rate/performance after a time-out, etc. The coach can then assess the strengths and weaknesses of the individuals and the team, or their opponents, and is able to make an attempt at correcting them.

This type of system is very easily changed to suit any team sport, redefining the playing surface, the number of players and the actions, and their outcomes, accordingly.

6.3.2 A NOTATION SYSTEM FOR VOLLEYBALL

The initial aim was to use a similar notation system to examine whether the length of the rally in volleyball had any relationship with the way in which the point was won or lost. It was hypothesised that if the rally was long, then the point would be less likely to finish on a powerful strike than if the rally was shorter. If the hypothesis was upheld then a deficiency in the fitness levels of the team would be highlighted, providing reliable knowledge to the coach.

Various general data were notated during the match, giving the score, the scoring team and the length of the rally (i.e. the number of times the ball crossed the net). Then the players' number, action and position on court was notated for each team during their final touch of the ball in the rally (i.e. the winning point and the losing point); a space was left for comments, such as fouls called, time-outs called and substitutions made.

The system was designed for post-event analysis, using video, enabling details such as comments to be made and simplifications, such as the length of the rally rather than a detailed analysis of the way the game was played throughout the rally. However, it was felt that the system could be adapted to analyse live matches.

Method

The fundamental elements in notation, i.e. position, player, action and time, are systematized below.

Position. Each side of the court was divided into six sections, these sections were all predetermined by the rule structure and dictate the general order in which the players must stand prior to the service (see Figure 6.11)

Players. The individual players were identified by the number displayed on their shirt.

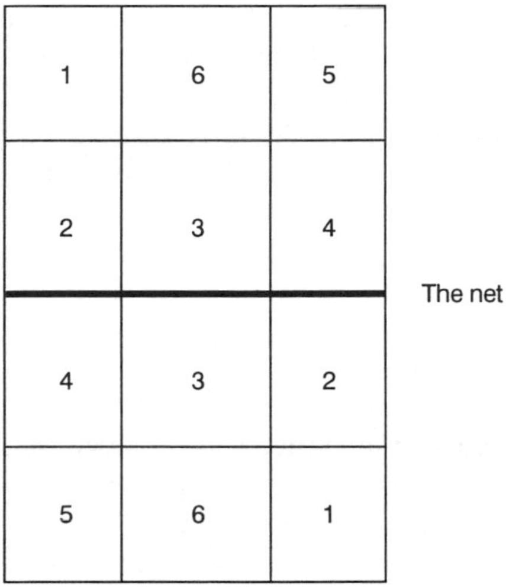

1	6	5
2	3	4
4	3	2
5	6	1

The net

Figure 6.11 Schematic representation of the volleyball court in order to define positions cells for a data gathering system.

Actions. The action of the player was notated using the following key:

R   serve

D   dig

S   set

K   spike

B   one-man block

BB   two-man block

BBB   three-man block

T   tip

An additional letter was occasionally used to give information about the outcome of the action. The letters used were:

N   into net, e.g. RF = serve into net.

O   out of court, e.g. KO = spike out of court.

F   attempted action but failed, e.g. DF = failed.

dig   or pick up the ball.

The letter M was used as 'miscellaneous', which enabled unusual actions, not catered for in the key, to be notated. It was usually accompanied by an explanation in the comments.

Time. It was decided that the actual ball-in-play time was not required in the notation system. However, the length of rally noted, the score, time-outs and substitutions made gave an indication of the order and speed at which the match was moving.

The information was collected on a notation sheet set out as a table. The score and the scoring team was noted. Then the length of the rally was determined, by simply counting the number of times that the ball crossed the net. When the rally was finished this information was recorded and the video was replayed to gather the information about the final points in the rally, comments were written if necessary and the score was adjusted in order to begin notating the next point. An example of the notation sheets is shown in Table 6.12.

The information in Table 6.12 shows that the 12th point was being played, the Canadians were winning 4–3 and serving. The rally was three shots long and the Canadians won the rally by a double block through position 3 involving Canadian players 4 and 1. The Korean spiker number 6, was blocked out whilst spiking diagonally from position 3, by the Canadian block. The Canadians won the point bringing the score up to 5–3.

Results

The set was notated (see Table 6.13) and the results analysed and tabulated. The raw data was split up into points won by the Canadian and Korean teams, and points lost. Percentages were calculated to analyse where points were won and lost by each team (Tables 6.14 and 6.15). Gaps left in the raw data indicated that this point had been won or lost by the team, when the opponents' touch of the ball was not significant.

Table 6.12   Example of the notation system used to analyse a volleyball match between Canada (C) and Korea (K).

No.	Score	Server	Net shots	Losing point			Winning point			Comments
				Player	Action	Position	Player	Action	Position	
12	4–3	C	3	6	K	3	4,1	BB	3	Diagonal spike
13	5–3	C								

Table 6.13 Data collected using the notation system from a volleyball match between Canada (C) and Korea (K).

No.	Score	Server	Net shots	Losing point Player	Action	Position	Winning point Player	Action	Position	Comments
1.	0–0	C	5	2	DF	4	9	K	3	
2.	1–0	C	3	2	K	4	1,9	BB	2	
3.	2–0	C	2	2	DF	41		K	4	
4.	3 0	C	1	C	RO	1				
5.	0–3	K	3	6	M	4		D	6	Ball out – off foot
6.	1–3	K	1		KN	5				
7.	2–3	K	2	11	DF	3		K	3	
8.	3–2	C	4	9	KO	1				
9.	2–3	K	3	1	DF	1	2	T	4	
10.	3–3	K	2	1	DF	2	5	K	4	
11.	3–3	K	4		K	3	4,5	BB	4	
12.	4–3	C	3	6	K	3	4,1	BB	3	Diagonal spike
13.	5–3	C	2		K	2	4,1	BB	4	
14.	6–3	C	2		K	4	4,1	BB	2	
15.	7–3	C	3	2	DF	2	3	K	3	
16.	8–3	C	2		DF	2		T	4	Foul against C-lifting
17.	3–8	K	3	7	M					Double tch C7 setting
18.	4–8	C	5	11	KN	4				
19.	8–4	K	3		DF	3		T	3	Ref changed decision
20.	4–8	C	2	11	DF	6	4	S	3	
21.	8–4	K	2		BBO	2	11	K	4	Rebound BB hit antenna – pt. K
22.	4–8	K	1	6	RO	1				
23.	8–4	C	3	11	K	2	11,6	BB	4	
24.	9–4	C	3	1	DF	6	1	T	3	
25.	4–9	K	4		BBN	2	9	K	4	
26.	9–4	C	2		DF	5	2	K	4	
27.	4–9	K	2	6	DF	5	9	K	3	K lost block
28.	9–4	C	2	12	DO	2				
29.	4–9	K	2	1,4,6	DF	5	1	K	3	K lost block
30.	9–4	C	2		BBBo	3	2	K	3	
31.	4–9	K	3	3	DF	5	9	K	2	

ABOUT THE MATCH NOTATED:

Women's International Volleyball Tournament.
Date – January 1987.
SEMI FINAL – Canada versus S. Korea
Notated from video.

Table 6.14   An analysis of the winning points played by both teams in the match between Canada and Korea, 1987.

	Canada		Korea	
	Number	%	Number	%
Serve	0	0	0	0
Dig	0	0	0	0
Set	1	6	0	0
Spike	8	47	9	60
Block	7	41	2	13
Tip	1	6	4	27
Total	17	100	15	100

Table 6.15   An analysis of the losing points played by both teams in the match between Canada and Korea, 1987.

	Canada		Korea	
	Number	%	Number	%
Serve	2	10	3	12
RN	0	0	1	4
RO	2	10	2	8
Dig	11	52	12	46
DF	8	37	10	38
DN	1	5	1	4
DO	2	10	1	4
Set	0	0	0	0
Spike	3	15	9	34
KBB	1	5	7	26
KN	1	5	1	4
KO	1	5	1	4
Block	5	23	2	8
Tip	0	0	0	0
Total	17	100	15	100

ABOUT THE TEAMS:

SOUTH KOREA
World Ranked No. 8.
Team of young players preparing for 1992 Olympics.

STAR PLAYERS:

1. KWOW YUN-HEE (Captain)
Age 17, Height 1.8 m
POS – outside attack (i.e. spiking through no. 4)

9. RYOU-YOUN SOO
Age 16, Height 1.83 m (tallest players in team)
POS – outside attack

7. KIM JU-RANG
Age 16, Height 1.70 m
POS – setter

CANADA
World Ranking No. 15.

STAR PLAYERS:

11. KRISTINE DRAKICH (Captain)
Age 22, Height 1.72 m
POS – outside attack

9. EILEEN KRAMCHYNSKY
Age 21, Height 1.81 m
POS – centre attack (i.e. spiking through no. 3)

6. HEATHER SAWYER
Age 24, Height 1.73 m
POS – setter

NOTATED 2nd SET Canada leading 1–0.

It can be seen by a simple analysis of the winning shots that the Canadian team won 44% of its points by blocking, compared with the Koreans who only succeeded with two blocks throughout the set (13% of shots won). This was due mainly to the height of each team. The Canadians, being taller, had a block that was far superior to that of the Koreans. This theory was reinforced by the percentage of points lost. The Korean team lost 26% of their points by their spikes being blocked out, compared with 5% of the Canadian team.

However, the Korean team won 60% of their points by spiking, which showed that they were a strong attacking team in this action, especially considering their size. The Korean team began to tip the ball over the top of the block and won 27% of their points in doing so. This change in tactics proved very effective as the Korean team lost no points whilst tipping the ball. This also showed that the Canadian team were relying on their block too much, as the ineffectiveness of the block cost the Canadian team 37% of their losing points (Pf – failing to pick up the ball).

As the Korean team were small and their block was inferior to that of the Canadians, then their corner and back court play should be improved to compensate for this physical disadvantage. The Koreans lost 38% of their points from failing to dig the ball after the spike.

The conclusions made were very simple and general; detailed statistical analysis is required to show if any of the results obtained would be significant. However, they do give an indication of the quantity of data obtained from a reasonably simple system.

By analysing the data obtained on individual players, an analysis could be formed of the performance of each player. Preferences by players for certain positions could be examined, as well as the system of attack and defence that the team operated.

6.3.3 A NOTATION SYSTEM FOR SOCCER

The aim of this notation system was to notate the distribution ability of a right full-back in soccer.

Method

Notation occurred each time the subject, the right full-back of Brook House FC, appeared to play or distribute the ball. The following symbols and meanings were used in order for the system to function:

- 'Clearances-' above symbols preceded by 'C', e.g. CF2 is a clearance by foot of between 10 and 30 yards (it should be noted that clearances were neither counted as completed or incompleted passes).

- 'Shots-' above symbols for feet or head preceded by 'F' for a goal and 'X' for a miss.

- 'Completed pass-' above symbols for feet, head or hand.

- 'Uncompleted pass-' above symbols for feet, head or hand, *circled*.

- The time elapsed of the half was also recorded at the end of each piece of information.

Therefore, an example of notated data is as follows:

CH3 12,37

This refers to a clearance by head of a distance of 30 yards or more, that occurred after 12 min 37 s of the half. These data were then recorded in columns on a prepared data collection sheet (see Table 6.16).

Results

The data was collected over 45 min (one half) of a 'local Sunday football league' match.

Table 6.16   Symbols for actions of a full-back in soccer.

Passes/clearances/shots	Distances	Symbols
By foot	<10 yards	F1
	10–30 yards	F2
	>10–30 yards	F3
By head	<10 yards	H1
	10–30 yards	H2
	>30 yards	H3
By hand	<10 yards	T1
(i.e. throw-in)	10–30 yards	T2
	>30 yards	T3

Match Information Date = 29/10/89   Start = 12.09 p.m.

First half of   Bow and Arrow FC   *versus*   Brook House FC
                (Black and white stripes)   (Royal blue and navy stripes)

Half-time score 1–3

The data were obtained by notating the first half of the above match and processing the data in a very simple way. From these results the following analysis was carried out.

Analysis

1. Number of touches of the ball = 29

2. Number of touches of the ball by each method:
   (i)   Number of foot contacts = 21
   (ii) Number of headed contacts = 3
   (iii) Number of throw-ins = 5

3. Percentage of touches by each method:
   (i)   Feet = 21/29 = 72.4%
   (ii) Head = 3/29 = 10.4%
   (iii) Throw-ins = 5/29 = 17.2%

4. Number of incomplete passes (i.e. errors), signified by circled symbol = 9

5. Number of errors by each method:
   (i)   Feet = 8
   (ii) Head = 0
   (iii) Throw-ins = 1

6. Percentage of errors by each method:
   (i)   Feet = 8/9 = 88.9%
   (ii) Head = 0/9 = 0%
   (iii) Throw-ins = 11.1%

7. Distribution at the various distances:
   (A) Total analysis
   (i)   Total < 10 yards = 14   [By foot = 12, By head = 1, Throw-in = 1]
   (ii) Total 10–30 yards = 11 [By foot = 5, By head = 2, Throw-in = 4]
   (iii) Total > 30 yards = 4   [By foot = 4, By head = 0, Throw-in = 0]
   TOTAL: 29

   Percentages of this total analysis (Ai–iii):
   Total < 10 yards = 48.3%
                   [By foot = 85.7%, By head = 7.1%, Throw-in = 7.1%]
   Total 10–30 yards = 37.9%
                   [By foot = 45.5%, By head = 18.2%, Throw-in = 37.4%]
   Total > 30 yards = 13.8%   [By foot = 100%]

   (B) Completed pass analysis (not including clearances):
   (i)   Total < 10 yards = 3   [By foot = 2, By head = 0, Throw-in = 1]
   (ii) Total 10–30 yards = 6 [By foot = 3, By head = 0, Throw-in = 3]
   (iii) Total > 30 yards = 2   [By foot = 2, By head = 0, Throw-in = 0]
   TOTAL: 11
   *Includes one successful attempt at goal

   Percentages of completed pass analysis (Bi–iii):
   Total < 10 yards = 27.3% [By foot = 66.7%, Throw-in = 33.3%]
   Total 10–30 yards = 54.6%   [By foot = 50%, Throw-in = 50%]
   Total > 30 yards = 18.2% [By foot = 100%]

   (C) Uncompleted pass analysis (not including clearances):
   (i)   Total < 10 yards = 6   [By foot = 6]
   (ii) Total 10–30 yards = 2 [By foot = 1, Throw-in = 1]
   (iii) Total > 30 yards = 1   [By foot = 1]
   TOTAL: 9

   Percentages of uncompleted pass analysis (Ci–iii):
   Total < 10 yards = 66.7%   [By foot = 100%]
   Total 10–30 yards = 22.2% [By foot = 50%, Throw-in = 50%]
   Total > 30 yards = 11.1%   [By foot = 100%]

8. Ratio: completed passes to total number of passes = 11/20 = 0.55
   Ratio: uncompleted passes to total number of passes = 9/20 = 0.45
   [NB, does not include clearances]

9. Clearance study:
   (A) Total number of clearances = 9

(B) Total number of clearances at each distance:
(i) Total < 10 yards = 5   [By foot = 4, By head = 1]
(ii) Total 10–30 yards = 3   [By foot = 1, By head = 2]
(iii) Total > 30 yards = 1   [By foot = 1]   Percentages of B(i–iii):
Total < 10 yards = 55.6%   [By foot = 80%, By head = 20%]
Total 10–30 yards = 33.3%   [By foot = 33.3%, By head = 66.7%]
Total > 30 yards = 11.1%   [By foot = 100%]

10. Outline of the subject's activity:

SECTION (min)		No. Touches	Successful	Unsuccessful	Clears
(i)	0–5	2	1	1	0
(ii)	5–10	2	0	1	0
(iii)	10–15	4	1	2	1
(iv)	15–20	4	1	1	2
(v)	20–25	3	3	0	0
(vi)	25–30	3	1	2	0
(vii)	30–35	1	0	0	1
(iix)	35–40	3	1	0	2
(ix)	40–45	4	3*	1	0
(x)	45–50	3	0	1	2

*Including one successful attempt at goal.

See Figures 6.12–6.15 for a visual representation of some of the data.

Discussion

Just one half of a soccer match does not produce anything like a significant
amount of data about which conclusions can be drawn, but this example
does give ideas about analysing and presenting data. A few statements can
be made about these interpretations. The majority of the full-back

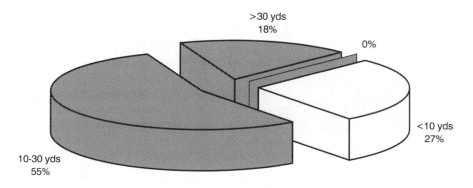

Figure 6.12   Representation of the number of completed passes.

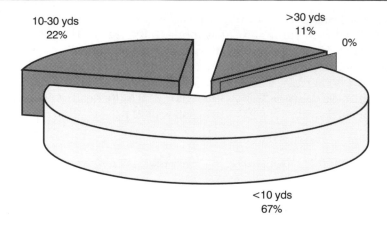

Figure 6.13   Representation of the number of incomplete passes.

'touches', 72.4%, were performed by the foot. However, this percentage led to a larger amount of errors, 88.9%, being by foot contact. There was a roughly equal distribution of passes performed over distances of less than 10 yards and between 10 and 30 yards, 48.3 and 37.9% respectively. Despite this almost equal distribution, the subject was twice as successful at passing over a distance of between 10 and 30 yards as one of less than 10 yards. This success over the intermediate distance (10–30 yards) is mirrored by the fact that the subject committed only one-fifth of the total errors committed over the distance. From the analysis it was found that the subject performed 10% more completed passes (not including clearances) than uncompleted passes (not including clearances).

Analysis of the clearances the subject performed shows that the

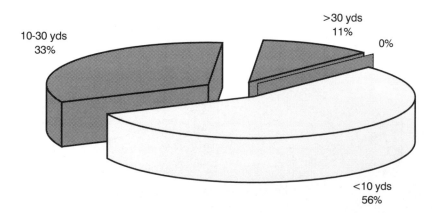

Figure 6.14   Representation of the clearances.

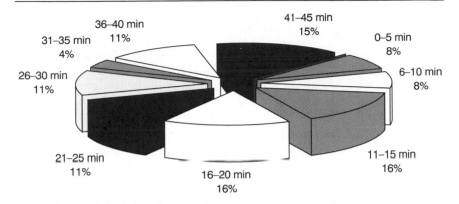

Figure 6.15   Representation of the percentage of activities throughout the first half.

majority were carried out over the short distance of less than 10 yards. As the 'direction of distribution' was not recorded (see adjustments) this aspect of clearance distance is difficult to interpret, but a partial explanation could be that the full-back plays near to the touchline and so a safe clearance will be over this touchline, which in many situations will be less than 10 yards from the point of play. The subject's intense periods of involvement were evenly spread throughout the half, with no one '5 min section' having no activity. A more general observation is of the small contribution that heading made to the subject's play, but this could be explained by the opposition employing two small forwards and subsequently not playing the ball to them in the air.

It would be interesting to see if these statements still held true with six to eight matches of data. Many of these points are somewhat subjective as they are made on the basis of only one short data collection session. It could be that all of the points made came about due to the context of the game, and a completely different set of remarks could have occurred if a different game had been notated.

The exercise did, however, produce some recommendations to improve the system.

Adjustments to the system

1. Divide foot passes into left foot or right foot passes. Therefore the present symbol would be proceeded by an 'L' or an 'R', e.g. FL = a left foot pass of 10 yards or less.
2. Notate fouls and indiscretions (i.e. bookings or sendings-off's).
3. Notate attempts on goal with a separate symbol = 'S', e.g. SFL, ! = a successful attempt at goal with the left foot less than 10 yards from

goal; SH, X = an unsuccessful attempt at goal with the head less than 10 yards from goal.

4. Notation of tackles could be introduced; but this is moving away from the aim of notating the 'distribution ability' of a full-back.

5. Notation with the aid of a grid. The grid could be designed by measuring the length and width of a pitch and dividing it into nine equal areas (see Figure 6.16), and then notation of positional data from where the full-back passes, and to where the passes go, becomes possible. This grid adjustment could lead to two methods of notating:

   (i) Produce printed sheets of the grid and for each piece of notation draw a line from the origin of the pass (i.e. position of full-back) to its destination, and on the same sheet include the appropriate symbol and time as before.

OR

   (ii) Similar to the original system notating in columns, the following type of codes could be used:

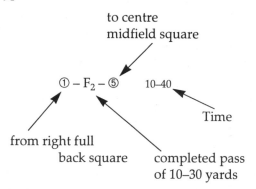

Method (i) would be more accurate as the exact position and not just the square would be notated. However, it would require one sheet for each piece of information notated. Also learning time would be much longer and 'logging time' for each action would be longer and more complicated.

6.3.4 A NOTATION SYSTEM FOR NETBALL.

A netball team consists of seven players. Each player has a limited area within which to operate. Every player is allocated a specific role in the game which corresponds to the area in which they operate. The object of the game is to attempt to score as many goals as possible. To achieve this requires team cohesion, co-operation and understanding between all the team members. A skilful game of netball relies on effective passing to maintain possession of the ball.

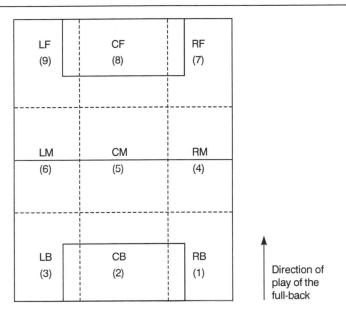

Figure 6.16   Schematic diagram of a soccer pitch showing suggested divisions of the playing area into a grid for notation.

Method

Before outlining the system, it is necessary to ensure that you understand the basic rules of the game.

Essential rules of netball

Like any other team game netball has its own specific set of rules which must be adhered to throughout the match. Before a system of notational analysis can be designed it is important to be familiar with these rules:

1. There is a 3 s limit on the time it takes a team member to pass the ball or attempt a shot at goal.
2. The ball must be caught or touched in each third of the court during play.
3. The centre pass must be caught or touched by a player allowed in the centre third of the court (Figure 6.17)
4. When a ball goes out of court it can only be thrown in by a player allowed in that particular area.
5. Only the goal-shooter or goal-attack can score a goal. The ball must also have been wholly caught within the goal circle.
6. A player must keep within the limits of area prescribed by her position.

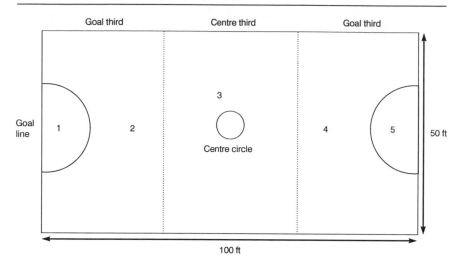

Figure 6.17 Schematic representation of the netball court for divisions of the playing surface.

Notation symbols

The symbols to be used will record the following:

1. The team member in possession of the ball and the position on the court where they received the ball.
2. What happens at the end of the passing sequence before reverting back to the centre pass or change of possession.
3. Out-of-court shots where the ball has been passed outside the side line.

Each player wears a vest with letters representing their roles (each one is self-explanatory):

GK	goal-keeper
GD	goal defence
WD	wing defence
C	centre
WA	wing attack
GA	goal attack
GS	goal shooter

The court was divided into five areas so that a simple view of the path of the ball can be deduced (Figure 6.17)

1	goal circle
2	goal third
3	centre third
4	goal third
5	goal circle

Each player has a prescribed playing area – these are designated in Table 6.17.

Actions

V   goal scored (should be followed by a centre pass).
X   goal attempted but missed.
O   out-of-court shot (the appropriate team is given a free throw from the side line where the ball went out).
C   centre pass (no court position number is added since it is always taken from within the centre circle).

Continued notation within the column implies a successful pass.

The record sheet

It is necessary for the recording sheet to contain descriptive details of the match or practices session so that the information obtained is available for analysis and future reference if required.

1. Match or practice session?
2. Venue.
3. Date.
4. (If possible) names of players.

The recording sheet consists of vertical columns under the headings of red and blue (referring to the team colours). Play is recorded in the

Table 6.17   Each player has designated areas within which they must play.

Player	Areas for team playing from area 1 towards area 5		
GK	1	2	
GD	1	2	3
WD	2	3	
C	2	3	4
WA		3	4
GA	3	4	5
GS		4	5

appropriate column according to the team in possession of the ball. Play is recorded from the top to the bottom of the column. The score is shown at the left side of each column.

Recording a sequence

Each sequence begins with the centre pass represented by the symbol 'C'. The centre pass is always taken from within the centre circle. Play continues and the player and position are notated. The sequence is completed when a goal is scored and represented by the symbol 'V'. An example of a record sheet is shown in Table 6.18

Results

The results (see Table 6.19) showed that the red ream were more successful at retaining possession once they had got it. The red team averaged three passes per possession and had only two passing errors. Both passing errors were caused by the red centre player passing the ball out-of-court.

The blue team had more possessions but that did not compensate for their passing errors since they only managed 1.6 passes per possession and incurred more passing errors. From this short example of data few conclusions can be drawn about the play – much more data is needed. However, the notation exercise enabled an assessment of the notation system. By examining the record sheet there are several factors that can be analysed without a great deal of effort:

1. The number of possessions by each team. A possession is defined as a single player or sequence of players following each other simultaneously in the team's column on the record sheet.

Table 6.18 Example of a record sheet for simple data gathering for notation of netball.

Score	Red	Blue	Score	Red	Blue
		C		O	
		WA 3		GD 4	
		GA 4		WD 3	
		GS 5		C3	
		X		O	GK 2
		GS 5			O
0–1		V		WA 3	
	C			C 3	
	WA 3			GA 2	
	C 2			GS 1	
	GS 1		2–1	V	
1–1	V				
	C			etc.	

Table 6.19   Data processed from a notated netball match (part only).

	Red	Blue
No. of possessions	7	10
No. of passes	21	16
Average sequence	21/7=3	16/10=1.6
No. of passing errors	2	4

2. Related to the number of possessions is the number of passing errors induced by a team and the frequency of passing errors by a particular player. To obtain a percentage of passing errors it would be necessary to evaluate the number of touches by that player. It is then also possible for the coach to assess whether the team is making good use of all the players in the team, although this is somewhat dependent on their accessibility at the time. The latter information would need to be combined with the coaches own subjective observations. A passing error would be defined as the ball changing possession or going out-of-court. A touch would be defined as the ball actually being caught and passed or must being touched as it travelled through the air.
3. It is possible to calculate the average number of passes in a sequence. This is important when assessing the path of the ball, particularly from the centre pass to an attempt at goal. A common strategy outlined in books is a three-pass attack down the centre although a two-pass attack is possible. The greater the number of passes incurred the greater the opportunity for defenders to break the attack.
4. A percentage success rate of goals by the goal shooter and goal attack can be calculated. It allows the coach to assess which, or if both, players need goal-shooting practice.
5. When analysing who attempted the most shots at goal it could be beneficial to work backwards and see the shots leading to the attempt. With sufficient data it may be possible to outline a common attacking strategy.

Although the record sheet appears 'simplistic', a great deal of information can be gleaned from it. It is possible to assemble a quick summary after the match. Given more time more detailed information may be extracted. Once the notation is sufficiently rehearsed it is easy to modify the system to take into consideration a number of other factors.

Possible improvements we could make include:

1. The court could be subdivided into smaller sections to outline a more accurate path of the ball, which can then be transferred to plans of play, e.g. this would be useful when tracing the path of the ball from centre pass – a common strategy advocated in coaching books is an

attack down the centre. By recording the team's patterns with their centre-pass, the coach can conclude whether the centre line attacking strategy is successful for them or whether the team tends to play more down one side than the other. On the other hand, having more position cells, will mean that more matches will have to be analysed to produce significant amounts of data in all the cells.

2. Players can be penalized for foot-faults, but this is not a common occurrence in experienced players so it would only be relevant when notating novices.

3. A throw-up is called for when a player of each team gains possession of the ball equally at the same time. The success of gaining possession by a particular team could be notated.

6.3.5 A NOTATION SYSTEM FOR RUGBY UNION – KICKING

The aim was to develop a notation system to notate kicking actions in rugby union.

Method

The data that needed to be recorded was:

1. The number of the player who kicked the ball.
2. The type of kick.
3. The area in which kick was made.
4. What was the initial outcome (whether it was for the home or away side).
5. Area in which the ball was regained.
6. How it was regained and whether it was immediate.
7. Whether it was a gain or loss of ground.

The position at which the kick was made was recorded using the cell codes shown in Figure 6.18. The players were notated by their shirt number.

The symbols

Before each symbol, the letter L or the letter R will be written. These represent whether the kick was made with the left foot or with the right foot, respectively.

- **Place kick (^).** This is when the ball is kicked from a stationary point on the ground, with the ball being placed on a tee of turf or sand (generally used for conversion, penalty and kick off).

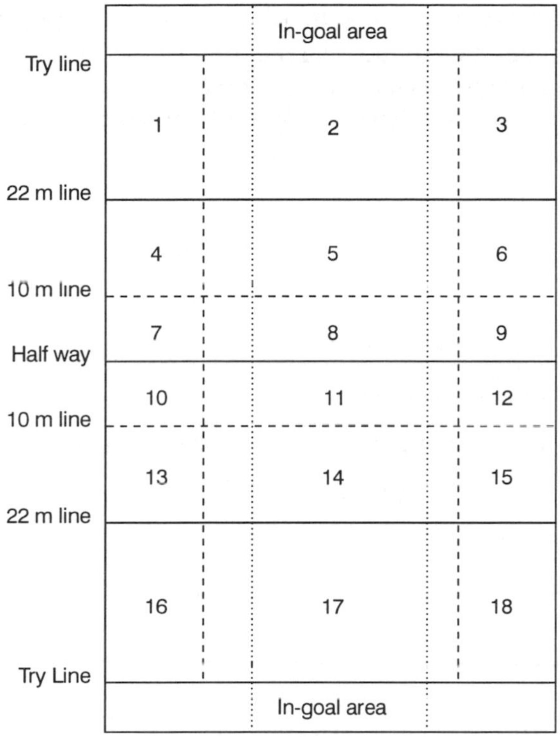

Figure 6.18 Schematic diagram of a rugby pitch to enable definition of the position cells for a notation system of kicking in the game.

- **Drop kick (v).** A drop kick is when the ball is kicked by the kicker, after being dropped by the kicker and at the instant of touching the floor (used for kick offs and goal attempts).
- **Grubber kick (m).** The grubber kick is used for tactical purposes to try and gain ground. The kicker kicks the ball out of his hands and along the floor with the point of contact of the ball with the floor being close to the kicker.
- **Chip kick (n).** This kick is performed when the opposition are coming up from defence, in a flat line. The ball is kicked over the head(s) of the oncoming opponent(s) and lands within 15 yards of being kicked.
- **Spiral kick (z).** The spiral kick is generally used as a clearance kick to touch as it is possible to get great distance with the kick. On kicking, the ball is kicked with the outside of the foot, which causes the ball to revolve. As a result the ball will travel further.
- **High kick (h).** This is a kick which is, as its name suggests, kicked high into the air and as far down the field as possible.

- **Fly hack (-).** This kick generally results from play of the ball. The ball is kicked along the ground, like the grubber kick, but instead of being kicked from the hands it is kicked off the floor.
- **Mis-kick (\).** This is where a kick is attempted but kicked incorrectly and as such its desired effect is not achieved.

Other symbols used:

*	possession had been regained immediately after the kick
C	the ball is caught by a particular player of that side
S	scrum awarded
L	line-out awarded
H	conversion/penalty, goal has been scored
D	drop-out has been awarded
I	interception
Wh	line-out was won
R	ball has been won from a ruck
F	free-kick has been awarded
Mp	missed penalty goal attempt
T	try has been scored
CD	charged slows kick
P	penalty
To or Ho	opposition has scored
Cm	a successful mark has been called

A sheet marked out in columns was used to record the data. A pre-recorded match (Cardiff versus New Zealand, 1989) was notated, for one team, by hand while watching a video of the match using the symbols and letters listed above, and also the areas of the field as shown in Figure 6.18. The video was rewound and the notation was repeated for the other team and recorded in the same way. From these tables various sets of information were taken for both sides. These included the number of times a certain kick was used. This was then compared with the percentage of the separate kicks that resulted in a gain/loss of yardage on repossession of the ball. Other sets of information included

1. Percentage success of the attempted spiral kicks, i.e. whether they made touch or not

2. Number of times possession was immediately regained following a kick
3. Whose half of the field the kicks and repossession took place.

From these results it was hoped to then show which side played the more effective kicking game and also which team had more territorial advantage during the game.

Results

The game that was notated was the first half of the Cardiff versus New Zealand game played at the National Stadium in Cardiff on 14 October 1989. The results of the notation are shown in Tables 6.20–6.22. From the data, the graphs in Figures 6.19 and 6.20 were constructed.

Table 6.22 shows that New Zealand also had the higher success rate for kicks that were aimed to touch. These data also demonstrate that the game was almost evenly matched in territorial terms for the first half,

Table 6.20 Summary data analysis of the kicking data for New Zealand from the first half of the rugby match between Cardiff and New Zealand, 1989.

	Types of kick							
	Place	Drop	Spiral	Grubber	Fly	Miss	High	Chip
No.	5	3	9	3	0	0	5	5
Per cent result in gain	80	66	66	100	0	0	80	0
Per cent result in loss	20	33	22	0	0	0	20	60

Table 6.21 Summary data analysis of the kicking data for Cardiff from the first half of the rugby match between Cardiff and New Zealand, 1989.

	Types of kick							
	Place	Drop	Spiral	Grubber	Fly	Miss	High	Chip
No.	4	3	15	3	1	0	3	0
Per cent result in gain	50	33	53	100	0	0	66	0
Per cent result in loss	25	33	13	0	0	0	0	0

Table 6.22   Summary data analysis of the spiral kicking data for Cardiff from the first half of the rugby match between Cardiff and New Zealand, 1989.

	New Zealand	Cardiff
Successful spiral kicks to touch (%)	89	60
Immediate repossession from kick	12	7
Kicked in:		
own half	21	23
opposition half	9	6
Repossessed in:		
own half	17	14
opposition half	13	15

with New Zealand having a slight advantage. The results show that the percentage success of gains in ground resulting from the majority of kicks were significantly better for New Zealand than Cardiff. Figures 6.19 and 6.20 as well demonstrate this comparison, but they also show some other interesting facts. They show that even though Cardiff used the spiral kick almost twice the amount that New Zealand did, the success rate

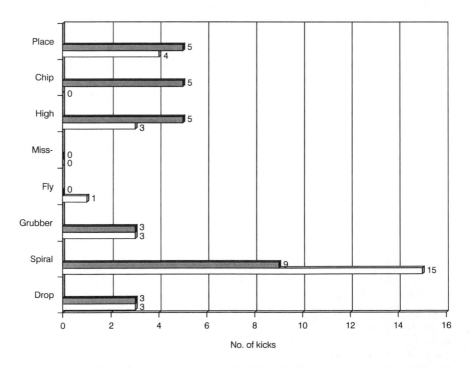

Figure 6.19   The kicking patterns of Cardiff and New Zealand in the first half (1989). ☐ Cardiff; ▨ New Zealand.

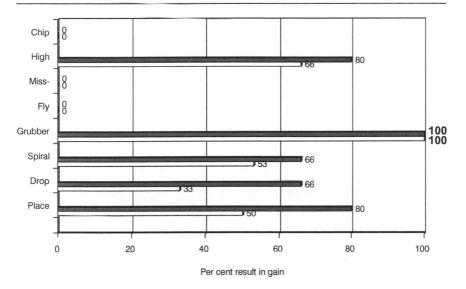

Figure 6.20   The distribution of kicks that gained ground in the match of Cardiff and New Zealand in the first half (1989). ☐ Cardiff; ▓ New Zealand.

for New Zealand was significantly higher than that of Cardiff. Both sides had a 100% success rate for gain of ground with the grubber kick whereas New Zealand, who chip kicked the ball five times, had a 0% success rate and a 60% fail rate for this kick.

Discussion

Once again the amount of data is small – this was a pilot study to test the system rather than make conclusions about the data, but the processing of these data suggest certain trends that this form of analysis can demonstrate.

The success rate for the spiral kick for New Zealand being higher than that for Cardiff could be due to the fact that New Zealand's kicks were mainly made by one player (No. 10) whereas with Cardiff the honours were shared (see Tables 6.18 and 6.19). It can therefore be suggested, from this notation, that to have a high success rate of kicks it is better policy to have one player kicking the ball. This is also supported with the success of the spiral kicks to touch.

The coach, for either side, could look at the results of the analysis and see that the most effective kick for his side is the grubber kick as it has a 100% success rate and as a result he could work on tactics around the grubber kick training. The notation also showed that either Cardiff have a good defence against the chip kick or that New Zealand are poor with it as they have a 60% failure rate and a 0% success rate with it. This would inform the New Zealand coach that the chip kick should be practised and drilled thoroughly in training to increase the success rate. The information gained for the kicks seems to go hand in hand with that of the territorial advantage, i.e. New Zealand had a better success rate of kicks and also a slight territorial advantage. This, however, is misleading because despite the facts that New Zealand were playing better than Cardiff, they were losing 9–3 at half time.

The main criticism of the system is that only one team can be notated at any one time. This is due to the extent of information that is written about the kick. To notate for both sides, either post-event analysis from video or two separate people using this system would have to be used. Another criticism is that some of the information used, such as how the ball was regained, is redundant and as such could be either dispensed with or improved to gain some further information about the game. The final criticism is that the divisions of the playing area are possibly too big; in certain situations it was difficult to determine whether a gain of yardage had been achieved. However, decreasing the size of the areas would make the notation more difficult and complex.

How to develop a computerized notation system

7

7.1 INTRODUCTION

The aim of this chapter is to build on the logical structure already created by the analysis of sport and the structuring of decision pathways, and then go on to explore and design flowcharts for computer programs. The next progression is to convert these flowcharts into sets of sequential instructions and hence into programs. If you are not familiar with any computing languages, this chapter should still be of use – for two reasons. If you are intending to learn to program there is no better way than having a specific goal for your first programs, but note that you will need help from other sources such as specific language textbooks and, almost certainly, the advice of an expert now and then. If you do not wish to gain these skills but are intending to use someone to do the programming for you, then this part of the book will prove invaluable in helping your communication with that expert. If you can already program, be patient with the simple approach; there are a number of very helpful pieces of advice, gained from years of experience (i.e. mistakes), hidden within these elementary programs.

The program examples are given mainly in BASIC as this is the most common computer language. Those who intend to use other languages can still benefit from the logic and experience present within the programs in this chapter, as the same principles will apply.

Examples of programs and parts of programs are given later in the chapter.

7.2 ADVANTAGES AND DISADVANTAGES OF MANUAL AND COMPUTERIZED NOTATION SYSTEMS

There are situations in which it is better to use computers to gather and process the required data, and there are others when the use of expensive hardware is inefficient. A good manual system, in a great many field situations, will do the job as quickly, more accurately and considerably more cheaply. Consider the advantages and disadvantages of both types of systems:

7.2.1 HAND NOTATION SYSTEMS

(a) Advantages

1. They are inexpensive.
2. They are easily portable, the venue does not normally affect their operation – they do not need power cables or batteries.
3. They are more accurate. This surprises a large number of people who assume that, because they are using computers, they are being more scientific and more accurate. Sadly this is not so. This is discussed more fully later.

(b) Disadvantages

1. The more sophisticated the system, the greater is the learning time involved in mastering the data collection. For example, the notation system developed to record a squash match by Sanderson and Way (1979) needed between 5 and 8 h of practise time before sufficient skills were gained to use the system in real-time.
2. The more sophisticated the system, the more data it will produce and consequently the more time that must be spent in processing that data. The system of Sanderson and Way, described above and in more detail in Chapter 5, produced such a mass of data that to process one match, lasting approximately 1 h, would take another 40–50 h of work.

7.2.2 COMPUTERIZED NOTATION SYSTEMS

(a) Advantages

1. They enable large sets of data to be processed very quickly and effortlessly, once the collection is completed. Hughes (1983) computerized the data processing side of the Sanderson–Way system, reducing the data processing time to 90 min, the time taken by the printer to print the graphs. Fortunately, the speed of printers has increased considerably, so the equivalent hardcopies (i.e. printout on paper) could be produced much more quickly now. Data presentation to the screen took only a matter of seconds.
2. Increasing sophistication of hardware has enabled the data coding and entry to become easier so much so that in some recent systems, even for complex games such as basketball or rugby, the learning time

is minimal. Specifically designed keyboards, e.g. Franks (1983) for soccer, and Alderson and Mackinnon (1985) for squash, make data entry for those sports involved very easy, but the large step forward in this field came with the use of the specialist 'bit-pads', e.g. Hughes and Feery (1986) for basketball, Sharp (1986) for table tennis, and Franks and Goodman (1986) for field hockey. More recently systems (Hughes and Clarke, A., 1995; Hughes and Clarke, S., 1995) have incorporated graphical user interfaces – the operator using a mouse to click on-screen icons to enter the data.

3. The developing quality of computer graphics is easing the sometimes difficult job of data presentation and, in turn, increasing the depth of analysis possible.

4. Some recent work (Franks, Johnson and Sinclair, 1988; Hughes, Franks and Nagelkerke, 1989; Hughes, 1994a, 1995) have used the computer in real-time analysis and stored the data sequentially, with a time base, enabling post-event time-based analyses, such as time-and-motion studies, and modelling.

5. The interfacing of computers with video decks enables the combination of the tasks of firstly analysing the data and then editing the video to enable the coach/athlete to view the relevant parts of the match. While entering the data into the computer in live play mode of the video, the computer places signals onto the second audio channel of the videotape, thus enabling the computer to find any required sequences later. This greatly reduces the time spent in going through tapes again and again to find the specific pieces of play.

(b) Disadvantages

1. Computers, and all the peripheral requirements such as visual display units, printers, disc drives, etc., are relatively expensive. The prices are continually decreasing, but compared to a hand notation system, the cost of a computerized system will always be a factor.

2. Computers are not as portable as they might seem. Their batteries tend to run down relatively quickly, so care must be taken to ensure a long enough battery life to notate a long event. What happens while the batteries are being changed (this usually necessitates the shut-down of the machine)? These problems are becoming less difficult as computer technology advances.

3. The data entry systems to computers, although improving all the time, will inevitably introduce extra sources of error that will not occur in hand systems. This is balanced to a certain extent in as much as the data processing will be error free, which is unlikely in a hand processed set of data.

There is a level of notation, in terms of either complexity of data gathering or data processing, above which it becomes profitable in time and expense to use computers.

Ultimately this decision must be made by the user, since it devolves onto subjective evaluation of time, accuracy, data storage and data presentation. When in doubt, always be prepared to consult with experts in either notation or computers, or preferably both.

7.3 CREATING THE FLOWCHARTS FOR THE PROGRAMS

The ease with which sports analysis flowcharts can be converted to sets of logical sequential instructions (programs) demonstrates the suitability of computers in the behavioural analysis of sports or any other structured activities. The first step in creating any programs is to create the flowcharts of the logical decisions to be made within the program. This logical pathway definition is the first step in sports analysis, it has to be completed before getting down to the job of deciding what data are to be notated. Consequently the logic is already there for a program of the game to be created. Consider the flowchart of basketball (see Figure 7.1), this is easily converted into sequential instructions and a simple example of a first attempt is shown in Figure 7.2.

7.4 SEQUENTIAL INSTRUCTIONS

Not many programmers will use sequential instructions as part of the process of creating programs, in fact not many use flowcharts. Although all programmers will pay lip service to creating the logical 'templates' from which they create their programs, few in practice are self-disciplined enough to use this necessary creative tool. In all teaching situations, and complex and advanced programming, this process is always followed. Sequential instructions do provide a logical step between the flowchart and the program that will make it easier for all readers to follow the logic involved in the designing of notation systems. It certainly makes it easier for us to understand the logical processes involved.

Let us examine the different 'blocks' within this set of instructions with a view to understanding the logic within each one.

Consider the following set of instructions.

```
10 Start.
20 Who is in possession?
30 Enter team.
```

This is the starting block, and asks for the team initially in possession. It enables later entry of the team in possession when situations arise that

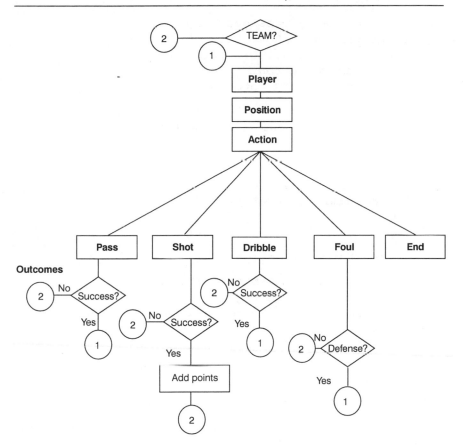

Figure 7.1   Flow chart of basketball.

bring about a change. In a more detailed analysis, this block would perhaps be preceded by another routine to include provision for entering all team and players' names, details of the substitutes, the venue, climactic conditions, officials names, competition, date, final score (if working from video), etc.

```
40 Enter position.
50 Enter player.
60 Enter choice of action.
```

This is the 'event entry section', the main data entry of the action – where it is happening, who is executing the action and what the action is. The set of instructions (the program) has to decide on the possible outcomes, with the help of the operator, of course.

```
70 If action was a pass goto 120
80 If action was a shot goto 100
90 If action was a dribble goto 160
100 If action was a foul goto 190
110 If action was END goto 999
```

Each of these instructions responds to whatever the operator entered at line 60, the Action, by sending the program to the line corresponding to

```
10 Start.
20 Who is in possession?
30 Enter team.

40 Enter position.
50 Enter player.
60 Enter choice of action.

70 If action was a pass goto 120
80 If action was a shot goto 100
90 If action was a dribble goto 160
100 If action was a foul goto 190
110 If action was END goto 999

120 Action — PASS, was it successful?
130 If YES then goto 40
140 If NO then CHANGE POSSESSION and then goto 40

150 Action — SHOT,
160 What was its value?
170 Was it successful?
180 If YES, increase score by requisite amount,
    CHANGE POSSESSION and goto 40.
190 If NO, which team won rebound?
200 Goto 40.

210 Action — DRIBBLE, was it successful?
220 If YES then goto 40
230 If NO then CHANGE POSSESSION and goto 40

240 Action — FOUL
250 Was it an offensive foul?
260 If YES then CHANGE POSSESSION and goto 40
270 If NO then goto 40

999 Stop
```

Figure 7.2   Sequential instructions for the game of basketball.

the Action, where the possible outcomes are explored. The last line of this section enables the operator to stop the program running.

```
120 Action — PASS, was it successful?
130 If YES then goto 40
140 If NO then CHANGE POSSESSION and then goto 40
```

The outcome of a pass is that if it was successful then the team retains possession; if it is not successful, they may lose possession. Line 130 responds to success by sending the program back to line 40, with the possession with the team who made the pass. Line 140, which will be reached if the answer to line 120 is NO, changes possession before returning the program to the event data entry section (line 40).

```
150 Action — SHOT,
160 What was its value?
170 Was it successful?
180 If YES, increase score by requisite amount,
    CHANGE POSSESSION and goto 40.
190 If NO, which team won rebound?
200 Goto 40.
```

Assume that the coach will be interested in knowing how many two- and three-point shots are attempted. In addition the program needs to know the value of the shot to advance the score by the requisite amount. Consequently line 160 poses the first question. If the shot is successful, then after the score has been advanced, possession will be changed and the program returned to the event data entry section. If the shot is not successful then there is a rebound situation, after which the program again is returned to line 40.

The other sections for the dribble and foul employ the same simple decision-making pathways.

It is now a matter of deciding which variables are going to be stored and then converting the sequential instructions into whichever computer language is to be used. Let us assume that the variables to be stored are position on the court at which the action takes place, the player involved in the action and the action itself. This will enable detailed analysis of the match with the data analysis program(s). In addition it will be useful to know how many successful and unsuccessful passes, shots and dribbles the team are making, to be processed as in-match data on the assumption that the analysis is being completed in real-time. The set of sequential instructions becomes as shown in Figure 7.3.

7.5 THE COMPUTER PROGRAM

A simple way of doing this in BASIC is shown below. The main point of this example is not the degree of sophistication of the programming, but

```
10 Start.
20 Who is in possession?
30 Enter team.
40 Enter position.
50 Enter player.
60 Enter choice of action.

65 Store data (position, player and action)in a file

70 If action was a pass goto 120
80 If action was a shot goto 100
90 If action was a dribble goto 160
100 If action was a foul goto 190
110 If action was END goto 999

120 Action — PASS, was it successful?
130 If YES then GOOD_PASS=GOOD_PASS+1; go to 300.
140 If NO then BAD_PASS=BAD_PASS+1
145 CHANGE POSSESSION and then go to 300.

150 Action — SHOT,
160 What was its VALUE?
170 Was it successful?
180 If NO goto 190

181 Successful SHOT
182 If VALUE=3 then goto 186
183 GOOD_SHOT2=GOOD_SHOT2+1
184 SCORE=SCORE+2
185 CHANGE POSSESSION and goto 300
186 GOOD_SHOT3=GOOD_SHOT3+1
187 SCORE=SCORE+3
188 CHANGE POSSESSION

189 Unsuccessful SHOT
190 If VALUE=2 then BAD_SHOT2=BAD_SHOT2+2
191 If VALUE=3 then BAD_SHOT3=BAD_SHOT3+3
192 Which team won rebound
200 Goto 300

210 Action — DRIBBLE, was it successful?
220 If NO then goto 230
221 GOOD_DRIB=GOOD_DRIB+1
222 goto 300
230 BAD_DRIB=BAD_DRIB+1
240 CHANGE POSSESSION and go to 300
```

```
240 Action — foul,
250 Was it an offensive foul?
260 If YES then CHANGE POSSESSION and goto 300
270 If NO then goto 300

300 OUTPUT TO SCREEN
310 PRINT values of GOOD_PASS, BAD_PASS, GOOD_SHOT2,
    GOOD_SHOT3, BAD_SHOT2, BAD_SHOT3, GOOD_DRIB and
    BAD_DRIB.
320 goto 40.
```

Note: This new section provides the update during the game in a very simple form; for example, it does not specify position or players.

```
999 STOP
```

Figure 7.3   Revised sequential instructions for the game of basketball

the ease with which the flowchart is transformed into the sequential instructions and they, in turn, are transformed into a computer language. The codes for position, shown in Figure 7.4(a), and action, Figure 7.4(b), are alphanumeric, whilst the numbers on the players' shirts will be used as identifying codes for the players (numeric).

Note that these keys form a solid block at the left hand side of the QWERTY keyboard, which can be looked upon as a simple representation of the court.

Although this example (Figure 7.4c) embodies a very simple approach to this problem, there are a number of lessons to be learnt from this programme. These can be summarized as:

Q	W	E	R
A	S	D	F
Z	X	C	V

Figure 7.4(a)   Divisions of the playing area for basketball.

Actions	Codes
Pass	P
Shoot	J
Dribble	L
Foul	M

Figure 7.4(b)   Action codes for basketball.

```
10  REM ********************
20  REM BASKETBALL PROGRAM
30  REM ********************
40  REM
50  REM WHO IS IN POSSESSION?
60  INPUT "ENTER TEAM IN POSSESSION";TEAM$
70
90  REM ENTER DATA
100
110 INPUT "POSITION";PO$

112 IF PO$="999" THEN GOTO 9999: REM THIS ENDS THE
    PROGRAM

120 INPUT "PLAYER";PL
130 INPUT "ACTION";A$
140
150 REM STORE DATA
160
170 REM THE NEXT LINES OPEN A STORAGE FILE AND THEN
    STORES (PRINTS) THE DATA IN THE FILE, AND THEN
    CLOSE THE FILE.
```

Note these file opening and closing instructions will be the most likely instructions to vary from machine to machine.

```
180 IF TEAM$="A" THEN OPEN "A-DATA.DAT" AS FILE 1,
    APPEND:GOTO 290
185 IF TEAM$="B" THEN OPEN "B_DATA.DAT" AS FILE 1,
    APPEND
```

Note: The different team data will be stored in two different files.

```
190 PRINT#1,PO$,PL,A$
200 CLOSE #1,
210
```

```
220 REM ROUTE CHOICE OF ACTION
230
240 IF A$="P" GOTO 300: REM THIS IS THE CODE FOR A
    PASS.
250 IF A$="J" GOTO 400: REM THIS IS THE CODE FOR A
    SHOT.
260 IF A$="L" GOTO 600: REM THIS IS THE CODE FOR A
    DRIBBLE
270 IF A$="M" GOTO 700: REM THIS IS A CODE FOR A FOUL
280
300 REM
310 REM PASS
320 REM
330 INPUT "WAS THE PASS SUCCESSFUL",ANSWER$
335 IF ANSWER$="N" THEN 350
340 IF ANSWER$="Y" THEN GOOD_PASS=GOODPASS+1: GOTO
    900
345 REM
350 REM UNSUCCESSFUL PASS
352 BAD_PASS=BAD_PASS+1
355 REM CHANGE POSSESSION, GOTO SCREEN OUPUT AND
    RETURN TO DATA INPUT
360 REM
370 IF TEAM$="A" THEN TEAM$="B":GOTO 900
380 TEAM$="A"
390 GOTO 900
392
400 REM SHOT SUB-ROUTINE
410
420 INPUT "WHAT WAS VALUE OF THE SHOT";VALUE
422 IF VALUE<2 OR VALUE>3 THEN GOSUB 2000:GOTO 420
430
440 INPUT "WAS IT SUCCESSFUL";ANSWER$
450 IF ANSWER$="YES" GOTO 500
460
470 REM UNSUCCESSFUL SHOT
472 IF VALUE=3 THEN 478
474 BAD_SHOT2=BAD_SHOT2+1
476 GOTO 480
478 BAD_SHOT3=BAD_SHOT3+1
480 INPUT "WHICH TEAM WON THE REBOUND";TEAM$
490 GOTO 900
492
500 REM SUCCESSFUL SHOT
```

```
502 REM
504 IF VALUE=2 THEN GOOD_SHOT2=GOOD_SHOT2+1
506 IF VALUE=3 THEN GOOD_SHOT3=GOOD_SHOT3+1
510 REM
512 REM INCREASE TEAM SCORES BY REQUISITE AMOUNT
514 REM
520 IF TEAM$="A" THEN SCORE_A=SCORE_A+VALUE:GOTO
    540
530 SCORE_B=SCORE_B+VALUE
540 REM
550 REM SCORE UPDATE
560 PRINT "CURRENT SCORE - TEAM A:";SCORE_A;" ::
    TEAM B:";SCORE_B
562 IF TEAM$="A" THEN TEAM$="B":GOTO 900
564 TEAM$="A"
570 GOTO 900
580
600 REM
610 REM DRIBBLE
620 REM
630 INPUT "WAS THE DRIBBLE SUCCESSFUL";ANSWER$
640 IF ANSWER$="N" GOTO 650
642 GOOD_DRIB=GOOD_DRIB+1
644 GOTO 900
645 REM
650 REM UNSUCCESSFUL DRIBBLE
652 BAD_DRIB=BAD_DRIB+1
655 REM CHANGE POSSESSION, GOTO SCREEN OUTPUT AND
    RETURN TO DATA INPUT
660 REM
670 IF TEAM$="A" THEN TEAM$="B":GOTO 900
680 TEAM$="A"
690 GOTO 900
700
900 REM
910 REM SCREEN OUPUT
920 REM
            930                              LET
A$="*****************************************
*************"
940 PRINT A$
950 PRINT A$
952 PRINT "            SHOTS           PASSESS
    DRIBBLES        "
```

```
954 PRINT A$
956 PRINT "     GOOD          BAD          GOOD          BAD
    GOOD          BAD"
958 PRINT A$
960 PRINT " 2pt.    3pt.      2pt.    3pt."
                   970                         PRINT
    TAB(4);GOOD_SHOT2;TAB(8);GOOD_SHOT3;TAB(12);
    BAD_SHOT2;TAB(16);BAD_SHOT3;TAB(24);GOOD_PASS;T
    AB(32);
    BAD_PASS;TAB(40);GOOD_DRIB;TAB(48);BAD_DRIB
980 PRINT A$
990
9999 END
```

Figure 7.4 (c) A simple example of a notational program in BASIC.

1. User protection – protecting the operator as much as possible from his/her mistakes and, possibly even more important, to protect the machine and the program from these mistakes.
2. In-match or post-event – whether the system is to be used in a live situation or with recordings with the facility of slow motion or replay.
3. Ergonomics of design – the design of the program so that the operation of the notation system is as ergonomically efficient as possible.
4. Type of data to be analysed – the way in which the analysis is to be processed will determine how the data will be collected.

Let us examine each in more detail.

7.5.1 USER PROTECTION

It is essential that when a program is constructed for notation purposes that it is even more 'user protective' than usual. 'User protective', in usual programming terms, means preventing the program from crashing and/or losing data and information in spite of any actions by the operator. Programs for notational analysis, however, have to be even more carefully designed and constructed. Obviously they must not crash – it is very frustrating to have notated a match for an hour, only to lose all the data because of a fault in the program. It is equally important that erroneous data must be minimized. There will obviously be human error in data entry that cannot be avoided, but what must be prevented is the entering of position instead of player or any other transposition of acceptable data. If this occurs early in the data collection, it will render unacceptable all the subsequent data. Consequently the above program would need to be modified in the following ways.

The first possible source of trouble could come in entering the initial team data. This is unlikely to cause the same problems as making a mistake after an hour of data entry, but it is best to develop the habit of preventing, where possible, any erroneous entries.

```
50 REM WHO IS IN POSSESSION?
60 INPUT "ENTER TEAM IN POSSESSION";TEAM$
70 IF TEAM$<>"A" OR TEAM$<>"B" THEN 50:   REM INPUT
   CHECK
```

Line 70 prevents the operator from entering any other alphanumeric variable other than 'A' or 'B'. The next possible problem is the most important one as it is the main data entry of the program and the part of the notation in which most of the pressure of data entry speed will apply. It is important to prevent the operator from entering data outside the permitted range of each variable, missing out one of the variables or repeating a variable (as can happen with some keyboards when the key is depressed for too long).

```
90 REM ENTER DATA
100
110 INPUT "POSITION";PO$
112 IF PO="999" THEN GOTO 9999: REM THIS ENDS THE
    PROGRAM
115 GOSUB 1000
```

(Here the program is sent to a sub-routine to check that the data entry falls within the range of the pitch divisions on the keyboard.)

```
1000 REM POSITION DATA CHECK
1010 REM
1020 IF PO$="Q" THEN RETURN
1030 IF PO$="W" THEN RETURN
1040 IF PO$="E" THEN RETURN
1050 IF PO$="R" THEN RETURN
1060 IF PO$="A" THEN RETURN
1070 IF PO$="S" THEN RETURN
1080 IF PO$="D" THEN RETURN
1090 IF PO$="F" THEN RETURN
1100 IF PO$="Z" THEN RETURN
1110 IF PO$="X" THEN RETURN
1120 IF PO$="C" THEN RETURN
1130 IF PO$="V" THEN RETURN
1140 GOSUB 2000: REM BEEP SUB-ROUTINE (SEE BELOW)
```

```
1150 GOTO 110
```

(The sub-routine 2000 is one that generates a 'beep' so that the operator will be aware of the error even if his/her attention is not upon the screen.)

```
2000 REM BEEP ROUTINE
2010 REM
2020 SOUND 37,.027
2030 RETURN
```

(This SOUND instruction will vary from machine to machine so check the manual of the machine being used.)

```
120 INPUT "PLAYER";PL
122 IF PL<1 OR PL>12 THEN GOSUB 2000:GOTO 120
```

The problem here is that although the idea of keeping the code for the players as a numeric variable is a good one in terms of design, if the operator inadvertently presses any key other than that with a number on it, in mistake, the program will crash with subsequent losses of data. A simple way round this problem is to have the numeric data entry accepted as alphanumeric variables, which will then accept either numerics or alphanumerics (and almost every other key) and then transform them back to numeric variables. This is simply done:

```
120 INPUT "PLAYER";PL$
121 LET PL=VAL(PL$)
122 IF PL<1 OR PL>12 THEN GOSUB 2000:GOTO 120
```

The simplest way to protect the action variable is to shift the program around slightly and modify the section where the program checks which action has been entered prior to going to the appropriate sub-routine.

```
130 INPUT "ACTION";A
140 REM ROUTE CHOICE OF ACTION
150
160 IF A$="P" GOSUB 250:GOTO 300: REM THIS IS THE
    CODE FOR A PASS.
170 IF A$="B" GOSUB 250:GOTO 400: REM THIS IS THE
    CODE FOR A SHOT.
180 IF A$="L" GOSUB 250:GOTO 600: REM THIS IS THE
    CODE FOR A DRIBBLE.
190 IF A$="M" GOSUB 250:GOTO 700: REM THIS IS THE
    CODE FOR A FOUL.
200 GOSUB 2000; REM IF THE PROGRAM REACHES HERE -
    MISTAKE
```

```
210 GOTO 130
240
250 REM STORE DATA
260
270 REM THE NEXT LINES OPEN A STORAGE FILE AND THEN
    STORES (PRINTS) THE DATA IN THE FILE, AND THEN
    CLOSE THE FILE.
280 IF TEAM$="A" THEN OPEN "A-DATA.DAT" AS FILE 1,
    APPEND:GOTO 290
285 IF TEAM$="B" THEN OPEN "B_DATA.DAT" AS FILE 1,
    APPEND
290 PRINT#1,PO$,PL,A$
292 CLOSE #1,
294 RETURN
```

The rest of the protective measures are to ensure that any subsequent data entry in the action sub-routines is within the range specified, usually 'YES' or 'NO', team 'A' or 'B', etc.

```
310 REM PASS
320 REM
330 INPUT "WAS THE PASS SUCCESSFUL, ANSWER 'Y' OR
    'N'";ANSWER$
335 IF ANSWER$="N" THEN 350
340 IF ANSWER$="Y" THEN GOOD_PASS=GOODPASS+1: GOTO
    900
345 GOSUB 2000: IF PROGRAM REACHES HERE - MISTAKE
346 GOTO 330
350 REM UNSUCCESSFUL PASS
430 REM SHOT SUB-ROUTINE
410
420 INPUT "WHAT WAS VALUE OF THE SHOT";VALUE
422 IF VALUE<2 OR VALUE>3 THEN GOSUB 2000:GOTO 420
430
440 INPUT "WAS IT SUCCESSFUL, ANSWER 'Y' OR
    'N'";ANSWER$
450 IF ANSWER$="Y" GOTO 500
452 IF ANSWER$="N" GOTO 470
454 GOSUB 2000:GOTO 440
460
480 INPUT "WHICH TEAM WON THE REBOUND";TEAM$
485 IF TEAM$<>"A" OR TEAM$<>"B" THEN GOSUB 2000:GOTO
    480
490 GOTO 900
610 REM DRIBBLE
```

```
620 REM
630 INPUT "WAS THE DRIBBLE SUCCESSFUL, ANSWER 'Y' OR
    'N'";ANSWER$
635 IF ANSWER$="Y" GOTO 642
640 IF ANSWER$="N" GOTO 650
641 GOSUB 2000: GOTO 635
642 GOOD_DRIB=GOOD_DRIB+1
644 GOTO 900
645 REM
650 REM UNSUCCESSFUL DRIBBLE
```

The complete program is collated and shown in the Appendix at the end of this chapter. All these changes are, in essence, basic checks to ensure that the operator's finger did not slip onto the wrong key. These and the other data entry checks above will not prevent the operator from making errors in the observational sense, i.e. entering the wrong position or identifying the wrong player. This observational type of error is inevitable in computerized systems, and manual systems for that matter. They must be eradicated as much as possible by practising with the system, ensuring a good overview and familiarising yourself with the players if possible. An additional check is to have the computer print to the screen the actual data entered so that the operator can confirm, at intervals, if this is the same as the data entry intended. It is also useful to have a 'data revision sub-routine', so that in the case of erroneous data being entered then the program can be halted and the data corrected. This is often difficult to do, especially in an in-match situation and the data is being down-loaded to files.

Each system must be validated to check that the data entered is the data recorded and processed, and an estimation made of the expected accuracy of the system in operation. This is discussed later in Section 7.8.

7.5.2. IN-MATCH OR POST-EVENT

The decision as to whether the system is to be used during a match, or post-event using video, must be made very early in the design stages. The reasons for this are obvious, inasmuch as if the data collection is to be completed in-match the system must be as 'streamlined' as possible. The data collection in this system is very simplistically designed, but for live in-match systems it may be necessary to be even more selective in deciding which data is to be collected. It is very difficult to collect all the information in a basketball match during the match. Dufour (1988) developed a system that enabled this, but it required two operators. If the system is to be used post-event, this does ease the pressure on collecting the data, since the use of replay, slow motion and freeze-frame enable as much detail as desired. It is still necessary to design the system as ergonomically as possible, otherwise the notation of the match may take a prohibitively long time.

7.5.3 ERGONOMICS OF DESIGN

It is essential that the data entry is made as economically as possible, even with systems that are being used post-event. There are a number of ways of doing this. First, each individual is always most comfortable with systems that they have designed – so if possible have a system designed to your own specifications of layout, coding and processing. Secondly, try to leave areas of the keyboard for specific 'types' of data entry, as in the basketball example for the court divisions, action variables and player numbers. Finally, attempt to design your program in such a way to reduce the number of times that the keys have to be struck to enter data. The above program is not well written in this sense at all and big improvements could be made. For example, the use of INPUT statement necessitates the entry of the item of data and in addition the strike of the 'ENTER' key, i.e. two strikes for each item of information. By using the GET statement, this second key strike is negated. In addition the action sub-routines could be designed to make data entry much easier; these improvements, and others, are discussed in the following sections.

7.5.4 TYPE OF DATA TO BE ANALYSED

The type of data to be collected and processed will determine the most economical way to record and store this information. In a number of situations the way in which the data is recorded will preclude certain ways of processing information from this data and, consequently, once again, decisions must be made at the planning stage that will determine what can and cannot be analysed from the notation system. Consider the example above of the basketball match. In this program a certain amount of data was processed during the match, numbers of good passes, bad passes, 2 point baskets, 3 point baskets, etc. If this were the only data stored, then any subsequent further examination of the patterns of play would not be possible. For example, it would be useful to know the distribution of assists amongst the players. This would not normally have been possible from this analysis; the program would have to be modified and, worse still, the match re-notated. Fortunately this program was designed to record all pertinent data in the match, which is not always the case. Further, this data was stored sequentially in file, albeit in a very raw format (lines 290–292). This does, however, enable the user of this program to complete further analyses on the data of any matches notated. In some situations this type of storage may not be possible, e.g. where microcomputers are working at the limit of their memory and the notation needs to be fast. In this situation, usually in-match but not always, dumping of data to a file is too time consuming and so the data has to be stored in the short term memory of the computer (usually called RAM) – this can fill up very quickly. So it pays to have a good idea what sort of analyses are to be completed, retaining as much flexibility as possible with respect to storage of match data. Remember, once the data has been processed, every coach will always respond – 'That's interesting, but what if we look at. . . '.

In certain situations some data forms have advantages over others, it is certainly worthwhile to familiarise yourself with as many types of data storage as possible. In addition some types of data would appear to be easier to handle and interpret by different individuals. Let us examine then some examples of data and the different ways it can be stored.

(a) Summary data and frequency counts

Summary data is usually simple totals and/or lists, but it can take on quite complicated dimensions when more complex analyses of team games are considered. The power of the computer, and its suitability for handling the types of data produced by notation, becomes evident once **arrays** are used, in conjunction with **loops**, for handling the data. Take for example the problem of entering the summary data at the start of a team game. Almost certainly the largest item of data to enter will be the players' names of each team. This can be done simply using an array and a loop:

```
100 FOR N=1 TO 12
110 PRINT "PLAYER"; N;
120 INPUT NAME$(N)
130 NEXT N
```

(Most computers require a DIMENSION statement with an array larger than ten, such as this – consult your manual, or local expert.)

This can be expanded very simply to embrace both teams:

```
100 DIM TEAM_NAME(2,12)
110 FOR T=1 TO 2
120 FOR N=1 TO 12
130 PRINT "ENTER NAME OF TEAM PLAYER";N
140 INPUT TEAM_NAME$(T,N)
150 NEXT N
160 NEXT T
```

With seven lines of program we are entering two team squads of twelve players each. Player shirt numbers can be handled in exactly the same way. The complexity of this type of approach is only limited by our imagination and only rarely by the machine. Those using computers that can handle three-dimensional arrays, or higher, can really simplify their programming. Consider the need within the program to enter the players' shirt numbers but to be able to refer to them, when required, by name.

```
100 DIM NAME$(2,12),NUMBER(2,12)
110 FOR T=1 TO 2
115 INPUT "TEAM NAME";TEAM$(T)
120 FOR N=1 TO 12
130 PRINT "ENTER NAME OF TEAM PLAYER";N
140 INPUT NAME$(T,N)
142 PRINT ". . . AND HIS NUMBER";
144 INPUT NUMBER(N)
150 NEXT N
160 NEXT T
```

It is easy then to build up the summary data of the match in this way. However, it is also a simple way of recording frequency counts or frequency distributions of actions with respect to players, or to playing areas, or both.

Consider the element of the basketball program in the example above which counted the number of good passes made by the team.

```
310 REM PASS
320 REM
330 INPUT "WAS THE PASS SUCCESSFUL, ANSWER 'Y' OR
    'N'";ANSWER$
335 IF ANSWER$="N" THEN 350
340 IF ANSWER$="Y" THEN GOOD_PASS=GOODPASS+1: GOTO
    900
345 GOSUB 2000: IF PROGRAM REACHES HERE - MISTAKE
346 GOTO 330
350 REM UNSUCCESSFUL PASS
```

More detailed information about this passing would be helpful – who is making these good passes? As at this stage of the program the variable PL will have the value of the player's number who made the pass. Consequently the player-distribution of good passes could be recorded by the following:

```
310 REM PASS
320 REM
330 INPUT "WAS THE PASS SUCCESSFUL, ANSWER 'Y' OR
    'N'";ANSWER$
```

```
335 IF ANSWER$="N" THEN 350
340 IF ANSWER$="Y" THEN
    GOOD_PASS(PL)=GOOD_PASS(PL)+1: GOTO 900
345 GOSUB 2000: IF PROGRAM REACHES HERE - MISTAKE
346 GOTO 330
350 REM UNSUCCESSFUL PASS
```

The output from this data can be easily displayed:

```
3000 REM GOOD_PASS OUTPUT
3010 REM
3020 CLS
3030 PRINT
     "*********************************************"
3040 PRINT "*    NAME    *   NUMBER   *    GOOD PASSES
     *"
3050 PRINT
     "*********************************************"
3060 FOR N=1 TO 12
3070 PRINT TAB(6);NAME$(N);TAB(17);NUMBER(N);TAB(34);
GOOD_PASS(N)
3080 PRINT
     "*********************************************"
3090 NEXT N
```

It is easy to make good passes, or shots, in open spaces, but much more difficult in closely marked space in your opponents' key, for example. This information, in the output part of the programme above, can be made more detailed by the inclusion of position on court. As the variable PO$ will have the value of the position on the court, this could be included in the arrays. Unfortunately the position code was chosen, for security reasons, to have alphanumeric codes, so this must first be changed back to a numeric coding, e.g.

```
4000 REM POSITION CODING SWITCH
4010 REM
4020 IF PO$="Q" THEN PO=1
4030 IF PO$="W" THEN PO=2
4040 IF PO$="E" THEN PO=3
4050 IF PO$="R" THEN PO=4
4060 IF PO$="A" THEN PO=5
4070 IF PO$="S" THEN PO=6
4080 IF PO$="D" THEN PO=7
4090 IF PO$="F" THEN PO=8
4100 IF PO$="Z" THEN PO=9
4110 IF PO$="X" THEN PO=10
```

```
4120 IF PO$="C" THEN PO=11
4130 IF PO$="V" THEN PO=12
4140 RETURN
```

Using this value of the pitch variable now, a two-dimensional array can be used to gather the distribution of passes in the playing area from player to player.

```
310 REM PASS
320 REM
330 INPUT "WAS THE PASS SUCCESSFUL, ANSWER 'Y' OR
    'N'";ANSWER$
335 IF ANSWER$="N" THEN 350
340 IF ANSWER$="Y" THEN
    GOOD_PASS(PL,PO)=GOOD_PASS(PL,PO)+1: GOTO 900
345 GOSUB 2000: REM IF PROGRAM REACHES HERE - MISTAKE
346 GOTO 330
350 REM UNSUCCESSFUL PASS
```

It is then a small step to use this type of two-dimensional array to obtain a pitch distribution of passes for each player, as in the field hockey example of Hughes and Cunliffe (1986).

Sometimes, if there is a large number of action variables, it might be better to use a different array name for each player, with the action variables and pitch specifications becoming the array dimensions. This can also be determined by the way the data is to be analysed. Again, it is immensely helpful to know where you are going before you set out.

> *Using frequency counts in this way is an efficient way of using the computer and a very informative way of analysing patterns of play, but when the data is stored in this way the SEQUENTIALITY of the data is lost. That is, there is no way of telling which pass preceded a shot on goal, or which tackle led to a change in possession, etc. If frequency counts are all that is required from your analysis, well and good. If further analysis of patterns of shots that led to winning shots (in tennis), or passes that led to a try (in rugby union), or work rates that preceded an error (in squash), it is necessary to record the data in some sequential form as well as the frequency arrays.*

(b) Sequential data

Using discrete data

One of the most interesting patterns in sport is that which differentiates between winners and losers. It is to this aspect that eventually the coach will turn. What pattern of play produces a basket opportunity, a shot at goal, a winner in tennis? Conversely, what patterns produce the error that enables a critical breakaway possession, that forces the pressure shot into the tin (in squash) or consistently fails to produce effective shooting opportunities. To analyse this type of information it is necessary to record not just the events of the game but also record the sequence of these events and, of course, their outcomes. In the above example, the basketball program, the data is stored in a sort of sequential form, but there could be problems in a detailed analysis in linking some of the actions with their outcomes, e.g. was a pass a good one or not? Even if the variable arrays GOOD_PASS and BAD_PASS were written to file, the sequentiality of the data would not be preserved. If this type of analysis is intended, then the data collection system must be designed with this in mind. Inevitably there are a number of ways of doing this. To remain with the example of the basketball program and the way that the data is being entered, the first step towards recording sequential data is to add to the action variables all that was previously labelled as 'outcomes'. In this way the storage of the sequential data, lines 290–292, will include all relevant data as long as the necessary action codes are sufficiently well designed.

```
290 PRINT#1,PO$,PL,A$
292 CLOSE #1,
294
```

The revised actions would then take the form shown in Figure 7.5. To use these actions/outcomes in the notation system will necessitate the definition of codes. It is tempting in these situations to use labels such as 'GP' for 'GOOD PASS' or 'BP' for 'BAD PASS', but that ease of association is paid for by having to hit two keys on the keyboard. It will almost certainly be better to assign a portion of the keyboard for actions and relabel the keys with temporary overlays. Even if the system is not going to be used in-match, the savings in time will be immense during the notation of a game.

Using data 'strings'

Another way of approaching this problem is to enter each phase of the play as one long continuous string variable, store it in this form and then operate on these strings within the data analysis programs. In our example of the basketball match, this type of string could be used for each possession by each team. Instead of printing each set of position, player, action to file, they are added to the growing string of possession:

```
130 INPUT "ACTION";A$
140 REM ROUTE CHOICE OF ACTION
150
```

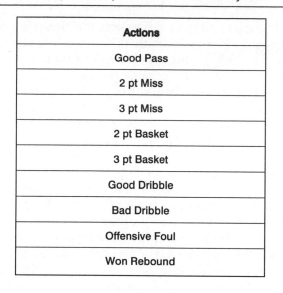

Actions
Good Pass
2 pt Miss
3 pt Miss
2 pt Basket
3 pt Basket
Good Dribble
Bad Dribble
Offensive Foul
Won Rebound

Figure 7.5 Revised action designations for basketball, including all the outcomes.

```
160  IF A$="P"  GOSUB 250:GOTO 300: REM THIS IS THE
     CODE FOR A PASS.
        *       *       *       *
        *       *       *       *
        *       *       *       *
        *       *       *       *
```

Plus the rest of the codes for Actions

```
        *       *       *       *
        *       *       *       *
        *       *       *       *
198  IF A$="Y" GOTO 270: REM THIS IS THE CODE FOR END
     OF POSSESSION, AND SENDS THE PROG TO FILE DUMP.
200  GOSUB 2000; REM IF THE PROGRAM REACHES HERE -
     MISTAKE
210  GOTO 130
240  REM
250  REM ADD TO POSSESSION STRING
251  REM
252  LET SUM$=SUM$+PO$+PL$+A$
260  RETURN
```

```
270 REM THE NEXT LINES OPEN A STORAGE FILE AND THEN
    STORES (PRINTS) THE DATA IN THE FILE, AND THEN
    CLOSE THE FILE.
280 IF TEAM$="A" THEN OPEN "A-DATA.DAT" AS FILE 1,
    APPEND:GOTO 290
285 IF TEAM$="B" THEN OPEN "B_DATA.DAT" AS FILE 1,
    APPEND
290 PRINT#1,SUM$
291 SUM$-""
292 CLOSE #1,
294 REM
295 REM CHANGE POSSESSION
296 REM
297 IF TEAM$="A" THEN TEAM$="B":GOTO 100
298 TEAM$="A"
299 GOTO 100
```

Lines 160–198 above include the new codes for actions and outcomes, discussed already, together with the code for END OF POSSESSION (line 198). This was arbitrarily assigned to the letter 'Y'. When any of the other actions/outcomes are entered the three variables, PO$, PL$ and A$, are all added to the string variable SUM$. When eventually the team lose possession, bad pass, losing a rebound, scoring a basket, etc., and the requisite key is hit (in this case 'Y'), then the program is directed to the file dump where the possession string consisting of all the actions within that possession is printed to file. This string is then 'emptied' (line 291) prior to returning to the data entry loop.

Note that although the variable PL$ is now treated as a string variable, numeric values can still be entered – it will require certain care in transforming these alphanumeric values back to numeric values in the position check sub-routine. This can be done very simply with the line:

```
120 INPUT "PLAYER";PL$
121 LET PL=VAL(PL$)
122 IF PL<1 OR PL>12 THEN GOSUB 2000:GOTO 120
```

In this way the different areas of the keyboard used will still facilitate data entry and reduce errors. The data file will now consist of a series of lines of data of the form:

A5KS6LD6KD6Y
Q8JC9LF7Y
D7Y
Q5MS5ID6LE7LD9PC4PD6PW7UW7Y

ETC.

The length of the line is determined by how many actions took place in that possession. The string consists of a series of sets of three codes: position, player and action. By knowing that these variables must occur in this order, and using operational statements such as LEFT$, RIGHT$, MID$ which enable dissection of long strings into shorter 'bit elements', the data can then be processed and classified very easily in any number of ways.

These two are the most commonly used methods of storing sequential data and some programs have utilized a mixture of both methods.

(c) Time-dependent data

As all computers have clocks integrated into their systems, the idea of creating time-related databases should not be too difficult in practice. The problem of realizing this idea, and its potential of then analysing actions and movements with reference to a time base, lies in the synchronizing of the notation of the event with the occurrence of the event itself. So time-dependent analyses using computerized notation have not been common. Hughes, Franks and Nagelkerke (1989) produced a system that they applied to squash, but it can be used for any sport. This system utilized a 'Power Pad' for data entry (see Section 7.6), together with a video special effects generator which mixed the actual picture of the playing area (in this case a squash court) with the simulated playing area (court) on the 'Power Pad'. This enabled accurate tracking of the players as they moved during the game. Accordingly accurate profiles of distances moved, velocities and accelerations of players can be obtained. This system was applied to differing standards of squash players (Hughes and Franks, 1991), enabling dynamic profiles of individual players to be defined. It was only used for research purposes.

Franks and Nagelkerke (1989), see Chapter 4, used the time base in the computer to enable accurate resolution of events on the videotape. This was achieved by programming the computer, which was integrated with the video deck, to implant time codes onto the second audio channel of the videotape. In this way, any event notated had a time code and could be found on the tape by means of that time code. This enabled the user to firstly analyse the important aspects of the game and then be able to replay each of those points in the game immediately.

This is certainly an area for development in the future as the technology of video, microcomputers and peripheral devices progresses.

7.6 ALTERNATIVE DATA ENTRY

To ease the data entry into the computer, reducing both learning time for a system and the actual notation time, a number of different ways of entering the data have been used. These can be summarized as follows:

1. Specifically built keyboards (Franks, 1983; Alderson and Mackinnon, 1985), see Chapter 4. These require a great deal of expertise both with computing hardware as well as the programming.
2. Touch-sensitive data pads (concept Keyboards or 'Power Pads'), see Chapter 4. These have been used to very good effect. They are relatively cheap, easy to program and enable quick, accurate data entry with little or no learning time.
3. Graphical user interfaces (GUI) – these have become very common (Hughes and Clarke, A., 1995; Hughes and Clarke, S., 1995) and, with the onset of Windows™- packages, they present a form of data entry with which most computer users are comfortable. The ease of programming in Visual BASIC make the use of this data interface very convenient and attractive for notation systems – see Chapter 5.
4. Voice entry (Taylor and Hughes, 1989; see Chapter 3). This is one of the developments that will arrive with time. The hardware is available now, but expensive and as yet not quite as sophisticated as required. However, given the rate at which computer developments progress, this statement could be wrong before this book reaches the press.

7.7 OUTPUT

In Chapter 5 it was stressed how important it was to ensure that the output of the system was simple and easily understood. This cannot be emphasized enough for computerized systems. Inevitably these type of systems are gathering more and more data, and consequently it is so much easier to produce masses of data and hence not only confuse the athlete or coach, but also put them off computerized data for life. Different approaches to this problem were given in Section 5.6.

7.8 VALIDATION AND RELIABILITY

All systems need validation, to ensure that they are accurately executing what they were designed to do. Computerized notation systems are generally validated by the following methods. First, notate a whole match, or section of a match, using the computerized system at the intended notation speed. This element of a game is then notated by hand very carefully, using replay or frame-by-frame analysis, where necessary, to ensure as accurate a record of the data as possible. The two sets of output data are then compared. It is assumed that the data from the hand notation will be 100% accurate and so it is a matter of comparing the data produced from the computerized system to see whether it is significantly different. There are two points to be made about the word 'significantly'. The limit of the accuracy can only be determined by the designer or user of the system; this will be dictated by the use to which it is to be put. Correct statistical procedures must be applied to test for the levels of significance; these will be determined by the form that the data takes in the output. This data format will also dictate, to a large extent, how the limits of accuracy can be estimated. In this situation it is advised that, unless you are very good at statistics, you consult an expert on statistics.

This data should also be tested for repeatability, i.e. the same operator repeats the notation, to demonstrate that the levels of accuracy are consistent – this is called **intra-observer reliability testing**.

In addition the system should be tested for **inter-observer reliability**. No matter how user friendly and how simple the data input system is, there is always an increase in the levels of skill the more one uses a system. An operator who has not used the system before should be introduced to the system and allowed the 'learning time' required to master the system. Once the operator feels that the system has been fully mastered, the same set of data (or perhaps another) is notated by the new operator, and this is again compared with the data output from the original operator and with that from the hand notation. If the data falls within the specified limits of accuracy then the system can be seen to be accurate irrespective of the operator. It may well be that this inter-observer reliability is not relevant – some systems require specific skills and a great deal of practice for them to be used fully (see the system of Franks and Goodman, 1986b, described in Chapter 4).

7.8.1 PROGRAM STABILITY CHECK

The operator will attempt to 'catch-out' the program by trying to enter wrong bands of data, i.e. position instead of player, etc. In addition the outcomes of certain actions must always be exclusive, e.g. a soccer goal cannot result from a throw-in. So the computer should be programmed not to accept this illogical type of data, and should tell the operator so. **Most importantly the program should not crash under any circumstances**. To avoid this all input situations should be examined very carefully. Basically this is a **systems' design check**.

7.8.2 DATA ENTERED IS ACCEPTED AND PROCESSED ACCURATELY

This is usually completed by creating some data or at least using a set of data of which there is a record. This is carefully entered into the computer, so that it is definitely entered accurately. This data is then processed to see if it provides the same analysis as that done by hand. This is a **systems' processing check**, testing the gathering and processing software and hardware. This should be 100% correct.

7.9 TYPES OF HARDWARE BEING USED

The different types of hardware being used fall into three groups. Originally, in the early 1980s, everybody was working on different computers. Fortunately there has been a 'coming together', partly due to a deliberate effort by the research workers in the field and partly due to market forces.

In America and Europe everybody is working on IBM machines or 'compatibles' – machines that work with the same software as IBM machines and are compatible with anything that runs on an IBM.

In Britain most early work was completed on the Acorn series of BBC machines. These were commissioned by the Department of Education for use in schools. All schools and colleges have these machines. In the mid-1970s a number of people working in computerized notation were brought together, along with top coaches, by the National Coaching Foundation (Sheffield, 1985) and in the course of this conference the BBC machine was accepted as the common medium. It was hoped that this would enable exchange of software, ideas, data and information in general. Most people are now switching to IBM and IBM-compatibles, and there are two reasons for this. First, the expected flood of ready made educational software for the BBC has not really satisfied the needs of the clientele, and secondly the new generation of PCs produced by IBM, and their imitators, offer so much more in terms of speed, memory size, integrated software and, most importantly, the price.

There has been a number of pieces of work involving mainframe computers (Hughes, 1983; Hughes and Charlish, 1986; Patrick and McKenna, 1986). Before the introduction of the new generation of PCs, it was sometimes necessary to use a mainframe because the amounts of data involved in notating some sports required large memory size. Although the reasons are still valid, it is more likely now that less and less work will be completed using this medium.

7.10 SUMMARY

Notational analysis is ideally suited for computerization, the logical analyses that must be completed for any hand notation system are very similar to the sort of logical structuring necessary for writing any program.

In writing your programs do not be too proud not to use the ideas developed by other people who have already completed work. Experience is a good teacher. Be prepared to consult any experts that you can contact – they will usually be only too happy to talk about their work, your work, anybody's work, etc. Their knowledge and help could save you weeks of work and, perhaps worst of all, wasted efforts.

Before commencing any data gathering, always run full system checks on your programs – be sure that your system really does do what you think and hope that it does. Remember that data gathering is relatively easy; it is producing sense from the data that is the most difficult task. Be prepared to sweat blood and tears over distilling your output until it produces meaningful information in a form that is comprehensible to anyone.

Finally, try to always keep in the forefront of your aims the original reasons why you wanted to create a notation system. With all the problems associated in writing computer programs, and the associate problems with the hardware, it is easy for your priorities to be changed for you because of other pressures.

APPENDIX. BASKETBALL PROGRAM IN BASIC

```
10 REM ********************
20 REM BASKETBALL PROGRAM
30 REM ********************
40 REM
50 REM WHO IS IN POSSESSION?
60 INPUT "ENTER TEAM IN POSSESSION";TEAM$
70
90 REM ENTER DATA
100
110 INPUT "POSITION";PO$
112 IF PO$="999" THEN GOTO 9999: REM THIS ENDS THE
    PROGRAM
115 GOSUB 1000
120 INPUT "PLAYER";PL
121 LET PL=VAL(PL$)
122 IF PL<1 OR PL>12 THEN GOSUB 2000:GOTO 120
130 INPUT "ACTION";A
140 REM ROUTE CHOICE OF ACTION
150
160 IF A$="P" GOSUB 250:GOTO 300: REM THIS IS THE
    CODE FOR A PASS.
170 IF A$="B" GOSUB 250:GOTO 400: REM THIS IS THE
    CODE FOR A SHOT.
180 IF A$="L" GOSUB 250:GOTO 600: REM THIS IS THE
    CODE FOR A DRIBBLE.
190 IF A$="M" GOSUB 250:GOTO 700: REM THIS IS THE
    CODE FOR A FOUL.
200 GOSUB 2000; REM IF THE PROGRAMME REACHES HERE -
    MISTAKE
210 GOTO 130
```

```
240
250 REM STORE DATA
260
270 REM THE NEXT LINES OPEN A STORAGE FILE AND THEN
    STORES (PRINTS) THE DATA IN THE FILE, AND THEN
    CLOSE THE FILE.
280 IF TEAM$="A" THEN OPEN "A-DATA.DAT" AS FILE 1,
APPEND:GOTO 290
285 IF TEAM$="B" THEN OPEN "B_DATA.DAT" AS FILE 1,
APPEND
290 PRINT#1,PO$,PL,A$
292 CLOSE #1,
294 RETURN
310 REM PASS
320 REM
330 INPUT "WAS THE PASS SUCCESSFUL, ANSWER 'Y' OR
    'N'"; ANSWER$
335 IF ANSWER$="N" THEN 350
340 IF ANSWER$="Y" THEN GOOD_PASS=GOODPASS+1: GOTO
    900
345 GOSUB 2000: IF PROGRAM REACHES HERE - MISTAKE
346 GOTO 330
350 REM UNSUCCESSFUL PASS
352 BAD_PASS=BAD_PASS+1
355 REM CHANGE POSSESSION, GOTO SCREEN OUPUT AND
    RETURN TO DATA INPUT
360 REM
370 IF TEAM$="A" THEN TEAM$="B":GOTO 900
380 TEAM$="A"
390 GOTO 900
392
400 REM SHOT SUB-ROUTINE
410
420 INPUT "WHAT WAS VALUE OF THE SHOT";VALUE
422 IF VALUE<2 OR VALUE>3 THEN GOSUB 2000:GOTO 420
430
440 INPUT "WAS IT SUCCESSFUL", ANSWER 'Y' OR 'N'";
    ANSWER$
450 IF ANSWER$="Y" GOTO 500
452 IF ANSWER$="N" GOTO 470
454 GOSUB 2000:GOTO 440
460
470 REM UNSUCCESSFUL SHOT
472 IF VALUE=3 THEN 478
```

```
474 BAD_SHOT2=BAD_SHOT2+1
476 GOTO 480
478 BAD_SHOT3=BAD_SHOT3+1
480 INPUT "WHICH TEAM WON THE REBOUND";TEAM$
485 IF TEAM$<>"A" OR TEAM$<>"B" THEN GOSUB 2000:GOTO
    480
490 GOTO 900
492
500 REM SUCCESSFUL SHOT
502 REM
504 IF VALUE=2 THEN GOOD_SHOT2=GOOD_SHOT2+1
506 IF VALUE=3 THEN GOOD_SHOT3=GOOD_SHOT3+1
510 REM
512 REM INCREASE TEAM SCORES BY REQUISITE AMOUNT
514 REM
520 IF TEAM$="A" THEN SCORE_A=SCORE_A+VALUE:GOTO 540
530 SCORE_B=SCORE_B+VALUE
540 REM
550 REM SCORE UPDATE
560 PRINT "CURRENT SCORE - TEAM A:";SCORE_A;" :: TEAM
    B:";SCORE_B
562 IF TEAM$="A" THEN TEAM$="B":GOTO 900
564 TEAM$="A"
570 GOTO 900
580
600 REM
610 REM DRIBBLE
620 REM
630 INPUT "WAS THE DRIBBLE SUCCESSFUL, ANSWER 'Y' OR
    'N'";ANSWER$
635 IF ANSWER$="Y" GOTO 642
640 IF ANSWER$="N" GOTO 650
641 GOSUB 2000: GOTO 635
642 GOOD_DRIB=GOOD_DRIB+1
644 GOTO 900
645 REM
650 REM UNSUCCESSFUL DRIBBLE
652 BAD_DRIB=BAD_DRIB+1
655 REM CHANGE POSSESSION, GOTO SCREEN OUTPUT AND
    RETURN TO DATA INPUT
660 REM
670 IF TEAM$="A" THEN TEAM$="B":GOTO 900
680 TEAM$="A"
690 GOTO 900
```

```
700
900 REM
910 REM SCREEN OUPUT
920 REM
930 LET
    A$="************************************************
    ***************"
940 PRINT A$
950 PRINT A$
952 PRINT "              SHOTS                    PASSESS
    DRIBBLES         "
954 PRINT A$
956 PRINT "      GOOD        BAD        GOOD        BAD
    GOOD       BAD"
958 PRINT A$
960 PRINT " 2pt.   3pt.     2pt.   3pt."
970 PRINT AB(4);GOOD_SHOT2;TAB(8);GOOD_SHOT3;TAB(12);
    BAD_SHOT2;TAB(16);BAD_SHOT3;TAB(24);GOOD_PASS;TAB
    (32); BAD_PASS;TAB(40);GOOD_DRIB;TAB(48);BAD_DRIB
980 PRINT A$
990
1000 REM POSITION DATA CHECK
1010 REM
1020 IF PO$="Q" THEN RETURN
1030 IF PO$="W" THEN RETURN
1040 IF PO$="E" THEN RETURN
1050 IF PO$="R" THEN RETURN
1060 IF PO$="A" THEN RETURN
1070 IF PO$="S" THEN RETURN
1080 IF PO$="D" THEN RETURN
1090 IF PO$="F" THEN RETURN
1100 IF PO$="Z" THEN RETURN
1110 IF PO$="X" THEN RETURN
1120 IF PO$="C" THEN RETURN
1130 IF PO$="V" THEN RETURN
1140 GOSUB 2000: REM BEEP SUB-ROUTINE (SEE BELOW)
1150 GOTO 110
```

(The sub-routine 2000 is one that generates a 'beep' so that the operator will be aware of the error even if his/her attention is not upon the screen.)

```
2000 REM BEEP ROUTINE
2010 REM
2020 SOUND 37,.027
```

`2030 RETURN`

(This SOUND instruction will vary from machine to machine so check the manual of the machine being used.)

`9999 END`

Analysis of coaching behaviour – a review

8

8.1 INTRODUCTION

Research into coaching effectiveness has increased over the last decade, and now analysis of planning, management, instruction and monitoring skills is occurring (Segrave and Ciancio, 1990). To direct this research, coaching effectiveness has drawn its theoretical framework from the teacher effectiveness domain where, in recent years, evaluation and analysis of teaching skills in the sport environment has steadily gained favour. Indeed, it is now suggested that teaching skills are a science and, therefore, amenable to systematic evaluation (Siedentop, 1991). The basis for this review, therefore, is provided by research into teacher effectiveness.

Four distinct areas are addressed in this review. The first two sections establish the background to modern research on teaching and, in particular, the development of systematic observation techniques as a means of generating valid and reliable information on teacher process variables. Intervention studies are then cited in the third section to detail the necessary contingencies for the effective use of systematic observation in the analysis and modification of instructional behaviour. The fourth section cites literature that presents a rationale for those verbal coaching behaviours that are considered most effective. Finally, an extensive bibliography of literature related to the research on coaching analysis is provided.

8.2 INSTRUCTION

Effective instruction is crucial to the pursuit of optimal sporting performance as the more effective the instruction, the more fully the instructor's role will benefit athlete performance. Such instruction requires the application of skills that range from the planning and organization of learning experiences, to the presentation of instructional and feedback information. Quantitative analysis of the instructional process promotes the objective assessment of instructional behaviour and provides information on variables deemed important in determining effectiveness. Systematic observation is an analytic process that can provide valid and reliable information on the key elements of effective instruction, and 'systematic observation instruments' can accurately describe instruction within the unique physical education and sport setting. Computer technology has enhanced the observation and analysis process as it allows for immediate summary and display of data, which offers the potential for the timely return of meaningful feedback on the observed teaching/coaching performance. The utility of systematic observation instruments as an intervention strategy has application to those in supervisory positions within education and sport organizations.

While it is not yet possible to assess completely the full range of skills needed for effective instruction, we should endeavour to assess specific skills where and when we can (Siedentop, 1991). To this end, research into the verbal behaviour of teachers and coaches in the act of instruction is widespread and has used student achievement as the criterion variable and a variety of teaching activities as the predictor variable. Studies using event recording have identified the percentage of contact time effective coaches give different verbal information (Tharp and Gallimore, 1976; Miller, 1992), and have assessed certain rates and ratios of verbal behaviours emitted by effective coaches (Lacy and Darst, 1985; Claxton, 1988; Segrave and Ciancio, 1990). As a result there is much pedagogic and motor learning literature available to direct the skills of effective verbal behaviour (e.g. Siedentop, 1991; Schmidt, 1988; Magill, 1989).

8.3 TEACHING AND COACHING EFFECTIVENESS

In the 1950s the American Educational Research Association stated that after 40 years of research into teacher effectiveness, during which a vast number of studies were carried out, few outcomes could be acknowledged that would advance teacher assessments or that could be employed in planning or improving teacher education programs (Dunkin and Biddle, 1974). The collection of teacher effectiveness data was described by Dunkin and Biddle (1974) as 'dust-bowl empiricism' as there appeared to be no rationale for what aspects of teacher behaviour were to be examined. Rink (1993) declared it 'a blind search for the universal qualities of good teaching'.

After years of fruitless search for effective teaching methodologies (Medley, 1979), the late 1950s saw a major shift in teacher effectiveness research, and the study of teaching was then organized to investigate the relationships between presage, context, process and product variables.

By the 1960s and early 1970s, the process of teaching (i.e. those variables concerned with the actual activities of classroom teaching) became the focus of attention and actual instances of instruction were observed. Researchers began to study what teachers did in the act of teaching, because teacher process variables (e.g. the skills of giving instruction, strategies for organization and provision of feedback) were shown to directly relate to teacher performance (Siedentop, 1991). For these skills to improve, Siedentop (1991) stated that teachers should have their teaching observed, receive regular feedback based on these observations, have goals to reach and be provided with the opportunity to improve.

The quality and accuracy of feedback given to the teacher is central to efforts to modify their instructional behaviour. A substantial body of evidence suggests that this feedback should be based on information gathered by systematic observation because intuitive observation is unlikely to be a powerful enough tool to account for improvement (Siedentop, 1991). Therefore systematic observation, which is the foundation on which modern research on teaching has been built, should also be the foundation upon which teaching skills are developed.

8.4 SYSTEMATIC OBSERVATION

Observation is a key element in efforts to improve teaching skills and the turning point for teaching research was the development of strategies for observing teachers as they taught. However, the observation and data collection process had to be sufficiently objective to give a reliable account of teacher behaviour, and not be susceptible to the distortion of suggestion and perception (Siedentop, 1991). This process was labelled the systematic observation of classroom behaviour, and it provided researchers with a method of obtaining objective, reliable and valid measures of instructional behaviour (Rink, 1993). Only through systematic observation will sufficiently reliable, accurate and consistent information be obtained to assess teacher effectiveness (Metzler, 1979; Siedentop, 1991).

Systematic observation permits a trained observer to use a set of guidelines and procedures to observe, record and analyse observable events and behaviours, with the assumption that other observers, using the same observation instrument, and viewing the same sequence of events, would agree with the recorded data. This process results in higher degrees of observer objectivity, and is not susceptible to the shortcomings of 'eyeballing', anecdotal recordings and rating scales (Metzler, 1981). While originally developed for use in traditional educational settings, these instruments have, in recent years, been adapted to study instructional behaviour in the sport environment (Tharp and Gallimore,

1976; Lacy and Darst, 1985; Claxton, 1988; Markland and Martinek, 1988; Segrave and Ciancio, 1990: Miller, 1992). To ease the process of data collection and analysis, researchers have recently used microcomputers as the data collection tool (Carlson and McKenzie, 1984; Hawkins and Wiegand, 1989; Briggs, 1991; Johnson and Franks, 1991).

The data obtained from systematic observation and recording can serve as information by which teaching skills can be improved. For example, classroom management and discipline are teaching skills deemed important and they have become a main focus for research (Luke, 1989). Through systematic observation, successful management techniques have been identified and these are now changing how physical education lessons are taught (Siedentop, 1991). Systematic observation has also produced valuable information on the concept of academic learning time–physical education [ALT-PE (Metzler, 1979)]. ALT-PE is a unit of time in which a student is engaged in physical education content suitable to their stage of development. Studies have denounced many teachers' use of class time, particularly the lack of time they afford to productive student participation (Metzler, 1989).

Observation systems are designed to produce information on specific teacher and student variables, and the specific system chosen should be tailored to the goals of the particular observation (Siedentop, 1991). For example, event recording, which gathers information relating to the frequency of event occurrence, may, in certain instances, be more informative than assessment by duration recording. Once the technique(s) best suited to achieve the observational goals is identified, a means and format for data collection must be chosen. Depending on the teacher behaviour being observed and the resources available to assist data collection, collection can occur in real-time or post-event (providing the session has been recorded on either audio or videotape), and can be achieved through hand notation or computer-assisted coding.

One of the first instruments used to observe instructional behaviour was the Flanders Interaction Analysis System (FIAS) (Flanders, 1960). It was designed to analyse verbal teaching behaviour under three major headings: teacher talk, student talk and silence/confusion. Following this lead within educational research, interactions in the physical education environment were analysed using similar methods. Such were the strengths of FIAS that several of the instruments developed for use in physical education were modifications of FIAS (Dougherty, 1970; Cheffers, 1972). Since the inception of systematic observation in physical education, numerous instruments have been designed to record information on different aspects of teacher behaviour. Darst, Zakrajsek and Mancini (1989) provide a compilation of observer systems specific to the physical education and sport environment.

Tharp and Gallimore (1976), were amongst the first to report observational data on coaching behaviour. They devised a ten-category system to observe UCLA basketball coach, John Wooden. This pioneer study sparked a host of similar studies designed to challenge and compare their findings (Lacy and Darst, 1985; Claxton, 1988; Segrave and Ciancio, 1990). Other instruments were developed to report information on varying areas of coaching effectiveness (Rushall, 1977; Sinclair, 1983; Franks et al., 1986; Markland and Martinek, 1988).

Franks, Johnson and Sinclair (1988) developed the Computerized Coaching Analysis System (CCAS) in an attempt to improve existing techniques for systematic observation in sport. One part of the three-component CCAS was the Coach Analysis Instrument (CAI): a computer-aided coaching system designed to analyse the verbal behaviour of the coach when organizing and instructing within a defined segment of practice. As well as producing a thorough quantitative analysis profile, reflective of every comment made during the observed practice, the system also reflected the content of the practice session and the performance needs of the athletes. Efficiency of the data collection method and the perceived utility of the instrument were also considered (see Johnson and Franks, 1991). The CAI was subsequently updated [CAI(II) (More et al., 1996)] to address the recommendations of Partridge and Franks (1991).

A systematic observation instrument must be sufficiently reliable that it can be assumed that changes in behaviour are in fact due to the teacher/coach, and not due to the observer. Pilot work (More et al., 1992) to test the reliability of the CAI(II) provided encouraging results in this regard. Intra-observer reliability coefficients far exceeded the 80% acceptable threshold (Rushall, 1977) in all dimensions of the instrument, indicating that once the instrument's operational definitions have been learned, observers attain a consistent level of coding using the CAI(II).

8.5 SYSTEMATIC OBSERVATION AND THE MODIFICATION OF BEHAVIOUR

> Having the opportunity to practise relevant skills with the provision for systematic feedback is the quickest way to develop skills in teaching. For a long time we have known this to be true for sport skills. It also appears to be true for teaching skills. (Siedentop, 1991)

Can instructional behaviour be modified? A review of the pertinent literature would suggest yes, given the appropriate contingencies. For example, Rink (1993) states that change can be expedited if attention is on one process variable and only a few teaching behaviours are selected for change at any one time. Siedentop (1984) states that enhancement in teaching performance can occur if the attention of the supervisor/educator is reinforcing to the trainee/coach. Counsel is given by Rink (1993), however, that changing behaviour is not easy, even when teachers are aware of both their behaviour and the changes they want to make.

Pedagogic literature of specific intervention studies provides evidence that behaviour can be modified/changed through systematic analysis (Borg, 1972; Werner and Rink, 1989; Grant, Ballard and Glynn, 1990). Initial study into pre-service training indicated that traditional supervisory methods could effect change on students' stress levels, ethics, appearance and confidence, but hardly any in the development of pedagogical skills (Paese, 1984). However, subsequent work carried out at Ohio State University (cited by Paese, 1984) showed that when their supervisors utilized systematic observation and goal-setting, those students could not only attain modification goals set by their supervisors, but they were able to maintain them at approximately 75% of the level achieved during intervention. Mancini et al. (1985), also reported that, based on observations of 201 pre-service teachers, teaching behaviour could be altered if supervisory feedback included the systematic analysis of their behaviour.

As those participating in this study had coached for several years, it was important to ascertain the success of intervention strategies designed to change the behaviour of experienced teachers/coaches. A review of intervention studies dealing with those experienced in instruction was undertaken but failed to find any studies relating specifically to the coaching environment, or to physical education teachers, after 1990. Nevertheless the studies to be reported generally support the contention that behaviour can be modified.

Whaley (1980) reported feedback on teaching performance to be successful in improving a variety of behaviours and proposed that it may be an unobtrusive method of increasing ALT-PE. Graphic feedback on ALT-PE categories was given to four high school physical education teachers with the expectation of improving their behaviour. Whaley (1980) concluded that, within the limitations of the study, no effect was found on the amount of content time, engaged time of students or motor responses of students. The changes reported in ALT-PE were associated with changes in activity rather than with intervention. It would appear that an intervention strategy that is solely graphic in nature is insufficient to create an increase in ALT-PE.

Event and duration recording was used by Ewens (1981) to assess the verbal behaviour of eight matched pairs of experienced elementary teachers. Following a baseline phase, where no significant differences between control and experimental groups were reported, planned intervention packages of self-assessment and goal-setting strategies were designed to increase positive specific feedback, corrective specific feedback, and the acceptance of student ideas in the experimental group. Results showed partial success as a significant difference was found between groups in all but the acceptance of student ideas. Similarly, only partial success was reported by O'Sullivan (1984), when assessing the effects of an in-service model of supervision on activity time, positive learning environment and student involvement. Feedback to teachers was provided in a series of conferences where strengths and weaknesses were discussed and strategies for improvement examined. O'Sullivan (1984) concluded that improvement in teacher performance could only occur when the environmental context within which teachers teach becomes supportive of their efforts towards instructional improvement. She implied that the intervention model would remain somewhat ineffective until teachers, in service, had incentive to improve and those at managerial level were held accountable for student learning. Clearly, this has inference for the context in which any intervention package or strategy is given, and the importance the participating teachers/coaches attach to the results of their behaviour.

Grant, Ballard and Glynn (1990) conducted a study on the amount of motor-on-task behaviour exhibited by the students of three experienced physical education teachers. Feedback was given to two of these teachers in the form of data generated by the Ohio State ALT-PE observation system. Their findings were that the intervention teachers were able to respond to feedback and modify their lessons so that the amount of student participation was increased. The results showed that these teachers increased the motor-on-task behaviour of their students by 15%, while the third teacher, not receiving feedback, showed no substantive differences in behaviour. An interesting feature of their methodology was the inclusion of interviews with the teachers to gain an insight into their perceptions of trying to modify behaviour. These interviews clearly revealed the teachers were unaware of their initial levels of behaviour and therefore insensitive to a need for change.

In conducting a single-subject analysis on the verbal behaviour of an experienced physical education teacher, McKenzie (1981) analysed three distinct and independent verbal behaviours: the use of 'OK', the use of first names and the use of positive specific feedback. Direct information feedback and goal-setting were the intervention components designed to modify and maintain improvement in these behaviours. Substantial positive change in the rates of all three behaviours was shown during intervention: OKs were reduced by 93%, the use of first names increased by 478% and the use of positive specific feedback increased by 1144%. Moreover, in a 12 month follow-up test, the use of OKs reduced further and, while decreasing slightly, the use of first names and positive specific feedback remained above that of baseline. While the behaviours targeted for change may appear rather cosmetic, and be somewhat independent of one another, the results suggest behaviour modification is possible.

The modification of instructional behaviour requires the systematic collection of valid and reliable information (Siedentop, 1991), and systematic observation instruments have been presented as the means by which sufficiently reliable data can be gathered to assess behaviour. The modification (or learning) of behaviour can then occur by using the data as direct feedback on teaching performance, as reinforcement of appropriate performance and as information in the form of directions and/or recommendations (Locke, 1984). This feedback process can oversee the 'fine-tuning' of existing instructional skills, as well as the understanding and acquisition of new skills.

Ocansey (1988) proposed a five-component guide to effectively oversee the modification of behaviour. The components were as follows:

1. Establish a baseline of teaching performance. Three observations are sufficient to establish a baseline, unless the data fail to show stability.
2. Select behaviours that need remediation or maintenance based on the baseline data.
3. Specify strategies to facilitate the remediation or maintenance of targeted behaviour(s).
4. Establish a criteria for evaluating performance of each targeted behaviour.
5. Indicate commencement and completion dates for the specified targeted behaviour(s).

These components provide an excellent framework to monitor the modification of behaviour; a framework that is to be adopted in this study.

8.6 IDENTIFICATION OF EFFECTIVE VERBAL COACHING STRATEGIES

McKenzie, Clark and McKenzie (1984), stated that 'an instructional strategy can be viewed as a particular arrangement of antecedents and consequences designed and implemented by a teacher to develop and control the behaviour of learners'. However, there are no stereotypical coaching strategies that will lead to success in all coaching environments, but rather that effective coaching behaviour is flexible and dependent on many aspects of the coaching environment (Cratty, 1983). The following section reviews literature on behaviours that can be analysed through the CAI(II), citing literature on effective verbal strategies from a range of learning contexts and identifying those coaching behaviours acknowledged as most effective.

Performance-related feedback are interactions directed at the athletic performance of the learners while behavioural feedback are interactions directed at the organization and social behaviour of the learners. 'More effective' physical education teachers spend more time instructing the proposed content of the lesson and providing performance-related feedback than do 'less effective' teachers (Phillips and Carlisle, 1983). Intuitively, this suggests that more effective teachers spend less time organizing the class and providing behavioural feedback. In respect to these findings, Mustain (1990) suggests that a necessity for increased amounts of behavioural feedback may reflect a lack of effective planning or result from poor organization and instruction. The implication for coaches is that they must seek solution to the origin of the problem, rather than increase behavioural feedback to maintain the learning environment. Doing so will allow them to spend a greater proportion of time giving performance-related instruction and feedback.

Schmidt (1988) stated that most researchers agree that feedback about the proficiency of an individual's response is the most important variable (except for practice itself) for motor learning. As coaches, by nature of their roles, are responsible for much of the augmented feedback received by athletes as they perform, it is crucial that the feedback they give reflect effective strategies identified in the literature. Current motor learning literature states that augmented feedback produces learning, not by the reward or punishment of responses, but by the provision of information about actions from a previous trial, and by suggestion of how to change subsequent trials (see Schmidt, 1988). Augmented feedback should, therefore, have informational content to direct the learner's attention to specific aspects of performance, as the allocation of attentional capacity is an important feature of skill acquisition (Magill, 1989).

Coaches, therefore, should ensure that their instructional feedback goes beyond simple reward or punishment (e.g. 'Nice job' or 'Not that way') and include some informational content (e.g. 'Nice job, but get more pace on the ball'). The information should reinforce the specific aspect(s) of performance that are 'correct', or should identify discrepancies between actual and desired response, so that 'incorrect' aspect(s) of performance can be modified. Thus, regardless of the quality of athlete performance, feedback should be enhanced by the inclusion of informational content, and comments that have no informational content, i.e. general and non-specific, should be limited.

While widely accepted that inclusion of information will provide for effective feedback comments, studies concerning the nature of this information are inconclusive. Markland and Martinek (1988) analysed the behaviour of high school varsity coaches and noted that the majority of feedback given by more successful coaches was 'corrective' in nature, given in reference to some error in performance. Tharp and Gallimore (1976), studied UCLA's highly successful basketball coach, John Wooden, and found that 'corrective' feedback, in the form of 'scold/reinstructions' outweighed 'praise' in the ratio of 2:1. Claxton (1988) compiled data on nine more or less successful high school tennis coaches and found that the more successful coaches indulged in less praise than less successful coaches. These studies would indicate, therefore, that effective coaches (as measured by their winning records) direct a large proportion of their feedback information towards aspects of performance that are performed incorrectly or inadequately.

Conversely, Miller (1992) analysed the behaviours of youth soccer coaches and noted that the 'praise' to 'scold' ratio was 6.7:1.5, indicating that these coaches spent a much higher proportion of time reinforcing correct behaviour than scolding incorrect behaviour. Lacy and Darst (1984) when analysing winning high school football coaches, observed that, across the entire season, praise was used over twice as much as scold. Segrave and Ciancio (1990) compared the profile of successful Pop Warner football coach with that of John Wooden (discussed earlier) and found that the former, Beau Kilmer, used twice as much praise as did Wooden.

The data from these selected studies suggest a differential use of feedback strategies commensurate with the age and ability of the athletes involved. In explaining Wooden's sparing use of praise, Tharp and Gallimore (1976) state that 'with players who are highly motivated towards specific goals, John Wooden did not need to hand out quick rewards on the practice court'. Level praise on the floor becomes virtually unnecessary with athletes at the élite collegiate. However, those that will form the athlete population in this study are neither at that age or ability level. Interestingly, Tharp and Gallimore (1976) note 'for students less motivated than Wooden's players social reward may be necessary as incentive to keep them in reach of instruction, modelling, feedback and other activities that do produce learning'. Thus, for those involved in this study an effective feedback strategy would be to concentrate on feedback that will reinforce correct performance, rather than use negative behaviours to stimulate the athletes. This is not to suggest that coaches eliminate feedback on incorrect performance, but rather develop a feedback strategy that favours providing information to reinforce correct actions (Sinclair, 1989).

The need for coaching comments to include informational content seems conclusive. Further, it would seem appropriate that the information given should pertain specifically to the skills and concepts that the drill is designed to improve. Information should specifically relate to the focus of the movement tasks being attempted (Mustain, 1990). For example, in a soccer drill designed to improve the skill of crossing, the coaching information should concentrate on the player's ability to gain the required pace, direction and flight of ball. The information should concentrate on the skill's mechanical and decision-making requirements and not dwell on information regarding ball reception or dribbling technique prior to cross delivery. While other aspects of performance will, instinctively, be commented upon, it is clearly desirable that the majority of skill-related comments concentrate on the key factors of the drill. To this end the decision to concentrate on specific 'key factors' should occur prior to the practice, to help ensure the coach's, and consequently the learner's, attention is focused on them.

In addition to being informational, skill-related feedback must also be accurate, yet not all teachers possess the ability to discriminate between actual and desired performance (Siedentop, 1991). Inaccurate evaluation of performance would clearly be inappropriate, and damaging to skill acquisition, so coaches must develop sufficient knowledge to accurately diagnose athletic performance.

If the movement task being attempted has low attentional demands that can be handled within capacity limits, then the information processing system can effectively attend to other tasks and stimuli at the same time. This, however, is not true if the task requires full allocation of our attention (see Magill, 1989, for Attention Capacity Theories). This feature of attentional capacity has clear implications for the coach. First, consideration must be given to different approaches of coaching high and low complexity skills, i.e. should the skill be practised in its entirety or should parts of it be practised? Secondly, consideration must be given to the timing of any verbal instruction or feedback. Because learners can only effectively process a limited amount of information at once, little benefit can be derived from coaching information if the task demand itself consumes most or all of the learner's attentional capacity. Markland and Martinek (1988) noted that successful high school volleyball coaches gave more immediate, terminal feedback than did less successful coaches – the inference being that successful coaches provide the majority of their feedback once the learner is free from the immediate attentional demands of performance. 'Immediate terminal' feedback was defined as 'feedback provided after the completed motor skill attempt and before participation in one or more intervening motor skill attempts'. This temporal location of feedback is supported in the motor learning literature. Schmidt (1988) states that during the delay between the learner's response and the provision of feedback, the active learner is engaged in processing information about the response. The learner's perception of the movement is thus retained so that when augmented feedback is received the two can be associated.

The frequency with which the athletes receive feedback is also an important feature in determining the effectiveness of verbal behaviour. Practice with the athletes receiving feedback after every performance (a schedule referred to as 100% relative frequency) has been shown to aid performance during acquisition, but to degrade learning relative to other feedback schedules (Swinnen *et al.*, 1990; Winstein and Schmidt, 1990). These findings provide empirical support for the 'guidance hypothesis', which suggests that immediate performance is facilitated because the subject is guided toward the target performance by the feedback, but that long-term retention (i.e. learning) is degraded because the athlete will rely on these guidance properties to perform correctly. The findings also provide support for Schmidt's (1988) contention that relative frequency should be large in initial practice to guide the athlete to enhanced performance, but systematically smaller as practice continues and so force the learner to engage in other processes to aid retention (e.g. detect ones own errors, attend to sensory feedback).

In the unique and dynamic setting of a team-sport practice, it is unrealistic to expect coaches to monitor the frequency with which they give feedback to individual athletes. A manageable schedule, therefore, would see the coach give many instances of individual feedback early in the practice drill but, thereafter, reduce the number of individual feedback comments and provide feedback judiciously to the whole group.

In teaching skills, particularly new skills, often the best way of communicating information is through a demonstration. Demonstrations (commonly referred to as modelling) can aid the learning of skills by accurately and skilfully portraying the critical features of the skill being taught (Magill, 1989). These demonstrations can occur before practice, to give the learners 'the idea of the movement' (Gentile, 1972), or during practice, to confirm and extend the learner's understanding of the task. McCullagh (1987), noted that provided the person is skilled in the act of demonstration, the athletes will learn from their coach or from one of their peers.

Demonstrations benefit learning by creating a representation of performance that can be copied. Cognitive mediation theory (Carroll and Bandura, 1987) suggests that the information conveyed in the demonstration is extracted via selective attention to the critical features of performance. This information is then transformed into symbolic codes that are stored in memory as internal models for action. This internal model is then, after rehearsal and organization, turned into a physical action, providing the required motivation and physical abilities are present. The cognitive representation not only guides the learner's response production, it also provides the standard against which feedback is compared.

By creating a representation of physical relationships (e.g. body parts, forces, speeds) demonstrations enhance the learner's understanding of the skill to be learned. Both slow-motion and real-time demonstrations are useful, although real-time demonstrations are more important in later stages to help the learner acquire the speed and flow characteristics of the movement (Scully, 1988). The demonstration should be accompanied by succinct verbal instructions, aimed at ensuring the learner's attention is directed to aspects of performance that will yield benefit (Mawer, 1990).

The theoretical literature stresses the importance of demonstrations being skilfully performed, but does not indicate the extent to which demonstrations should focus on 'correct' or 'incorrect' performance. Studies of coaching behaviour, however, have shown that successful coaches tend to give more demonstrations of correct performance than of incorrect performance (Lacy and Darst, 1985; Claxton, 1988; Segrave and Ciancio, 1990). Results suggest that demonstrations account for 3.4–6.1% of all coaching behaviours and that demonstrations of correct performance outnumber those of incorrect performance by approximately 3:1. The studies by Lacy and Darst (1985), and Segrave and Ciancio (1990), also showed that the use of demonstration decreased as the season progressed (3.3 to 1.8%, and 7.4 to 2.7% of all behaviours respectively), while Miller (1992), working with youth soccer coaches, found no such drop off. This latter study could perhaps indicate, that with younger athletes, there is a greater need for demonstrations to enhance the coaching process.

This review of literature has centred on the effectiveness of comments considered to be skill related. However, those comments considered non-skill related, that is organizational, behavioural, effort or non-specific, also contribute to the quality of the learning environment. With the exception of organizational comments, all non-skill comments should carry a measure of intent to motivate the learner towards the coach's demands. For example, the coach may use an enthusiastic tone to generate more effort or a forceful tone to deal with an incident of misbehaviour. Both of these strategies increase the likelihood of the learner becoming more productive.

The coach is the individual responsible for establishing the climate of the learning environment. While there is no empirical support that a positive climate (i.e. friendly, reinforcing) enhances student learning, it is clear that a negative climate is detrimental to learning (Soar and Soar, 1979). It is, therefore, apparent that when maintaining productive behaviour, demanding effort or providing motivation, the majority of comments should be positive in nature (i.e. constructive, reinforcing) to increase the effectiveness of the learning environment.

8.7 SUMMARY

Research into coaching has been able to draw on the physical education pedagogy literature in much the same way as research in teaching physical education has drawn upon the findings of mainstream educational research (Hastie, 1992). As a result, all instructors within the sport environment have available to them an extensive and growing knowledge base from which to make decisions about their practice. However, despite research identifying practices of effective instruction that are clearly linked to indices of student achievement, and studies producing an optimistic database for the modification of behaviour, little effort has been made to make behaviour modification the central issue in most teacher and coach education programs. Siedentop (1984) contends that this is because 'the old argument between education and training is currently being decided in favour of education', despite there being little evidence to support the cognitivist position that education provides a deeper, broader and more lasting teaching ability.

If teacher and coach programs are to consider intervention methods as part of 'training' oriented education and/or certification, continued study into the utility of systematic observation and the modification of behaviour is required.

8.8 EXTENDED BIBLIOGRAPHY OF COACHING ANALYSIS LITERATURE

This bibliography is included separately to the rest of the references of the book, as it is intended as a supplemental reading list to anyone who wishes to extend their reading in this specific subject area.

Borg, W.R. (1972) The minicourse as a vehicle for changing teacher behavior: a three-year follow-up. *Journal of Educational Psychology*, **63**(6), 572–579.

Briggs, J.D. (1991) The physical education systematic observation program (PE-SOP): an application oriented, computerized systematic observation program. *The Physical Educator*, Fall, 151–156.

Carlson, B.R. and McKenzie, T.L. (1984) Computer technology for recording, storing, and analyzing temporal data in physical activity settings. *Journal of Teaching in Physical Education*, **4**(1), 24–29.

Carroll, W.R. and Bandura, A. (1987) Translating cognition into action: the role of visual guidance in observational learning. *Journal of Motor Behavior*, **19** (3), 385–398.

Cheffers, J.T.F. (1972) The validation of an instrument designed to expand the Flanders system of interaction analysis to describe non-verbal interaction, different varieties of teacher behavior and pupil response. Unpublished doctoral dissertation. Temple University.

Claxton, B. (1988) A systematic observation of more and less successful high school tennis coaches. *Journal of Teaching in Physical Education*, **7**, 302–310.

Cook, T.D. and Campbell, D.T. (1979) *Quasi-Experimentation: Design and Analysis Issues for Field Settings.* Houghton Mifflin, Boston, MA.

Cratty, B.J. (1983) *Psychology in Contemporary Sport.* Prentice-Hall, Englewood Cliffs, NJ.

Darst, P.W., Zakrajsek, D.B. and Mancini, V.H. (1989) *Analyzing Physical Education and Sport Instruction*, 2nd edn. Human Kinetics, Champaign, IL.

Donahue, J.A., Gillis, J.H. and King, K. (1990) Behavior modification in sport and physical education: a review. *Journal of Sport Psychology*, **2**, 311–328.

Dougherty, N.J. (1970) A comparison of command, task and individual program styles of teaching in the development of physical fitness and motor skills. Unpublished doctoral dissertation. Temple University.

Dufour, W. (1993) Computer-assisted scouting in soccer. In T. Reilly, J. Clarys and A. Stibbe (Eds), *Science and Football II.* E. & F.N. Spon, London, pp. 160–166.

Dunkin, M.J. and Biddle, B.J. (1974) *The Study of Teaching.* Holt, Reinhart and Wilson, New York.

Ewens, B.L. (1981) Effects of self-assessment and goal setting on verbal behavior of elementary physical education teachers. *Dissertation Abstracts International*, **42**, 2559-A.

Flanders, N. (1960) *Interaction Analysis in the Classroom: A Manual for Observers.* University of Minnesota Press, Minneapolis, MN.

Franks, I.M., Sinclair, G.D., Thomson, W. and Goodman, D. (1986) Analysis of the coaching practice. *SPORTS*, January.

Franks, I.M., Johnson, R.B. and Sinclair, G.D. (1988) The development of a computerized coaching analysis system for recording behavior in sporting environments. *Journal of Teaching in Physical Education*, **8**, 23–32.

Grant, B.C., Ballard, K.D. and Glynn, T.L. (1990) Teacher feedback intervention, motor-on-task behavior, and successful task performance. *Journal of Teaching in Physical Education*, **9**, 123–139.

Hastie, P.A. (1992) Towards a pedagogy of sports coaching: research directions for the 1990's. *International Journal of Physical Education*, **29**(3), 26–29.

Hawkins, A.H. and Wiegand, R.L. (1989) West Virginia University teaching evaluation system and feedback taxonomy. In P.W. Darst, D.B. Zakrajsek and V.H. Mancini (Eds), *Analyzing Physical Education and Sport Instruction.* Human Kinetics, Champaign, IL, pp. 277-293.

House, A.E., House, B.J. and Campbell, M.B. (1981) Measures of inter-observer agreement: calculation formulas and distribution effects. *Journal of Behavioral Assessment*, **3**(1), 37–57.

Johnson, R.B. (1988) Determining the reliability of a computerized coach analysis instrument. Unpublished masters dissertation. University of British Columbia.

Johnson, R.B. and Franks, I.M. (1991) Measuring the reliability of a computer aided systematic observation instrument. *Canadian Journal of Sport Science*, **16**(1), 45–57.

Kazdin, A.E. (1978) Methodological and interpretive problems of single-case experimental designs. *Journal of Consulting and Clinical Psychology*, **46**(4), 629–642.

Lacy, A.C. and Darst, P.W. (1985) Systematic observation of winning football coaches. *Journal of Teaching in Physical Education*, **4**, 256–270.

Locke, L.F. (1984) Research on teaching teachers: where are we now? *Journal of Teaching in Physical Education*, Monograph 2, Summer.

Luke, M. (1989) Research on class management and organization: review with implications for current practice. *Quest*, **41**, 55–67.

Magill, R.A. (1989) *Motor learning: Concepts and applications.* Wm.C. Brown, Ames, IA.

Mancini, V.H., Wuest, D.A. and van der Mars, H. (1985) Use of instruction and supervision in systematic observation in undergraduate professional preparation. *Journal of Teaching in Physical Education*, **5**, 22–33.

Markland, R. and Martinek, T.J. (1988) Descriptive analysis of augmented feedback given to high school varsity female volleyball players. *Journal of Teaching in Physical Education*, **7**, 289–301.

Mawer, M. (1990) It's not what you do – it's the way that you do it! Teaching skills in physical education. *British Journal of Physical Education*, Summer, 307–312.

McCullagh, P. (1987) Model similarity effects on motor performance. *Journal of Sports Psychology*, **9**, 249–260.

McKenzie, T.L. (1981) Modification, transfer, and maintenance of the verbal behavior of an experienced physical education teacher: a single-subject analysis. *Journal of Teaching in Physical Education*, Introductory Issue, 48–56.

McKenzie, T.L., Clark, E.K. and McKenzie, R. (1984) Instructional strategies: influence on teacher and student behavior. *Journal of Teaching in Physical Education*, Winter, 20–28.

Medley, D. (1979) The effectiveness of teachers. In P. Peterson and H. Walberg (Eds), *Research on Teaching: Concepts, Findings and Implications.* McCutchan, Berkeley, CA.

Metzler, M. (1979) The measurement of academic learning time in physical education. Unpublished doctoral dissertation. The Ohio State University, Columbus. OH.

Metzler, M. (1981) A multi-observational system for supervising student teachers in physical education. *The Physical Educator*, **3**, 152–159.

Metzler, M. (1989) A review of research on time in sport pedagogy. *Journal of Teaching in Physical Education*, **8**(2), 87–103.

Miller, A.W. (1992) Systematic observation behavior similarities of various youth sport soccer coaches. *The Physical Educator*, **49**, 136–143.

More, K.G., Franks, I.M., McGarry, T. and Partridge, D. (1992) Analysis of coaching behaviors: the effectiveness of using a computer-aided system. Paper presented to the *Canadian Society for Psychomotor Learning and Sport Psychology*, Saskatoon, Saskatchewan.

More, K.G., Franks, I.M., McGarry, T. and Partridge, D. (1993) Computer-aided analysis of coaching intervention: a test of intra and inter observer reliability. Paper presented to the *Association for the Advancement of Applied Sport Psychology*, Montreal, Quebec.

Mustain, W.C. (1990) Are you the best teacher you can be? *Journal of Physical Education, Recreation and Dance*, February, 69–73.

Ocansey, R. (1988) An effective supervision guide for supervisors: a systematic approach to organizing data generated during monitoring sessions in student teaching. *The Physical Educator*, **45**(1), 24–29.

O'Sullivan, M.M. (1984) The effects of inservice education on the teaching effectiveness of experienced physical educators. *Dissertation Abstracts International*, **44**, 1724-A.

Paese, P.C. (1984) Student teacher supervision: where we are and where we should be. *The Physical Educator*, **41**, 90–94.

Partridge, D. and Franks, I.M. (1991) Changing coaching behaviors in a sport environment by means of computer aided observation. Paper presented to the *Canadian Society for Psychomotor Learning and Sport Psychology*, London, Ontario.

Phillips, D.A. and Carlisle, C. (1983) A comparison of physical education teachers categorized as most and least effective. *Journal of Teaching in Physical Education*, **2**(3), 55–67.

Ratliffe, T. (1986) The influence of school principals on management time and student activity time for two elementary physical education teachers. *Journal of Teaching in Physical Education*, **5**, 117–125.

Rink, J. (1993) *Teaching Physical Education for Learning*. Mosby, St Louis, MO.

Rupert, T. and Buschner, C. (1989) Teaching and coaching: a comparison of instructional behaviors. *Journal of Teaching in Physical Education*, **9**, 49–57.

Rushall, B.S. (1977) Two observation schedules for sporting and physical education environments. *Canadian Journal of Applied Sport Science*, **2**, 15–21.

Schmidt, R.A. (1988) *Motor Control and Learning: A Behavioral Emphasis*. Human Kinetics, Champaign, IL.

Scully, D. (1988) Visual perception of human movement: the use of demonstrations in teaching motor skills. *British Journal of Physical Education*, Research Supplement 4.

Segrave, J.O. and Ciancio, C.A. (1990) An observational study of a successful Pop Warner football coach. *Journal of Teaching in Physical Education*, **9**, 294–306.

Siedentop, D. (1984) The modification of teacher behavior. In M.P. Pieron and G Graham (Eds), *Sport Pedagogy*. Human Kinetics, Champaign, IL, pp. 3-19.

Siedentop, D. (1991) *Developing Teaching Skills in Physical Education*, 3rd edn. Mayfield, Mountain View, CA.

Sinclair, G.D. (1989) Feedback analysis profile. In P.W. Darst, D.B. Zakrajsek and V.H. Mancini (Eds), *Analyzing Physical Education and Sport Instruction*. Human Kinetics, Champaign, IL, pp. 361-368.

Soar, R.S. and Soar, R.M. (1979) Emotional climate and management. In P.L. Peterson and H.J. Walberg (Eds) *Research on Teaching: Concepts, Findings, and Implications*. McCutchan, Berkeley, CA.

Swinnen, S.P., Schmidt, R.A., Nicholson, D.E. and Shapiro, D.C. (1990) Information feedback for skill acquisition: instantaneous knowledge of results degrades learning. *Journal of Experimental Psychology: Learning, Memory, and Cognition*, **16**(4), 706–716.

Tharp, R.G. and Gallimore, R. (1976) What a coach can teach a teacher. *Psychology Today*, **25**, 75–78.

Wampold, B.E. and Furlong, M.J. (1981) The heuristics of visual inference. *Behavioral Assessment*, **3**, 79–92.

Werner, P. and Rink, R. (1989) Case studies of teacher effectiveness in second grade physical education. *Journal of Teaching in Physical Education*, **8**, 280–297.

Whaley, G.M. (1980) The effect of daily monitoring and feedback to teachers and students on academic learning time-physical education. *Dissertation Abstracts International*, **41**, 1477-A.

Winstein, C.J. and Schmidt, R.A. (1990) Reduced frequency of knowledge of results enhances motor skill learning. *Journal of Experimental Psychology: Learning, Memory, and Cognition*, **16**(4), 677–691.

Summary and conclusions

In this chapter the main points of constructing and/or using notation systems, either hand or computerized, are reviewed.

WHY USE FEEDBACK?

Coaching intervention has traditionally been based upon subjective observations of athletes. However, several recent studies have shown that such observations are not only unreliable but also inaccurate. Although the benefits of feedback and KR are well accepted, the problems of highlighting, memory and observational difficulties result in the accuracy of subjective coaching analysis and feedback being limited. Video analysis has been shown to benefit the most advanced athletes but care must be taken when providing this form of feedback to any other standard of performer. On a practical level therefore, problems arise for the coach when considering the use of video feedback. The major problem is that of identifying the 'critical elements' of successful athletic performance, identifying the key events to the players.

To overcome these problems analysis systems have been devised. In developing these systems it is necessary to define and identify the critical elements of performance, and then devise an efficient data entry method, such that, in certain situations, a trained observer could record these events in real-time. When the demands of the complexity of the systems are such that real-time notation is not possible, then post-event analysis has been completed using the slow motion and replay facilities afforded by video. The benefits of using computers to record human athletic behaviour in this way can be summarized in terms of speed, efficiency and objective accuracy.

The use of systematic observation instruments provides researchers with a method of collecting behavioural data on both the coach and the athlete. These data can be analysed and processed in a variety of ways to provide a descriptive profile that can be used for giving both the athlete and the coach feedback about their actions. Advances in both computer and video technology can make this observation process more efficient and also provide the coach with audiovisual feedback about their interactions with athletes.

ANALYSIS OF SPORT

Logical analysis of the form and function of the events taking place in a sport is necessary before any analysis can take place. Franks and Goodman (1986) outlined three steps in forming any analysis system:

TASK 1: Describe your sport from a general level to a specific focus.

TASK 2: Prioritize key factors of performance.

TASK 3: Devise a recording method that is efficient and easy to learn.

By elucidating tasks 1 and 2, the creation of a notation system becomes an easy and logical progression. Practising these logical definitions is not difficult but it is a skill that becomes easier and easier with practice.

The more complex the sport, e.g. team games like soccer or American football, then the more care that must be taken in deciding exactly what is required of the system – which units of the team, or individuals, are to be analysed, which actions and events have the most relevance, etc.

The next step in analysis logic is to decide the level at which the analysis will take place. If it is a team game, then what units of the team are going to be analysed? Or are individuals to be monitored? Or the whole team? This type of decision does not apply in individual sports, but the level or degree of detail of output must be decided – and it is vital that these decisions are made early in the analytical process.

WORK ALREADY COMPLETED – LESSONS TO LEARN

HAND NOTATION SYSTEMS

Hand notation systems are in general very accurate but they do have some disadvantages. The more sophisticated systems involve considerable learning time. In addition, the amount of data that these systems produce can involve many person-hours of work in processing them into forms of output that are meaningful to the coach, athlete or sports scientist. Even in a simple game like squash the amount of data produced by the Sanderson–Way system of notation required 40 person-hours of work to process one match.

The introduction of computerized notation systems has enabled these two problems, in particular the data processing, to be tackled in a positive way. Used in real-time analysis or in post-event analysis in conjunction with video recordings, they enable immediate, easy access to data. They also enable the sports scientist to present the data in graphical forms more easily understood by the coach and athlete. The increasing sophistication and reducing cost of video systems has greatly enhanced the whole area of post-event feedback, from playback with subjective analysis by a coach to detailed objective analysis by means of notation systems.

COMPUTERIZED NOTATION SYSTEMS

To summarize the developments in computerized notational analysis, one can trace the innovative steps used in overcoming the two main problems of dealing with computers – data input and data output.

The initial difficulty in using a computer is entering information. The traditional method is using the QWERTY keyboard. However, unless the operator possesses considerable skills, this can be a lengthy and boring task. By assigning codes to the different actions, positions or players, that have some meaning to the operator then the key entry can be easier. The next step is to assign areas of the keyboard to represent areas of the pitch, numbers for the players, and another section of the keyboard for the actions (see Hughes and Cunliffe, 1986). An alternative to this approach to his problem is to use a specifically designed keyboard (Franks, Goodman and Miller, 1983a,b; Alderson and McKinnon, 1985), that has key entry designed ergonomically to meet the particular needs of the sport under analysis.

The major innovation, however, in this area, that eased considerably the problems of data entry both in terms of skill requirements and learning time was the introduction of the digitization pad. In Britain most workers have utilized the concept keyboard (Hughes and Feery, 1986; Sharp, 1986; Treadwell, 1988) whilst in Canada, Ian Franks, at his Notational Analysis Centre at University of British Columbia, Vancouver, has utilized another pad that has the trade name 'Power Pad' (Franks *et al.*, 1986). These are programmable, touch-sensitive, pads, over which one can place an overlay that has a graphic representation of the pitch and aptly labelled keypad areas for the actions and the players. This considerably reduces the skill required for fast data entry and the learning time required to gain this level of skill. More recently, data entry has been via graphical user interfaces, using the mouse to point and click at icons, etc. to enter information into the computer – a system made popular and familiar by the Windows™- software. Although ergonomically not as efficient as the concept keyboard method of entering data, it does have the advantages of not having to buy extra hardware for your computer, as well as the familiarity of use by most computer users.

A recent innovation expected to develop into a commercially competitive method of entering information is the development of voice-interactive systems to introduce data into the computer. Although Taylor and Hughes

(1988) were severely limited by the amounts of funding for their research, they were still able to demonstrate that this type of system can and will be used by the computer 'non-expert'. Although systems are expensive at the moment, computer technology is an environment of rapidly decreasing costs, even as the technology races ahead, so one can expect that this will be the next big step forward in the use of computers, in general, and sports systems, in particular.

Notational analysis, whilst having been the platform for considerable research, has its foundations in practical applications in sport. In these situations, it is imperative that the output is as immediate as possible and, perhaps more important, clear, concise and to the point. Consequently, the second strand of innovation that one can trace through the development of different systems is that of better output.

The first systems produced tables and tables of data, incorporated with statistical significance tests, that sport scientists had difficulty in interpreting; pity the coach or the athlete attempting to adopt these systems. Some researchers attempted to tackle the problem (Sanderson and Way, 1977), but not everyone would agree that this type of presentation was any easier to understand than the tables of data. Representations of frequency distributions across graphics of the playing area (Hughes *et al.*, 1988), traces of the path of the ball prior to a shot or a goal (Hughes and Cunliffe, 1986; Franks and Nagelkerke, 1989) and similar ploys have made the output of some systems far more attractive and easier to understand. The system developed by Hughes and McGarry specifically tackled this problem and produced some three-dimensional colour graphics that presented the data in a compact form, very easy to assimilate. Finally, the computer-controlled video, interactive systems (Franks, Nagelkerke and Goodman, 1989) present the users of analysis systems the potential of immediate analysis combined with the visual presentation of the feedback of the action.

FUTURE DEVELOPMENTS IN NOTATIONAL ANALYSIS

In terms of technological development, notational analysis will undoubtedly move as rapidly as the developments in computer technology and video technology as we approach the 21st century. There are two developments that will almost certainly happen over the next few years. The first will be the development of 'all-purpose', generic software. Work in some centres has almost reached this point now. Another technological advance that will make computerized notation more easily handled by the non-specialist will be the introduction of 'voice-over' methods of data entry. Taylor and Hughes (1988) have demonstrated that this is possible now, but relatively expensive at present day prices. These are expected to drop rapidly over the next couple of years and voice-interaction should therefore be a natural extension of any computing hardware system.

The integration of both these technological developments with computerized-video feedback will enable both detailed objective analysis of competition and the immediate presentation of the most important elements of play. Computerized systems on sale now enable the analysis, selection, compilation and re-presentation of any game on video to be processed in a matter of seconds. The coach can then use this facility as a visual aid to support the detailed analysis. Franks (1988) devised a more detailed model of the feedback process that could be possible with this type of technology.

As these systems are used more and more, and larger databases are created, a clearer understanding of each sport will follow. The mathematical approach, typified by Eom (1988) and McGarry and Franks (1994, 1995), will make these systems more and more accurate in their predictions. At the moment the main functions of the systems are analysis, diagnosis and feedback – few sports have gathered enough data to allow prediction of optimum tactics in set situations. Where large databases have been collected (e.g. soccer and squash), models of the games have been created and this has enabled predictive assertions of winning tactics. This has led to some controversy, particularly in soccer, due to the lack of understanding of the statistics involved and their range of application. Nevertheless, the function of the systems could well change, particularly as the financial rewards in certain sports are providing such large incentives for success.

DEVELOPING HAND NOTATION SYSTEMS

Make sure the you have a clear idea of what it is you are trying to analyse before you start. If possible you should also know what your output is going to be and the form it will take. Being able to do this, of course requires a great deal of experience of notation within that particular sport. This is not possible, but the more planning done beforehand, the more fruitless hours saved.

Keep the data collection system as simple as possible for as long as possible. If it does need to become more complex then add an extra routine at a time. Before adding another make sure that the new system works fully.

If you are going to use statistics to test your data for significant differences, etc., then again be sure of the procedures that you are going to use before you start collecting the data. Most statistical tests will require minimum amounts of data, so this will determine how many matches, etc., you must notate.

If your data is to be presented to others, as is usually the case, take great care to fit the format and style of presentation to the people to whom you are attempting to communicate. Always remember that because you have been wrestling with this type of data for some time now, what seems simple and obvious to you can be very confusing to others. If in doubt, always err on the side of simplicity.

WRITING COMPUTERIZED SYSTEMS

Notational analysis is ideally suited for computerization – the logical analyses that must be completed for any hand notation system are very similar to the sort of logical structuring necessary for writing any program.

In writing your programs do not be too proud to use the ideas developed by other people who have already completed work. Experience is a good teacher. Be prepared to consult any experts that you can contact – they will usually be only too happy to talk about their work, your work, anybody's work, etc. Their knowledge and help could save you weeks of work and, perhaps worst of all, wasted efforts. Always work through flowcharts and sets of sequential instructions towards your final conversion into whichever programming language you are to use. The time spent on these logical progressions is well invested, and will, in most situations, eventually save time and effort during the debugging and validation stages of programming.

Before commencing any data gathering, always run full system checks on your programs – be sure that your system really does do what you think and hope that it does. Remember that data gathering is relatively easy, it is producing sense from the data that is the most difficult task. Be prepared to sweat blood and tears over distilling your output until it produces meaningful information in a form that is comprehensible to anyone.

Finally, always try to keep in the forefront of your aims the original reasons why you wanted to create a notation system. With all the problems associated in writing computer programs, and the associate problems with the hardware, it is easy for your priorities to be changed for you because of other pressures.

WHERE TO FIND HELP

A word of advice can save hours, if not days, of wasted effort, but how do you find help? Are there any experts locally that can help you? The International Society of Notational Analysis was formed in 1991 with the aim of creating a communications forum for people interested in notational analysis. The Society has a register of members and is going through the process of accrediting experts in notational analysis. The secretarial base of the Society is:

Dr Mike Hughes
Centre for Notational Analysis
University of Wales Institute Cardiff
Cyncoed
CARDIFF CF2 6XD
Wales

If you get in touch with the Society, then they will be able to advise you of the experts in your locale and their respective areas of expertise in notational analysis.

References

Alderson, J., Fuller, N. and Treadwell, P. (1990) *Match Analysis in Sport: A 'State of Art' Review.* National Coaching Foundation, Leeds

Alexander, D., McClements, K. and Simmons, J. (1988). Calculating to win. *New Scientist,* 10 December, 30–33.

Ali, A.H. (1988) A statistical analysis of tactical movement patterns in soccer. In T. Reilly, A. Lees, K. Davids and W. Murphy (Eds), *Science and Football.* E. & F.N. Spon, London, pp. 302–308.

Ali, A.H. (1992) Analysis of patterns of play of an international soccer team. In T. Reilly (Ed.), *Science and Football II.* E. & F.N. Spon, London.

Andrews, K. (1985) A match analysis of attacking circle play. *Hockey Field,* **72,** 199–201.

Baacke, H. (1982) Statistical match analysis for evaluation of players' and teams' performances. *Volleyball Technical Journal,* **VII,** 45–56.

Barham, P.J. (1980) A systematic analysis of play in netball. *Sports Coach,* **4**(2), 27–31.

Bate, R. (1988) Football chance: tactics and strategy. In T. Reilly, A. Lees, K. Davids and W. Murphy (Eds), *Science and Football.* E. & F.N. Spon, London, pp. 293–301.

Benesh, J. and Benesh, R. (1956) *Reading Dance – The Birth of Choreology.* Souvenir Press, London.

Beynon, S. (1995) A computerized analysis of field hockey. Unpublished Dissertation. Cardiff Institute.

Borrie, A., Mullan, M., Palmer, C. and Hughes, M. (1994) Requirements in netball: an example of the benefits of an inter-disciplinary approach to sports science support. *Journal of Sports Science,* **12**(2), 81.

Bouthier, D., Barthed, D., David, B. and Grehaigne, J.F. (1996) Tactical analysis of play combinations in rugby union with video-computer technology – rationalising French 'flair'. In M.D. Hughes (Ed.), *Notational Analysis of Sport – I & II.* UWIC, Cardiff, pp. 135–144.

Brooke, J.D. and Knowles, J.E. (1974) A movement analysis of player behaviour in soccer match performance. *British Proceedings of Sport Psychology,* 246–256.

Brown, D. and Hughes, M. (1995) The effectiveness of quantitative and qualitative feedback in improving performance in squash. In T. Reilly, M.D. Hughes and A. Lees (Eds), *Science and Racket Sports.* E. & F.N. Spon, London, pp. 232–237.

Byra, M. and Scott, A. (1983) A method for recording team statistics in volleyball. *Volleyball Technical Journal*, **VII**, 39–44.

Carter, A. (1996) Time and motion analysis and heart rate monitoring of a back-row forward in first class rugby union football. In M.D. Hughes (Ed.), *Notational Analysis of Sport – I & II*. UWIC, Cardiff, pp. 145–160.

Chervenjakov, M. and Dimitrov, G. (1988) Assessment of the playing effectiveness of soccer players. In T. Reilly, A. Lees, K. Davids and W. Murphy (Eds), *Science and Football*. E. & F.N. Spon, London, pp. 288–292.

Church, S. and Hughes, M.D. (1986) Patterns of play in Association Football – a computerized analysis. Communication to *First World Congress of Science and Football*, Liverpool, 13–17 April.

Croucher, J. S. (1996) The use of notational analysis in determining optimal strategies in sports. In M. Hughes (Ed.), *Notational Analysis of Sport – I & II*. UWIC, Cardiff, pp. 3–20.

Dagget, A. and Davies, B. (1982) Physical fitness: a prerequisite for the game of hockey. *Hockey Field*, **70**(1), 12–15.

Darst, P. W. (Ed.) (1983) *Systematic Observation and Instrumentation for Physical Education*. Leisure Press, New York.

Docherty, D., *et al.* (1988) Time–motion analysis related to the physiological demands of rugby. *Journal of Human Movement Studies*, **14**, 269–277.

Dodds, P. and Rife, F. (1981) A descriptive-analytic study of the practice field behaviour of a winning female coach. Master's Thesis. Iowa State University.

Doggart, L., Keane, S., Reilly, T. and Stanhope, J. (1993) A task analysis of Gaelic Football. In T. Reilly, J. Clarys and A. Stibbe (Eds), *Science and Football II*. E. & F.N. Spon, London, pp. 186–189.

Downey, J.C. (1973) *The Singles Game*. E.P. Publications, London.

Dowrick, P. W. (1991) *Practical Guide to Using Video in the Behavioural Sciences*. John Wiley, New York.

Dufour, W. (1992) Observation techniques of human behaviour. In T. Reilly (Ed.), *Science and Football II*. E. & F.N. Spon, London, pp. 160–166

Du Toit, P. (1989) Time motion analysis of Rugby Union. Presentation at the World Congress of Notation of Sport, Burton, Wirral, November.

Elliott, B.C. and Smith, J.R. (1983) Netball shooting – a statistical analysis. *Sports Coach*, **7**(1), 29–36.

Ellis, H. (1984) Practical aspects of face memory. In G. Wells and E. Loftus (Eds), *Eyewitness Testimony – Psychological Perspectives*. Cambridge University Press, Cambridge, pp. 13–37.

Embrey, L. (1978) Analysing netball matches. *Sports Coach*, **2**(3), 35–38.

Eom, H.J. (1988) A mathematical analysis of team performance in volleyball. *Canadian Journal of Sports Science*, **13**, 55–56.

Eom, H.J. (1989) Computer-aided recording and mathematical analysis of team performance in volleyball. Unpublished Masters' Thesis, UBC., Vancouver.

Franks, I.M. (1988) Analysis of Association Football. *Soccer Journal*, September/October, 35–43.

Franks, I.M. (1992) Computer technology and the education of soccer coaches. In T. Reilly (Ed.), *Science and Football II*. E. & F.N. Spon, London.

Franks, I.M. (1993) The effects of experience on the detection and location of performance differences in a gymnastic technique. *Research Quarterly for Exercise and Sport*, **64**(2), 227–231

Franks, I.M. (1996) The science of match analysis. In T. Reilly (Ed.), *Science and Soccer*. E. & F.N. Spon, London, pp. 363–375.

Franks, I.M. (1997) Use of feedback by coaches and players. In T. Reilly, J. Bangsbo and M. Hughes (Eds), *Science and Football III*. E. & F.N. Spon, London, pp. 267–278.

Franks, I.M. and Goodman, D. (1984) A hierarchical approach to performance analysis. *SPORTS*, June.

Franks, I.M. and Goodman, D. (1986a) A systematic approach to analyzing sports performance. *Journal of Sports Science*, 4, 49–59.

Franks, I.M. and Goodman, D. (1986b) Computer-assisted technical analysis of sport. *Coaching Review*, May/June. 58–64.

Franks, I. M. and Maile, L. J. (1991) The use of video in sport skill acquisition. In P.W. Dowrick (Ed.), *Practical Guide to Using Video in the Behavioural Sciences*. John Wiley, New York.

Franks, I.M. and Miller, G. (1986) Eyewitness testimony in sport. *Journal of Sport Behavior*, 9, 39–45.

Franks, I.M. and Nagelkerke, P. (1988) The use of computer interactive video technology in sport analysis. *Ergonomics*, 31(99), 1593–1603.

Franks, I.M., Elliot, M. and Johnson, R. (1985) Paper presented at the *Canadian Psycho-motor Conference*, Montreal, October.

Franks, I.M., Goodman, D. and Miller, G. (1983a) Analysis of performance: qualitative or quantitative. *SPORTS*, March.

Franks, I.M., Goodman, D. and Miller, G. (1983b) Human factors in sport systems: an empirical investigation of events in team games. *Proceeding of the Human Factors Society 27th Annual Meeting*, Vol. 1, Norfolk, Virginia, pp. 383–386.

Franks, I.M., Goodman, D. and Paterson, D. (1986) The real time analysis of sport: an overview. *Canadian Journal of Sport Science*, 11, 55–57.

Franks, I.M., Johnson, R and Sinclair, G.D. (1988) The development of a computerized coaching analysis system for recording behaviour in sporting environments. *Journal of Teaching Physical Education*, 8, 23–32.

Franks, I.M., Nagelkerke, P. and Goodman, D. (1989) Computer controlled video: an inexpensive IBM based system. *Computers in Education*, 13(1), 33–44.

Franks, I.M., Wilson, G.E. and Goodman, D. (1987) Analyzing a team sport with the aid of computers. *Canadian Journal of Sport Science*, 12, 120–125.

Franks, I. M., Wilberg, R. B. and Fishburne, G. T. (1982) The process of Decision Making: An application to Team Games. *Coaching Science*, 12–16.

Franks, I.M., Sinclair, G.D., Thomson, W. and Goodman, D. (1986) Analysis of the coaching process. *SPORTS*, January.

Fitts, M. and Posner, M. (1967) *Human Performance*. Brooke/Cole, California.

Fuller, N. (1990) Computerized performance analysis in netball. Interim report to the National Coaching Foundation, Leeds.

Gardiner, G. (1984) Beaten by statistics: possible problems with the Canadian Olympic team selection guidelines. Unpublished MSc degree thesis. University of British Columbia, Vancouver.

Garganta, J. and Goncalves, G. (1996) Comparison of successful attacking play in male and female Portuguese national soccer teams. In M.D. Hughes (Ed.), *Notational Analysis of Sport – I & II*. UWIC, Cardiff, pp. 79–84

Gerisch, G. and Reichelt, M. (1993) Computer- and video-aided analysis of football games. In T. Reilly, J. Clarys and A. Stibbe (Eds), *Science and Football II*. E. & F.N. Spon, London, pp. 167–173.

Goodman, D. and Franks, I.M. (1994) The computer and the hockey coach. *Proceedings of the International Ice Hockey Coaching Symposium*, Cavalese, Italy, May.

Grehaigne, J.R., Bouthier, D. and David, B. (1996) Soccer: the players' action zone in a team. In M.D. Hughes (Ed.), *Notational Analysis of Sport – I & II*. UWIC, Cardiff, pp. 61–68

Handford, C. and Smith, N.C. (1996) Three touches and it's over: addressing the problems of performance analysis in volleyball. In M.D. Hughes (Ed.), *Notational Analysis of Sport – I & II*. UWIC, Cardiff, pp. 205–212.

Harris, S. and Reilly, T. (1988) Space, teamwork and attacking success in soccer. In T. Reilly, A. Lees, K. Davids and W. Murphy (Eds), *Science and Football*. E. & F.N. Spon, London, pp. 322–328.

Harris-Jenkins, E. and Hughes, M.D. (1995) A computerized analysis of female coaching behaviour with male and female athletes. In: Reilly, T., Hughes, M.D. and Lees, A. (Eds.) *Science and Racket Sports*. E. & F.N. Spon, London, pp. 228–231.

Hastie, P.A. (1990) Models of videotape use in sports settings. *Physical Education Review*, **13**(2), 101–108.

Herbert, P. and Tong, R. (1996) A comparison of the positional demands of wingers and back row forwards using movement analysis and heart rate telemetry. In M.D. Hughes (Ed.), *Notational Analysis of Sport – I & II*. UWIC, Cardiff, pp. 177–182.

Herborn, R. (1989) Video analysis of Association Football: the long ball theory. Unpublished undergraduate dissertation. Cardiff Institute of Higher Education, Cardiff.

Hughes, C. (1973) *Football Tactics and Teamwork*. E.P. Publishing, Wakefield.

Hughes, M.D. (1985) A comparison of the patterns of play of squash. In I.D. Brown, R. Goldsmith, K. Coombes and M.A. Sinclair (Eds), *International Ergonomics '85*. Taylor & Francis, London, pp. 139–141.

Hughes, M.D. (1986) A review of patterns of play in squash. In J. Watkins, T. Reilly and L. Burwitz (Eds) *Sports Science*. E. & F.N. Spon, London, pp. 362–369.

Hughes, M.D. (1988) Computerized notation analysis in field games. *Ergonomics*, **31**(11), 1585–1592.

Hughes, M.D. (1993) Notational analysis of football. In T. Reilly, J. Clarys and A. Stibbe *Science and Football II*. E. & F.N. Spon, London, pp. 151–159.

Hughes, M.D. (1994) A time-based model of the activity cycles in squash, with different scoring systems, and tennis, on different surfaces. *Journal of Sports Science*, **13**(1), 85.

Hughes, M.D. (1995a) Using notational analysis to create a more exciting scoring system for squash. In G. Atkinson and T. Reilly (Eds), *Sport, Leisure and Ergonomics*. E. & F.N. Spon, London, pp. 243–247.

Hughes, M.D. (1995b) Notational Analysis of racket sports. In T. Reilly and M. Hughes (Eds), *Science and Racket Sports*. E. & F.N. Spon, London, pp. 249–256.

Hughes, M.D. (1996a) Computerized notation systems in sport. In M.D. Hughes (Ed.), *Notational Analysis of Sport – I & II*. UWIC, Cardiff, pp. 21–26.

Hughes, M.D. (Ed.) (1996b) *Notational Analysis of Sport – I & II*. UWIC, Cardiff.

Hughes, M.D. (Ed.) (1997) *Notational Analysis of Sport – III*. UWIC, Cardiff.

Hughes, M.D. and Billingham, N. (1986) Computerized analysis of patterns of play in field hockey. *National Conference of Psychology*. Patiala, India.

Hughes, M.D. and Charlish, F. (1988) The development and validation of a computerized notation system for American football. *Journal of Sports Sciences*, **6**, 253–254.

Hughes, M.D. and Clarke, A. (1994) Computerized notational analysis of the effects of the law changes upon patterns of play of international teams in rugby union. *Journal of Sports Science*, **12**(2), 181.

Hughes, M.D. and Clarke, S. (1995) Surface effect on patterns of play of elite tennis players. In T. Reilly, M. Hughes and A. Lees (Eds), *Science of Racket Sports*. London E. & F.N. Spon, pp. 272–278.

Hughes, M.D. and Cunliffe, S. (1986) Notational analysis of field hockey. *Proceedings of the BASS Conference*, Birmingham University, September.

Hughes, M.D. and Feery, M. (1986) Notational analysis of basketball. *Proceedings of BASS Conference*, Birmingham University, September.

Hughes, M.D. and Franks, I.M. (1991) A time–motion analysis of squash players using a mixed-image video tracking system. *Ergonomics*, **37**(1), 23–29.

Hughes, M.D. and Hill, J. (1996)An analysis of referees in the men's Rugby Union World Cup, 1991. In M.D. Hughes (Ed.), *Notational Analysis of Sport – I & II*. UWIC, Cardiff, pp. 161–167.

Hughes, M.D. and Knight, P. (1995) A comparison of playing patterns of elite squash players, using English scoring to point per rally scoring. In T. Reilly, M. Hughes and A. Lees (Eds), *Science of Racket Sports*. E. & F.N. Spon, London, pp. 257–259.

Hughes, M.D. and McGarry, T. (1989) Computerized notational analysis of squash. In M.D. Hughes (Ed.) *Science in Squash*. Liverpool Polytechnic, pp. 183–205.

Hughes, M.D. and Nicholson, A. (1986) Analysis of tactics in inland dinghy racing. *Proceedings of the BASS Conference*, Birmingham University, September.

Hughes, M.D. and Spurle, T. (1995) An analysis of the variables that determine the dismissal of opening batsmen in test cricket between England and Australia. *Journal of Sports Science*, **12**(1), 180.

Hughes, M.D. and Sykes, I. (1994) Computerized notational analysis of the effects of the law changes in soccer upon patterns of play. *Journal of Sports Science*, **12**(1), 180.

Hughes, M.D. and Tillin, P. (1994) An analysis of the attacking strategies in female elite tennis players at Wimbledon. *Journal of Sports Science*, **13**(1), 86.

Hughes, M.D. and White, P. (1996) An analysis of forward play in the men's Rugby Union World Cup, 1991. In M.D. Hughes (Ed.), *Notational Analysis of Sport – I & II*. UWIC, Cardiff, pp. 183–192.

Hughes, M.D. and Williams, D. (1988) The development and application of a computerized Rugby Union notation system. *Journal of Sports Sciences*, **6**, 254–255.

Hughes, M. D., Franks, I.M. and Nagelkerke, P. (1989) A video-system for the quantitative motion analysis of athletes in competitive sport. *Journal of Human Movement Studies*, **17**, 212–227.

Hughes, M.D., Kitchen, S. and Horobin, A. (1996) An analysis of women's international rugby union. In M.D. Hughes (Ed.), *Notational Analysis of Sport – I & II*. UWIC, Cardiff, pp. 125–133.

Hughes, M.D., Robertson, K. and Nicholson, A. (1988) An analysis of 1984 World Cup of Association Football. In T. Reilly, A. Lees, K. Davids and W. Murphy (Eds), *Science and Football*. E. & F.N. Spon, London, pp. 363–367.

Hutchinson, A. (1970) *Labanotation – The System of Analysing and Recording Movement* Oxford University Press, London.

Ichiguchi, M. (1981) Analysis of techniques in World amateur wrestling games Greco-Roman in 1979. *Bulletin, School of Physical Education, Tokai University*, **11**, 53–58.

Ichiguchi, M. and Iwagaki, S. (1981) Analysis of techniques in World amateur wrestling games Greco-Roman in 1979. *Bulletin, School of Physical Education, Tokai University*, **11**, 85–94.

Ichiguchi, M., Ogawa, K. and Iwagaki, S. (1978) Analysis of techniques in Wrestling games. *Bulletin, School of Physical Education, Tokai University*, **8**, 45–56.

Ichiguchi, M., Ogawa, K. and Iwagaki, S. (1979) Analysis of techniques in Wrestling games. *Bulletin, School of Physical Education, Tokai University*, **9**, 93–107.

Ichiguchi, M., Kasai, S., Nishiyama, T., Takenouchi, T., Mitsukuri, T. and Saito, M. (1978) A basic study on recording method and information analysis of wrestling games. *Bulletin, School of Physical Education, Tokai University*, **8**, 31–43.

Jinslian, X., Xiaoke, K., Yamanaka, K. and Matsumoto, M. Analysis of the goals in the 14th World Cup. In T. Reilly, J. Clarys and A. Stibble (Eds), *Science and Football II*. E. & F.N. Spon, London, pp. 203–205.

Johnson, R.B. (1987) A reliability test of the computerized coaching analysis system. Unpublished Masters' thesis. University of British Columbia, Vancouver.

Kawai, K. (1996) Development of a computerized notational analysis system of soccer allowing for accurate reproduction of plays and feedback effects In M.D. Hughes (Ed.), *Notational Analysis of Sport – I & II*. UWIC, Cardiff, pp. 257–266.

Kenyon, G.S. and Schutz, R.W. (1970) Patterns of involvement in sport: a stochastic view. In G.S. Kenyon (Ed.), *Contemporary Psychology of Sport*. Athletic Institute, Chicago, IL, pp. 23–45.

Knapp, B.J. (1963) *Skill in Sport – The Attainment of Proficiency*. Routledge and Kegan Paul, London.

Laban, R. (1975) *Laban's Principles of Dance and Music Notation*. McDonald and Evans, London.

Lacy, A.C. and Darst, P.W. (1985) Systematic observation of behaviours of winning high school head football coaches. *Journal of Teaching in Physical Education*, 4(4), 256–270.

Ladany, S.P. and Machol, R.E. (Eds) (1977) *Optimal Strategies in Sports*. North Holland, Amsterdam.

Lanham, N. (1993) Figures do not cease to exist because they are not counted. In T. Reilly, J. Clarys and A. Stibbe (Eds), *Science and Football II*. E. & F.N. Spon, London, pp. 180–185.

Larder, P. (1988) *Rugby League Coaching Manual*. Kingswood Press, London.

Lewis, M. and Hughes, M.D. (1988) Attacking play in the 1986 World Cup of Association Football. *Journal of Sport Science*, **6**, 169

Longville, J., Allen, C. and Hughes, M. (1996) Shooting opportunities in netball. In M.D. Hughes (Ed.), *Notational Analysis of Sport – I & II*. UWIC, Cardiff, pp. 227–234.

Luhtanen, P.H. (1993) A statistical evaluation of offensive actions in soccer at world cup level in Italy, 1990. In T. Reilly, J. Clarys and A. Stibbe (Eds), *Science and Football II*. E. & F.N. Spon, London, pp. 215–220.

Lyons, K. (1988) *Using Video in Sport*. Springfield Books, Huddersfield.

Lyons, K. (1992) The use of notational analysis in sport. *In Touch*, Autumn.

Lyons, K. (1996) Lloyd Messersmith. In M.D. Hughes (Ed.), *Notational Analysis of Sport – I & II*. UWIC, Cardiff, pp. 49–58.

Maclean, D. (1992) Analysis of the physical demands of international rugby union. *Journal of Sport Science*, **10**(3), 285–296.

MacDonald, N. (1984) Avoiding the pitfalls in player selection. *Coaching Science Update*, 41–45.

Marascuilo, L.A. and Busk, P.L. (1987) Loglinear models: a way to study main effects and interactions for multidimensional contingency tables with categorical data. *Journal of Counseling Psychology*, **34**, 443–455.

Mayhew, S.R. and Wenger, H.A. (1985) Time-motion analysis of professional soccer. *Journal of Human Movement Studies*, **11**, 49–52.

McCann, A., Treadwell, P. and Baker, J.S. (1996) A notational analysis system for evaluation of karate performance. In M.D. Hughes (Ed.), *Notational Analysis of Sport – I & II*. UWIC, Cardiff, pp. 245–248.

McDonald, M. (1984) Avoiding the pitfalls of player selection. *Coaching Science Update*, 41–45.

McGarry, T. and Franks, I.M. (1994) A stochastic approach to predicting competition squash match-play. *Journal of Sports Sciences*, **12**, 573–584.

McGarry, T. and Franks, I.M. (1995) Modeling competitive squash performance from quantitative analysis. *Human Performance*, **8**(2), 113–129.

McGarry, T. and Franks, I.M. (1996) Analysing championship squash match play: In search of a system description. In S. Haake (Ed.) *The Engineering of Sport*. Balkema, Rotterdam, pp. 263–269.

McGarry, T. and Franks, I.M. (1996) In search of invariance in championship squash. In M.D. Hughes (Ed.), *Notational Analysis of Sport – I & II*. UWIC, Cardiff, pp. 281–288.

McKenna, M.J., Patrick, J.D., Sandstrom, E.R. and Chennells, M.H.D. (1988) Computer-video analysis of activity patterns in Australian rules football. In T. Reilly, A. Lees, K. Davids and W. Murphy (Eds), *Science and Football*. E. & F.N. Spon, London, pp. 274–281.

McKenzie, T.L. and Carlson, B.R. (1984) Computer technology for exercise and sport pedagogy: recording, storing and analyzing interval data. *Journal of Teaching in Physical Education*, **3**, 17–27.

McNamara, M. (1989) Match analysis of women's hockey. Unpublished undergraduate dissertation. Cardiff Institute of Higher Education, Cardiff.

Messersmith, L.L. and Corey, S. (1931) The distance traversed by a basketball player. *Research Quarterly*, **II**(2), 57–60.

Metzler, M.W. (1984) ALT-PE micro computer data collection system/version 1.0 [Computer program]. Metzsoft, Blacksburg, Virginia.

Miller, B. and Edwards, S. (1983) Assessing motor performance in hockey: a field based approach. Paper presented at *British Society of Sports Psychology Conference*, Birmingham, February.

Miller, G.N. (1988) Observational accuracy in sport. Unpublished Masters' thesis. University of British Columbia, Vancouver.

Miller, B.P. and Winter, E. (1984) Specificity and netball performance. *Report for the All England Netball Association*, June.

More, K.G. (1994) Analysis and modification of verbal coaching behaviour: the utility of a data driven intervention strategy. Unpublished Masters' dissertation. University of British Columbia, Vancouver.

More, K.G. and Franks, I.M. (in press) Analysis of verbal coaching behaviour: the utility of a data driven intervention strategy. *Journal of Sports Sciences*.

More, K.G., McGarry, T., Partridge, D. and Franks, I.M. (in press) A computerized assisted analysis of verbal coaching behaviour in soccer. *Journal of Sports Sciences*.

Morris, P. and Bell, H. (1985) An analysis of individual performance in hockey. *Carnegie Research Papers*, **1**(7), 18–22.

Nicholson, A. (1996) Commercialisation and the future success of sports notation. In M.D. Hughes (Ed.), *Notational Analysis of Sport – I & II*. UWIC, Cardiff, pp. 255–256.

O'Hare, M. (1995) In a league of their own. *New Scientist*, 30 September, 30–35.

Ohashi, J., Togari, H., Isokawa, M. and Suzuki, S. (1988) Measuring movement speeds and distances covered during soccer matchplay. In T. Reilly, A. Lees, K. Davids and W. Murphy (Eds), *Science and Football*. E. & F.N. Spon, London, pp. 329–333.

Oliveira, J. (1996) Playing two on two. A descriptive study of young basketball players aged 13–14. In M.D. Hughes (Ed.), *Notational Analysis of Sport – I & II*. UWIC, Cardiff, pp. 221–226.

O'Shea, R. (1992) An analysis of the tries scored in the 1991 Rugby World Cup. Unpublished undergraduate dissertation. Cardiff Institute of Higher Education, Cardiff.

Otago, L. (1983) A game analysis of the activity patterns of netball players. *Sports Coach*, **7**(1), 24–28.

Palmer, C., Hughes, M. and Borrie, A. (1994) Centre pass patterns of play of successful and non-successful international netball teams. *Journal of Sports Science*, **12**(2), 181.

Palmer, C., Borrie, A., Burwitz, L., Whitby, D. and Broomhead, L. (1996) Development of a computerized real time match analysis system for netball. In M.D. Hughes (Ed.), *Notational Analysis of Sport – I & II*. UWIC, Cardiff, pp. 249–254.

Partridge, D. and Franks, I.M. (1989a) A detailed analysis of crossing opportunities from the 1986 World Cup (Part I). *Soccer Journal*. May/June, pp. 47–50.

Partridge, D. and Franks, I.M. (1989b) A detailed analysis of crossing opportunities from the 1986 World Cup (Part II). *Soccer Journal*. June/July, pp. 45–48.

Partridge, D. and Franks, I.M. (1993) Computer-aided analysis of sport performance: an example from soccer. *The Physical Educator*, **50**, 208–215.

Partridge, D. and Franks, I.M. (1996) Analyzing and modifying coaching behaviours by means of computer aided observation. *The Physical Educator*, **53**, 8–23.

Partridge, D., Mosher, R.E. and Franks, I.M. (1993) A computer assisted analysis of technical performance – a comparison of the 1990 world cup and intercollegiate soccer. In T. Reilly, J. Clarys and A. Stibbe (Eds), *Science and Football II*. E. & F.N. Spon, London, pp. 221–231.

Patrick, J.D. and Mackenna, M.J. (1988) CABER – a computer system for football analysis. In T. Reilly, A. Lees, K. Davids and W. Murphy (Eds), *Science and Football*. E. & F.N. Spon, London, pp. 267–273.

Penner, D. (1985) Computer volleyball stats. *Volleyball Technical Journal*, **VIII**, 116–127.

Pollard, R., Reep, C. and Hartley, S. (1988) The quantitative comparison of playing styles in soccer. In T. Reilly, A. Lees, K. Davids and W. Murphy (Eds), *Science and Football*. E. & F.N. Spon, London, pp. 309–315.

Potter, G. (1996a) Hand notation of the 1994 soccer World Cup. In M.D. Hughes (Ed.), *Notational Analysis of Sport – I & II*. UWIC, Cardiff, pp. 113–122.

Potter, G. (1996b) A case study of England's performance in the five nations championship over a three year period (1992–94) In M.D. Hughes (Ed.), *Notational Analysis of Sport – I & II*. UWIC, Cardiff, pp. 193–202.

Potter, G. and Carter, A. (1995) Performance at the 1995 Rugby World Cup. In C. Tau (Ed.), *Rugby World Cup 1995*. International Rugby Football Board, Bristol.

Potter, M. (1985) Notation of Schoolgirl Netball. Unpublished undergraduate dissertation. Bedford College of Higher Education.

Purdy, J.G. (1974) Computer analysis of champion athletic performance. *Research Quarterly*, **45**, 391–397.

Purdy, J.G. (1977) Computers and sports: from football play analysis to the Olympic games. In S.P. Ladany and R.E. Machol (Eds), *Optimal Strategies in Sports*. Amsterdam, North Holland, pp. 196–205.

Reep, C. and Benjamin, B. (1968) Skill and chance in association football. *Journal of the Royal Statistical Society, Series A*, **131**, 581–585.

Reep, C., Pollard, R. and Benjamin, B. (1971) Skill and chance in ball games. *Journal of the Royal Statistical Society*, **134**, 623–629.

Reilly, T. (ed) (1996) *Science and Soccer*. E. & F.N. Spon, London.

Reilly, T. and Thomas, V. (1976) A motion analysis of work-rate in different positional roles in professional football match-play. *Journal of Human Movement Studies*, **2**, 87– 97.

Reilly, T., Clarys, J. and Stibbe, A. (Eds) (1993) *Science and Football II*. E. & F.N. Spon, London.

Reilly, T., Hughes, M. and Lees, A. (1995) *Science and Racket Sports*. London, E. & F.N. Spon.

Reilly, T., Lees, A., Davids, K. and Murphy, W. (Eds) (1988) *Science and Football*. E. & F.N. Spon, London.

Rebelo, A.N. and Soares, J.M.C. A comparative study of time-motion analysis during the two halves of a soccer game. In M.D. Hughes (Ed.), *Notational Analysis of Sport – I & II*. UWIC, Cardiff, pp. 69–73.

Rico, J. and Bangsbo, J. (1996) Coding system to evaluate actions with the ball during a soccer match. In M.D. Hughes (Ed.), *Notational Analysis of Sport – I & II*. UWIC, Cardiff, pp. 85–90.

Ross, D., Bird, A.M., Dosdy, S.G. and Zoeller, M. (1985) Effects of modelling and videotape feedback with knowledge of results on motor performance. *J.H.M.*, **4**, 149–157.

Russell, D. (1986) A study of passing movements in relation to strikes at goal in Association Football. Unpublished undergraduate dissertation. Bedford College of Higher Education.

Sanderson, F.H. (1983) A notation system for analysing squash. *Physical Education Review*, **6**, 19–23.

Sanderson, F.H. and Way, K.I.M. (1977) The development of an objective method of game analysis in squash rackets. *British Journal of Sports Medicine*, **11**, 188

Schutz, R.W. (1970a) Stochastic processes: their nature and use in the study of sport and physical activity. *The Research Quarterly*, **41**, 205–212.

Schutz, R.W. (1980) Sport and mathematics: a definition and delineation. *Research Quarterly for Exercise and Sport*, **51**, 37–49.

Schutz, R.W. and Gessaroli, M.E. (1987) The analysis of repeated measure designs involving multiple dependent variables. *Research Quarterly for Exercise and Sport*, **58**, 132–149.

Schutz, R.W. and Kinnsey, W.J. (1977) Comparison of North American and international Squash scoring systems – a computer simulation. *Research Quarterly*, **48**, 248–251.

Sharp, R. (1986) Presentation: *Notation Workshop in the Commonwealth Games Conference on Sport Science*, Glasgow.

Stanhope, J. and Hughes, M.D. (1996) An analysis of scoring in the 1991 Rugby Union World Cup for men. In M.D. Hughes (Ed.), *Notational Analysis of Sport – I & II*. UWIC, Cardiff, pp. 167–176.

Steele, J. R. and Chad, K. E. (1991) Relationship between movement patterns performed in match play and in training by skilled netball players. *Journal of Human Movement Studies*, **20**(6), 249–278.

Steele, J. R. and Chad, K. E. (1992) An analysis of movement patterns of netball players during match play: implications for designing training programmes. *Sports Coach*, **15**(1), 21–28.

Suinn, R.M. (1980) *Psychology in Sport – Methods and Applications*. Burgess, New York, USA.

Taylor, S. and Hughes, M.D. (1988) Computerized notational analysis: a voice interactive system. *Journal of Sport Sciences*, **6**, 255.

Templin, D.P. and Vernacchia, R.A. (1995) The effect of highlight music videotapes upon the game performance of intercollegiate basketball players. *The Sport Psychologist*, **9**, 41–50.

Thornton, S. (1971) *A Movement Perspective of Rudolph Laban*. McDonald and Evans, London.

Tiryaki, G., Cicek, S., Erdogan, A.T., *et al.* (1996) The analysis of the offensive patterns of the Switzerland soccer team in the World Cup, 1994. In M.D. Hughes (Ed.), *Notational Analysis of Sport – I & II*. UWIC, Cardiff, pp. 91–98.

Tavares, F. (1996) Decision-making in basketball: a computer assisted video-test for evaluation. In M.D. Hughes (Ed.), *Notational Analysis of Sport – I & II*. UWIC, Cardiff, pp. 213–220.

Treadwell, P.J. (1987) Computer aided match analysis of selected ball-games (soccer and rugby union). In T. Reilly, A. Lees, K. Davids and W. Murphy (Eds), *Science and Football*. E. & F.N. Spon, London, pp. 282–287.

Treadwell, P.J. (1992) The predictive potential of match analysis systems for rugby union football. In T. Reilly, (Ed.), *Science and Football II*. E. & F.N. Spon, London.

Treadwell, P.J. (1996) Building knowledge in sports science: the potential of sports notation. In M.D. Hughes (Ed.), *Notational Analysis of Sport – I & II*. UWIC, Cardiff, pp. 43–48.

Tuckwell, M., Longville, J., Allen, C. and Hughes, M.D. (1996) Defensive patterns of play from the centre pass in netball In M.D. Hughes (Ed.), *Notational Analysis of Sport – I & II*. UWIC, Cardiff, pp. 235–242.

Underwood, G, and Macheath, J, (1977) Video analysis in tennis coaching. *British Journal of Physical Education*, **8**(5), 136–138.

Van der Mars, H. (1989) Observer reliability: issues and procedures. In P W Darst *et al.* (Eds), *Analyzing Physical Education and Sport Instruction.* Human Kinetics, Champaign, Illinois.

Wade, A. (1967) *The F.A. Guide to Training and Coaching.* Heinemann, London.

Wilson, G. (1987) A case for hockey statistics. *Hockey Field*, **74**(5), 161–163.

Wilson, G. (1987) A case for hockey statistics: as seen through the eyes of a computer. *Hockey Field*, **74**(6), 191–194.

Winkler, W. (1988) Match analysis and improvement of performance in soccer with the aid of computer controlled dual video systems (CCDVS). In T. Reilly, A. Lees, K. Davids and W. Murphy (Eds), *Science and Football.* E. & F.N. Spon, London.

Winkler, W. (1993) A new approach to the video analysis of tactical aspects of soccer. In T. Reilly, J. Clarys and A. Stibbe (Eds), *Science and Football II.* E. & F.N. Spon, London, pp. 368–372.

Winkler, W. (1996a) Computer-controlled assessment- and video-technology for the diagnosis of a player's performance in soccer training. In T. Reilly, J. Clarys and A. Stibbe (Eds), *Science and Football II.* E. & F.N. Spon, London, pp. 73–80.

Winkler, W. (1996b) Computer/video analysis in German soccer. In M. Hughes (Ed.), *Notational Analysis of Sport – I & II.* UWIC, Cardiff, pp. 21–26.

Winterbottom, W. (1959) *Soccer Coaching.* The Naldrett Press, Kingswood.

Withers, R.T., Maricic, Z., Wasilewski, S. and Kelly, L. (1982) Match analyses of Australian professional soccer players. *Journal of Human Movement Studies*, **8**, 158–176.

Yamanaka, K., Hughes, M. and Lott, M. (1993) An analysis of playing patterns in the 1990 World Cup for association football. In T. Reilly, J. Clarys and A. Stibbe (Eds), *Science and Football II.* E. & F.N. Spon, London, pp. 206–214.

Young, D.E. and Schmidt, R.A. (1992) Augmented feedback for enhanced skill acquisition. In G.E. Stelmach and J. Requim (Eds), *Tutorials in Motor Behaviour II.* Amsterdam, North Holland, pp. 677–694.

Index